PALGRAVE STUDIES IN THEATRE AND PERFORMANCE HISTORY is a series devoted to the best of theatre/performance scholarship currently available, accessible, and free of jargon. It strives to include a wide range of topics, from the more traditional to those performance forms that in recent years have helped broaden the understanding of what theatre as a category might include (from variety forms as diverse as the circus and burlesque to street buskers, stage magic, and musical theatre, among many others). Although historical, critical, or analytical studies are of special interest, more theoretical projects, if not the dominant thrust of a study, but utilized as important underpinning or as a historiographical or analytical method of exploration, are also of interest. Textual studies of drama or other types of less traditional performance texts are also germane to the series if placed in their cultural, historical, social, or political and economic context. There is no geographical focus for this series and works of excellence of a diverse and international nature, including comparative studies, are sought.

The editor of the series is Don B. Wilmeth (EMERITUS, Brown University), Ph.D., University of Illinois, who brings to the series over a dozen years of experience as editor of a book series on American theatre and drama, in addition to his own extensive experience as an editor of books and journals. He is the author of several award-winning books and has received numerous career achievement awards, including one for sustained excellence in editing from the Association for Theatre in Higher Education.

Also in the series:

Undressed for Success by Brenda Foley
Theatre, Performance, and the Historical Avant-garde by Günter Berghaus
Theatre, Politics, and Markets in Fin-de-Siècle Paris by Sally Charnow
Ghosts of Theatre and Cinema in the Brain by Mark Pizzato
Moscow Theatres for Young People by Manon van de Water
Absence and Memory in Colonial American Theatre by Odai Johnson
Vaudeville Wars: How the Keith-Albee and Orpheum Circuits Controlled the Big-Time and Its Performers by Arthur Frank Wertheim
Performance and Femininity in Eighteenth-Century German Women's Writing by Wendy Arons
Operatic China: Staging Chinese Identity across the Pacific by Daphne P. Lei
Transatlantic Stage Stars in Vaudeville and Variety: Celebrity Turns by Leigh Woods
Interrogating America through Theatre and Performance edited by William W. Demastes and Iris Smith Fischer
Plays in American Periodicals, 1890–1918 by Susan Harris Smith

Representation and Identity from Versailles to the Present: The Performing Subject by Alan Sikes
Directors and the New Musical Drama: British and American Musical Theatre in the 1980s and 90s by Miranda Lundskaer-Nielsen
Beyond the Golden Door: Jewish-American Drama and Jewish-American Experience by Julius Novick
American Puppet Modernism: Essays on the Material World in Performance by John Bell
On the Uses of the Fantastic in Modern Theatre: Cocteau, Oedipus, and the Monster by Irene Eynat-Confino
Staging Stigma: A Critical Examination of the American Freak Show by Michael M. Chemers, foreword by Jim Ferris
Performing Magic on the Western Stage: From the Eighteenth-Century to the Present edited by Francesca Coppa, Larry Hass, and James Peck, foreword by Eugene Burger
Memory in Play: From Aeschylus to Sam Shepard by Attilio Favorini
Danjūrō's Girls: Women on the Kabuki Stage by Loren Edelson
Mendel's Theatre: Heredity, Eugenics, and Early Twentieth-Century American Drama by Tamsen Wolff
Theatre and Religion on Krishna's Stage: Performing in Vrindavan by David V. Mason
Rogue Performances: Staging the Underclasses in Early American Theatre Culture by Peter P. Reed
Broadway and Corporate Capitalism: The Rise of the Professional-Managerial Class, 1900–1920 by Michael Schwartz
Lady Macbeth in America: From the Stage to the White House by Gay Smith
Performing Bodies in Pain: Medieval and Post-Modern Martyrs, Mystics, and Artists by Marla Carlson
Early-Twentieth-Century Frontier Dramas on Broadway: Situating the Western Experience in Performing Arts by Richard Wattenberg
Staging the People: Community and Identity in the Federal Theatre Project by Elizabeth A. Osborne
Russian Culture and Theatrical Performance in America, 1891–1933 by Valleri J. Hohman
Baggy Pants Comedy: Burlesque and the Oral Tradition by Andrew Davis
Transposing Broadway: Jews, Assimilation, and the American Musical by Stuart J. Hecht

Transposing Broadway

Jews, Assimilation, and the American Musical

Stuart J. Hecht

palgrave
macmillan

TRANSPOSING BROADWAY
Copyright © Stuart J. Hecht, 2011.

All rights reserved.

First published in 2011 by
PALGRAVE MACMILLAN®
in the United States—a division of St. Martin's Press LLC,
175 Fifth Avenue, New York, NY 10010.

Where this book is distributed in the UK, Europe and the rest of the world, this is by Palgrave Macmillan, a division of Macmillan Publishers Limited, registered in England, company number 785998, of Houndmills, Basingstoke, Hampshire RG21 6XS.

Palgrave Macmillan is the global academic imprint of the above companies and has companies and representatives throughout the world.

Palgrave® and Macmillan® are registered trademarks in the United States, the United Kingdom, Europe and other countries.

ISBN 978-1-349-29503-6   ISBN 978-1-137-00174-0 (eBook)
DOI 10.1057/9781137001740

Library of Congress Cataloging-in-Publication Data

Hecht, Stuart Joel, 1955–
   Transposing Broadway : Jews, assimilation, and the American musical / by Stuart J. Hecht.
      p. cm.—(Palgrave studies in theatre and performance history)
   Includes bibliographical references and index.

   1. Musicals—United States—History—20th century. 2. Jews—Cultural assimilation—United States. 3. Jews—United States—Ethnic identity. I. Title. II. Series.

ML1711.H34 2011
792.6089′924073—dc22   2011017726

A catalogue record of the book is available from the British Library.

Design by Newgen Imaging Systems (P) Ltd., Chennai, India.

First edition: November 2011

10 9 8 7 6 5 4 3 2 1

Transferred to Digital Printing in 2012

Contents ❦

Acknowledgments	vii
1. Introduction: Broadway as a Cultural Ellis Island	1
2. Hello, Young Lovers: Assimilation and Dramatic Configurations in the American Musical	15
3. The Melting Pot Paradigm of Irving Berlin	41
4. How to Succeed	61
5. Cinderellas	103
6. Turns of the Century: Dreams of Progress, Dreams of Loss	131
7. Fiddler's Children	179
8. Lovable Monsters: An Epilogue	201
Notes	205
Representative Bibliography	221
Index	227

Acknowledgments

I wish to thank the following people for their encouragement, conversation, and advice in writing this book: Howard S. Becker, Ted Chapin, Charles Combs and Nancy Kindelin, Moshe and Susan Dworkin, Philip Furia, Ida Golden and Jacob Hecht, Seymour Greene, Robert Gross, Jennie Rose Halperin, Jacob Hecht, Mark Eden Horowitz, James Kolb, Jeffrey Martin, Edna Nahshon, Heather Nathans, Cantor Robert Scher, Alezah Weinberg, Barry Weissler, and Stephen Whitfield. Let me also thank my Boston College Theatre Department colleagues, especially Scott T. Cummings, John H. Houchin, and Crystal Tiala, and Boston College for providing both a Research Grant and sabbatical leave. I also thank the Theatre Division of the Library of Congress as well as the curators of the New York Public Library's Billy Rose Theatre Collections' invaluable video archive. I also thank the students in my American Musical Theatre course over the years for helping me discover and learn.

A special thank you to Don Wilmeth for his guidance, understanding and faith, and to Samantha Hasey, my Palgrave editor, for her on-going help and support.

I also thank my parents Edith and Emanuel Hecht for raising us with the arts, both high and low, to my sister Nancy, and to my eldest sister Alice who sat at the piano and made me sing show tunes.

Finally I thank my wife Shirah for her knowledge, insight, and support. Fittingly, "shirah" is Hebrew for song or poem—music and words, thoughts, and feeling. It is to her that I lovingly dedicate this book.

1. Introduction: Broadway as a Cultural Ellis Island

Coming to America

From the 1910s on, America's Broadway musical was developed primarily by Jews. Reflecting their own adjustments to American life, and that of their increasingly Jewish audience, these artists shaped the musical into a form that illustrated their concerns, promoted their values, and, above all, provided a setting for the ongoing discussion of how outsiders might gain access to America and its "Dream" of acceptance and success.

Broadway is identified with New York City. In the years that the musical evolved, Jews formed an increasing percentage of the city's population, in large part due to the great wave of immigration from Eastern Europe that begun in the 1880s. In 1870, 60,000 Jews lived in New York constituting 4 percent of the city's population; in 1900 there were 580,000, representing 11 percent. By 1920, 1,643,000 Jews lived in New York, forming fully 29 percent of the city. Furthermore, as the *Encyclopedia Judaica* notes:

> It is safe to say that from the 1920s on Jews formed a disproportionately high percentage of New York's theatergoers, music listeners, book purchasers, and art collectors. One rough estimate placed Jews at 70% of the city's concert and theater audience during the 1950s.[1]

Consequently, the Broadway musical reflected a primary audience that was increasingly composed of Jews. It makes sense that Jewish issues and tastes be found in shows leading up to, and including, what is regarded as the musical's "golden age." This dynamic was accentuated by the fact that the vast majority of Broadway's leading creative lights were predominantly Jews, who in many ways understandably shared their audience's values and concerns.

Assimilation or Acculturation?

One of the primary cultural challenges for newcomers to America was assimilation. It seemed necessary to lose Old Country ways—behavior, appearance, language, culture—and take on those of America in order to succeed. But how did one do that? And to what degree did one try to hold on to one's identity in the process?

There is a subtle but important distinction often made between "assimilation" and "acculturation." The former suggests that one loses oneself entirely in the American "melting pot," that one's ethnicity yields to a new secular amalgam formed in the American crucible. "Acculturation" suggests that one preserves his or her identity and take on only the outer trappings of being American when participating in public life. The image sometimes given for the latter, in contrast to "the melting pot," is that of "the salad bowl," where America is formed by the harmonious interaction of differing, still distinctive, ethnicities.

Each immigrant had to negotiate for himself or herself the manner and degree to which they were willing to adopt American ways. A measure of personal transformation was required to participate fully in the larger, secular American society. Immigrant-generation Jews living in New York City exuberantly attended Yiddish theatre productions, the most common subject of which was the painful conflict between older immigrant parents suffering at their children's preference to adopt American ways at the cost of their traditional ethnic upbringing.[2]

Immigrant children were natural actors. They spoke Yiddish at home and English on the street; they practiced traditional religious rites in synagogue and then learned American history in English-speaking public schools. What they did not know they imitated; there was nothing worse than being ridiculed by peers for being a "greenhorn," which is to say, a person still showing Old World ignorance of modern American ways. Jewish parents, despite their laments, pushed their children to succeed; they recognized America's possibilities and wanted their children to do better than they themselves. Success was to be achieved through education: a good education meant a good job and the chance to climb out of the ghetto. So children were paradoxically encouraged to imitate American culture and language as it was the cultural price of admission to the best schools and, ultimately, access to the dominant White Anglo-Saxon Protestant society.[3]

While professions such as law and medicine were idealized, one route out of the tenement was through entertainment. Anti-Semitism kept Jews out of many occupations. This was not restricted to Jews; many immigrant groups experienced comparable prejudice. "Irish need not apply" was commonly listed in want ads, and there was much antipathy toward Italian immigrants as well. Irish, and then Jews, found show business not restrictive, especially the popular entertainments performed in New York City with its diverse population and audience. The 1880s Irish vaudeville team of Harrigan and Hart offered sketches of ethnic New York life featuring competing working-class nationalities in knock-about comedies. They proved so popular that politicians knew better than to hold meetings on nights when the duo performed. A decade later, the Jewish Weber and Fields operated in Harrigan and Hart's footsteps, presenting themselves as "Dutch" comedians, a definition encompassing the German or Jewish, sufficiently vague as to not turn away customers of any ilk.[4] A decade later the Irish George M. Cohan teamed up with the Jewish producer Sam H. Harris, to create a formidable producing organization. In the 1920s, Harris, having broken amicably with Cohan, now joined the Jewish Irving Berlin in a like partnership. [5]

A Note on Assimilation and Jewish Humor

Where Weber and Fields differed from Harrigan and Hart was in their love of parody. Every year they produced a revue that included within it a send-up of a then-popular Broadway hit, with an off-kilter title. Hence, for instance, they called their version of Rostand's *Cyrano de Bergerac*, "*Cyrano de Bric-a-Brac*." It is an age's old theatrical device, dating back at least to the Greeks. Minstrel shows also often included skits that similarly spoofed current hits. Jews themselves long performed travesties of the Queen Esther story on Purim. So though they did not invent the parody, Jews certainly embraced it and practiced it in various forms of American entertainment, including the musical.

The tendency of Jewish musical artists toward such send ups was at some level a reaction against the pressure to assimilate. Humor and iconoclasm are often self-protective devices. Jewish humor ranged from violently anarchistic chaos, such as the Marx Brothers' *Animal Crackers*, to the adoring tweak, such as Mel Brooks' *The Young Frankenstein*. *Of Thee I Sing* represents a middle ground as a satire of the American political system that is both caustic and, because of its underlying patriotism, paradoxically affectionate.

Cohan and Herbert

The Jewish influence on Broadway was built upon a bedrock foundation already established by the Irish. Most important were two artists, contrasting sharply in substance and style: George M. Cohan and Victor Herbert. Cohan was primarily a vaudevillian, a top-notch song and dance man armed with bowler and cane, known for his kangaroo strut and singing out the of side of his mouth. Cohan wrote catchy, often patriotic, songs designed to appeal to everyday tastes, fit into stirring melodramas of his own design, usually starring himself. He was all bravado and nonstop energy, loud and urban like New York itself. Herbert on the other hand was a classically trained musician, a cello prodigy wed to a Metropolitan Opera star, who composed operettas along classical lines, complete scores resistant to the then common practice of interpolating hit songs randomly into the musical mix. Where Cohan was the popular "low," Herbert was the European-influenced "high" shaping early shows. Where Cohan wrote and starred in the raucous *Little Johnny Jones* and introduced his song "I'm a Yankee Doodle Dandy," Herbert composed and conducted his genteel *Babes in Toyland* with its lyrically nostalgic hit, "Toy Land." Their two artistic worlds, though both sprung from Irish roots, would remain apart until Jewish composers and writers found ways to unite the high with the low to shape the musical into a cohesive whole. But the story of that will come later.

Why "Ellis Island?"

This book's thesis is that Jews shaped the musical, aside from its entertainment value, to represent their grappling with the promise of the American Dream and the methods of assimilation that might help one achieve it. At some level the standard book musical became a sort of tacit blueprint on how to make it in America. It provided countless examples of outsider characters (suggesting ethnic peoples) trying to gain access to success and usually having to transform themselves in order to do so. Similarly, those same shows demonstrated to America itself how it might accommodate those newcomers. Thus the shows evolved into a sort of paradigm, an instructional mechanism demonstrating methods for the integration of the new into their new nation. The characters and the stories might change from show to show, but this basic dynamic is usually present thematically.

Broadway musicals were created mostly by Jews and often featured Jewish characters (whether acknowledged as such or not).[6] Elements of this first appear in the 1910s and reach their pinnacle with the book musicals of the musical's "golden age" of the 1940s and 1950s and into the mid-1960s. Written primarily with the New York audience in mind, which by the 1920s was increasingly Jewish, these shows celebrated the process by which America came to absorb its newcomers into the fold.

What is remarkable is that in the decades to follow, other groups found access to the American mainstream through use of the same paradigmatic model. Just as Jews shaped the musical to help them integrate, so too did later "fringe" groups similarly use it to comparable ends. In the 1960s, it was youth culture; in the 1970s it was American skepticism. The same musical model has been used subsequently by blacks, women, gays, and Latino/Latinas in subsequent years. Hence, I call Broadway musicals our "cultural Ellis Island" as it provides access to U.S. culture not unlike how Ellis Island once welcomed immigrants to America's New York shores. Keep in mind that Ellis Island's immigration officers also turned some away, while also often altering or even replacing difficult-sounding ethnic names into more familiar, American-sounding ones, easier for Americans to pronounce and remember, even if original names were then lost and forgotten.

Musicals and the Mainstream

There is value to studying Broadway musicals in particular when considering the theatre's impact on transforming American beliefs. Broadway is not responsible for making change, but it has encouraged and supported larger cultural efforts to do so. Primarily commercial, Broadway is an ostensibly conservative entertainment form. Shows that trumpet harsh political extremes rarely find a home on Broadway, nor are they intended to do so. Shrill topics usually only appeal to the choir, to those already sharing comparable beliefs. That is not to suggest they have no value or purpose, only that they impact a relatively smaller audience and endure only so long as their cause remains immediate. Theatre rarely leads the times; instead it tends to reflect the times, as Shakespeare pointed out in *Hamlet*.[7] In part this is practical since it takes time to write plays and go through the long, arduous process of trying to get them developed and staged. By the time a work does find the stage the events that originally inspired it are usually long gone. If it survives it is because it most often addresses larger, more universal issues rather than the problems of a particular time and place.

Broadway's commercialism makes it generally slow to change, hesitant to get too far ahead of its audience's tastes or beliefs for fear of losing paying customers. Most musicals are written with the New York audience in mind, even today. As early as the mid-nineteenth century, New York theatre entrepreneurs were intent on shipping their shows nationally to generate greater profit. Such work was of a quality sufficient to replace local theatrical efforts and assert urban tastes on increasingly national audiences. But the savvy vaudevillian knew how to adjust his or her material to fit local beliefs; what flew in New York may well not work in Poughkeepsie or Peoria, let alone Topeka or Tulsa.

However, it is a mistake to think the Broadway musical incapable of influencing social change. Its very conservative nature granted it special privilege with mainstream audiences. Because it usually shunned controversy, when a Broadway show did include controversial subject matter, that subject tended to find more ready acceptance. And as that show then toured nationally, it introduced that same "new" worldview to a still broader audience. That is not to say a show found acceptance in every region, but it certainly stood a far better chance of having its worldview gain some measure of acceptance than would a less commercial show with a more combative guise. Mainstream audiences might avoid attending a gay show like *Boys In the Band* or *Love! Valour! Compassion!* but be far less adverse to seeing *La Cage Aux Folles* because of its being light entertainment. Musicals implicitly promise a safety net to their audiences, assuring them that they need not take what is onstage as anything more than escapism. Yet by seeing a show like *La Cage Aux Folles* they are acknowledging the existence of gay life and its inclusion in the American landscape, not only culturally but socially, and perhaps even politically as well.

Broadway musicals have long measured their success not in aesthetic terms but rather by the length of their run. To some degree this implies a correlation between a show's duration and its degree of artistry, suggesting there is integrity in broad public approval. Regardless of relative aesthetic value, the number of performances is certainly a measure of mainstream audience acceptance. The longer a show runs means that a greater number and variety of people have seen it; truly successful hits brag of successful runs in foreign countries. This could be seen as asserting a multicultural appeal or could be seen as a form of American colonialism. Either way, such international success indicates broad acceptance—and hence approval—for the given musical and for its content. Here lies the Broadway musical's special power to influence change.

Consider Jerry Herman

Change did not happen all at once. It evolved over time in a pattern of gradual risk-taking, reflecting a steady opening-up of American sensibilities.

Introduction   7

For instance, after writing several revues, in 1961 Jerry Herman wrote *Milk and Honey*, which celebrated the founding of the State of Israel by having a group of Jewish American widows experience romance while visiting the still-fledgling state.[8] Producers clearly felt confident enough in the subject matter to risk investment; that the show ran for almost two years on Broadway proved them right. Herman then followed with several shows more conventional in subject matter (like *Hello, Dolly!*, *Mame*) establishing him as a prominent mainstream musical composer/lyricist. This "mainstream" reputation probably served him well in convincing producers to risk investing in his 1983 show, *La Cage Aux Folles*, which initially ran for over six years. So Herman, who is both Jewish and gay, dared to introduce to Broadway a show about Israel and then, twenty years later, introduced a show about gay life complete with cross-dressing. His shows may rely on conventional Broadway devices, but he is pioneering in his use of subject matter.

Is the Broadway musical then subversive? No. It is more a matter of its producers gauging the theatre-going public's frame of mind and taste. The "shocking" innovations a show may present are a risk, but a calculated risk. That risk is made by artists in association with business people, by innovators and by those more conservative who invest, both to support theatrical arts, and also hoping to make money. Again, commercial theatre follows and can validate more than it can genuinely innovate. Consider that Leon Uris's 1958 novel *Exodus* was a bestseller about the founding of the State of Israel, followed two years later by a hit Hollywood film of the same name. This no doubt offered evidence of sufficient positive interest in the topic to warrant the creation of *Milk and Honey*. Similarly, the French film *La Cage Aux Folles* had already had a successful run as a popular movie in America, again demonstrating the acceptability of its subject matter and the commercial appeal of the story itself. Once successfully done on Broadway, those topics tend to have a still greater degree of validation nationally, signaling their integration into mainstream American culture and life.

Still, Herman set the stage for other shows to come. In 1983 Herman composed the defiant "I am What I Am," sung as an anthem of gay pride. A decade later Jonathan Larson's musical *Rent* could feature in the song "Take Me or Leave Me" a chorus of "Take me for what I am," a confident declaration of gay sexuality. The former song is celebratory but also political; the latter asserts a gay self-worth that has become a cultural given.

Jewish Musicals as Democratic

Jewish composers and lyricists were inherently democratic. Why? Because they feared being viewed as outsiders and hence created shows that promoted diversity. It was not that they invented staged "variety"—that came from the nineteenth-century variety shows that later evolved into vaudeville. American popular entertainment long favored the diverse. Minstrel shows and vaudeville regularly included all sorts of performers and acts: singers, dancers, comics, animal acts, and so forth. P. T. Barnum's American Museum exhibited a panoply of freaks and the public adored it.

Rather, Jews embraced variety and embellished it in their musicals. Perhaps the key hallmark of an American book musical is its democratic makeup. They usually feature a broad range of characters, each with at least one distinctive song that reflects who they are and what they believe. And just as each character has his or her distinctive voice, so too do the music and words tend to express their individuality. Take *Oklahoma!* as an example: just as Laurie is different from Ado Annie, or Curly from Jud, so too do the substance and style of their songs markedly differ. This became a major characteristic of the American musical, as compared, for instance, with British book musicals, which tend to be more operatic, featuring more homogenous music, lacking comparable individuality.

One reason Jews may have proved comfortable creating multiple characters and sounds is because of their own experience adopting American ways. An immigrant's day was spent trying to master the language and behaviors of the dominant culture, striving to transform so that they might fit in better. Consequently, they became adept at placing themselves in others' shoes, speaking through others' voices, defining themselves by testing the mettle of others.

Listening to the music of a Richard Rodgers or an Irving Berlin, one is amazed at their transformative ability; they were chameleon composers, musical "actors" who could write music to define any sort of on-stage character, echo any culture's sound. However, they did so within their own Americanized vernacular. Rodgers' music for *The King and I* is not authentically Siamese, but it effectively captures the sense of the place for American ears. Or contrast Berlin's urbane song "Cheek to Cheek" to his hillbilly "Doin' What Comes Naturally." Both Rodgers and Berlin had enormous range and could also find just the right sounds for those specific characters in those specific situations.

Jewish tradition tends to promote empathy. The Passover seder urges Jews to imagine the plight of their enslaved forbearers and urges them to identify with others who suffer. The religion itself tends to promote trying to fix the world, to do what one can to make it a better place. Perhaps that tradition of empathy contributed to seeing things from others' points of view, which in turn informed Jewish playwrights, composers, and lyricists.

The tradition of identifying with others who suffer also drew Jews to identify with America's blacks. Furthermore, Jewish liturgical music had much in common with black music, with its musical laments and heart-wrenching grace notes. Both peoples shared the blues. Similarly, Jewish *Klezmer* music joined with black honky-tonk in shaping American jazz. All would find their way into Broadway scores.

Consequently, the score of an American book musical usually resembles a mixed bouquet of flowers. Each song is distinctive, each is complete in and of itself, and yet they function best collectively, complementing each other to form a cohesive, multifaceted whole. It is much like American city life, composed of multiple types, working together for their collective benefit, hence democratic.

Jews and Lyrics

Irving Berlin never completed school and was on the street at age thirteen. He accompanied his family from Russia at age four. Most likely the family spoke Yiddish at home, Hebrew at *shul*; English was not Berlin's native language. And yet Berlin's song lyrics demonstrate great range and sophistication.

One wonders what the Lower East Side of New York must have sounded like to a newcomer. English itself must have sounded garbled; greenhorns struggled to pick up words, then sentences, then phrases, trying to piece together meanings, needing to in order to survive. The teenage Berlin would have heard the equally strange sounds of a polyglot of different languages, from multiple nationalities, each with different intonations and rhythms, barely understood sing-songs of sound, searching intently for hints to their meaning. Add to that the fierce sounds of tough street slang, abbreviated and to the point. Meanwhile, trolleys rattled by, autos honked, vendors bellowed out their sales spiels, and densely packed masses noisily competed for attention and space. No wonder an Ira Gershwin, though educated, had an ear for the musicality of slang, and no wonder his brother George thought to include taxi horns in his otherwise classically orchestrated "An American in Paris." It resonates in Lorenz Hart's lyric in Hart and Richard Rodgers' first hit, "Manhattan": "And tell me what street, compares with Mott Street in July? Sweet pushcarts gently, gliding by." Lumbering pushcarts were anything but "sweet," and Hart fully expected his audience familiar enough to get the joke.

Jews are people of the Book. Torah study favors sharp analysis and inventive insights, with subtle understandings of the multiple possible meaning of words and phrases. There is playfulness to this type of study, a pleasure taken in clever word-play. To pray was to chant, to rhythmically sway to the familiar Hebrew prayers, finding meaning in both words and in the tempos of that recitation. Words and music. The Jewish liturgical word is *Nusach*, which is to say it is logogenic. Jewish prayer and music grow out of the meaning and sound of the sacred words. The joy in liturgical language and music no doubt spilled out into the secular settings as Jewish youngsters grew up to be the composers and lyricists of Broadway musicals.[9] Where there are words there are also ideas and hence issues to discuss and explore. Lyricist Yip Harburg liked to say, "Words make you think thoughts. Music makes you feel a feeling. But a song makes you feel a thought."[10]

The Major and the Minor

Reflecting centuries of grief, Jewish music favors the minor key. In music, major keys are cheerful; minor keys ache. Major keys are optimistic and confident; minor keys are mournful and filled with angst. Major keys are more about narrative than emotion; minor keys are more about emotion than narrative. Major keys express relief; minor keys indulge in feelings. Major keys assert that all is well, that we are off the hook; minor keys find a grief that underscores our ties to others, our fundamental shared humanity. Major keys rouse us to battle; minor keys allow us to weep.

Prior to 1900 most popular American songs employed melodies in major keys. Songs placed emphasis on a lengthy verse, on the telling of a story; the chorus was relatively brief. Think of all those Stephen Foster songs; even the most sentimental are couched primarily in major keys. It was the music of nineteenth-century America: active, confident, largely external and proud. It is the music of those who get things done, not those who linger and dwell.

In the early twentieth century, Jewish songwriters began to have hits writing songs in the minor key. Irving Berlin was famous for writing heart-wrenching ballads, designed to bring a tear to the eye. Such songs pared down the verses and placed greater musical emphasis on the repeated chorus. Storytelling was thus diminished and the "moral of the story," found in the chorus, drew listeners forward. The outcome became more prominent than the story, the emotion more than the intellect. You can hear it even in an upbeat song of Berlin's: the words to his "Blue Skies" are cheerful and optimistic, but the bass line drops steadily downward, creating a sad melody in contrast to the upbeat lyrics. The tension between the happy outlook and the musical lament makes for a certain depth and complexity heretofore unknown in American popular song.

It might be that the sudden success of minor key popular songs was because they were different and new. It might also be that their popularity reflected the sharp percentile rise in Jewish population, hence creating a substantial buying public for those songs. But the popularity of the songs transcended the boundaries of New York City and even America itself; they truly touched a universal nerve and endured.

It is interesting that the word "major" means primary, that which is the norm, which is favored and preferred. In contrast, the word "minor" means less important, that which is the exception, not the rule, which is used only sparingly and hence marginalized. By the same token, "major" here reflects the values of the dominant culture. It suggests power, the might of the majority. In this context the word "minor" reflects the values of those far less important, those who are at the will of the majority and its values, those who are minorities, who live on society's fringe.

Transposing Broadway

I call this book "transposing Broadway." "Transposing" is most often a musical term meaning changing the key of a pre-existing melody. Songs are usually transposed in order to fit a singer whose vocal range cannot handle the song's original key, either because the song as written is too high or too low in pitch.

This has certain power implications. Those auditioning for a Broadway show are most often rejected outright if their voices do not work for the score, whether under consideration for primary roles or for the chorus. However, the producers might waive that requirement if they wanted a particular star performer for their show. In that case the music might be adjusted (i.e. transposed) to fit their voice, or, as in the case of Rex Harrison in *My Fair Lady*, the songs were even originally written to accommodate that singer's vocal limitations. In other words, for those who lack leverage it is expected that their voice must fit the score. It is only when performers have leverage that transposing is even considered.

A variation of transposing would be to take a melody written in a major key and then redefine it by playing it in a minor key. Thus a familiar song like "Twinkle, Twinkle, Little Star," which is cheerfully written in a major key, when transposed into a minor key essentially becomes the stirring "Hatikvah," the national anthem of the State of Israel.

"Transposing" does not mean inventing. It rather means adjusting and adapting. Such alterations redefine the meaning and hence the impact of the original song. Composers write music in a particular key because that key has particular musical associations and meanings. It usually matters if something is written in, say, the key of B as opposed to being written in the key of F sharp. Change the key and you change the meaning.

Irving Berlin could only play the piano in one key and so used a specially designed piano. It had a lever which, when pulled, changed the musical key even as Berlin hit the same notes on the keyboard. This speaks to the man's limitations as a musician and also to his ingenuity and perhaps even his values. If the chosen singer was unable to sing in the original key then Berlin was perfectly willing to adjust his music to fit them. To Berlin songwriting was always a business first. As we will explore later, Berlin himself was more willing than most to abandon his born ways in order to become Americanized: he was happy to "transpose" the key, drop songs that did not work, and, in like manner, redefine his own ethnic identity.

But to Berlin it was never a one-way street; it was always a mutually negotiated transaction. To elaborate on the analogy, yes, Berlin pulled his piano's magic lever, adjusting his work to others' needs, but in return this allowed others to be able to sing his songs. And by singing his songs, not only did Berlin gain acceptance, fame, and fortune, he also transformed the musical tastes of a nation.

"Transposing" is thus not limited to musical settings—it can apply to any aesthetic or culture. While an Irving Berlin changed the face of American song, he and his predominantly Jewish peers similarly changed the face of the American musical. And since that was and is a commercial form requiring widespread acceptance, in some respects one could argue that those changes in the musical altered the American's view of themselves. This included redefining who and what constituted being "American."

As we move through the twentieth century and into the twenty-first century we see that this pattern continues even today. The Broadway musical stage remains an important setting for redefining the American character. The methodologies and forms invented and implemented by past

Jewish musical theatre artists live on both through the works of new generations of Jewish composers, lyricists, and librettists, as well as through those of other once-fringe groups who emulated (knowingly or not) the Jewish example, whether black, Latin, female or gay.

Transposing Broadway is the story of "transposing" the style and sounds of our music, a process that is ongoing. It is the story of transposing how musicals are constructed aesthetically and of how characters and subject matter have changed demographically to reflect the changing ethnic face of its audience. *Transposing Broadway* is thus the story of an ever-changing nation.

Methodology

This book is essentially dramaturgical in approach. Topics are examined through the study of representative shows and analyzed according to how they work onstage for both the immediate audience and for the larger community which that audience represents.

I use a montage approach here, more than a strictly narrative approach. By analogy, fans of musicals may know the difference between a book musical and a concept musical. The book musical broke through as the dominant musical form in 1943 with *Oklahoma!* The form is characterized by being essentially a narrative play with music, in which the story unfolds chronologically. Similarly, the concept musical broke through as a popular new form in 1970 with *Company*. The concept musical introduces a central idea or dynamic and each scene illuminates a different aspect of that dynamic. It is thus more montage than narrative. This book is assembled in like manner, with each chapter addressing a different dimension of the issue of assimilation and the musical. Furthermore, because those aspects do differ, I use a variety of scholarly methodologies to dissect how a given aspect may work. Whether drawing from Diaspora studies or sociology, from literary analysis or social history, from performance studies or directorial practice, my fundamental approach remains essentially dramaturgical in nature.

2. Hello, Young Lovers: Assimilation and Dramatic Configurations in the American Musical ◈

PART ONE: WINNING COMBINATIONS

Oscar Hammerstein is rightfully applauded for his life-long contributions to the American musical theatre. From his earliest efforts as librettist and lyricist working with the likes of Sigmund Romberg and Jerome Kern, through to his last phase when he teamed with composer Richard Rodgers, Hammerstein enjoyed enormous prestige, acceptance, and respect. He is also rightfully remembered for his proclivity for forming believable characters and promoting a humanistic agenda, be it the anti-prejudicial statements found in *South Pacific* or the political and social dilemmas faced by the King of Siam. And while he is sometimes lampooned for his overly folksy depictions and sometimes awkward or sugary wordplay, the underlying integrity of his work endures, as witnessed by the regular revivals of his and Rodgers' shows, as well as his masterwork with Kern, *Show Boat*.

Richard Rodgers and Oscar Hammerstein II have regularly been credited with the complete integration of the musical, creating the "musical play" out of what had been "musical comedy," initiating the dominance of book musicals and the musical's corresponding "golden age." Beginning with *Oklahoma!* (1943) this era lasted roughly for twenty years, only to be eventually toppled by the emergence of rock and roll and later the so-called concept musicals of the 1970s. However, if you place Rodgers and Hammerstein within the larger context of their times, other patterns emerge, as evident in their works, which in turn influenced not only the content but the form of the book musical itself.

What is in their subject matter and overall structure that enables Golden Age musicals to endure? Was there a dramatic formula such shows used that in part explains both their commercial viability as well as their universal appeal?

I believe that the story of the book musical's rise directly corresponds to the generational integration of urban ethnic groups into American culture and society. More specifically, I think the musical reflects the efforts by New York City's predominantly, though not exclusively, Jewish immigrant population to assimilate to American life, as they gradually gained acceptance and affluence.

The Canon, Threesomes, and Foursomes

There is a canon of musicals that are revived on a regular basis, even though those shows are decades old. They are all book musicals, essentially "musical plays" rather than "musical comedies," and the majority of them were created between 1945 and 1965. This includes the major works of Rodgers and Hammerstein, some by Lerner and Loewe, some Frank Loesser, and a smattering of works by other leading lights: *Kiss Me Kate*, *Annie Get Your Gun*, *Show Boat*, *West Side Story*, *The Music Man*, *Gypsy*, *Pal Joey*, *Damn Yankees*, and so on. There are other prominent musicals that are not often revived, usually because the books have grown dated, and hence are not on this list.

It is also true that in recent years some revivals feature reworked books, to make them more topical or less offensive, particularly in the portrayal of minorities. But most musicals have not needed drastic changes to story or characters in order to be revived.

There are many earlier classics that are never revived, despite possessing outstanding scores from musical theatre luminaries. Most come from the era of "musical comedy" and feature words and music by the likes of the Gershwins, Jerome Kern, Cole Porter, Irving Berlin, Rodgers, and Hart. When efforts are made to return to such material, an entirely new book is written, as was the case for *Crazy for You*. But aside from *Anything Goes*, most musical comedies from the 1920s and 1930s are kept on the shelf, unproduced, even though songs from those shows are considered popular classics and endure on their own.

Hence, a primary determinant for whether or not a show endures is its book. Almost every show in the "canon" is a book musical, suggesting that it is the story that enables the work to hold up over time. The relative quality and enduring universality of that book also determines the degree to which it can still function effectively on stage today.

But from where did the book musical come, and what are the components that enable it to still work? My journey led me well beyond the realm of musical theatre to believe that there is a direct relationship between how the Jewish population of New York City assimilated and evolved during the first half of the twentieth century, and how its strategies for upward mobility and acceptance were played out on the New York musical stage. Hence, the book musical reflects efforts to gain acceptance and recognition; its very dramaturgical structure is an expression of those broader societal dynamics and shifts, and certain dynamics of which still apply today and enable the form's perpetuation.

Musical Formations: Vaudeville and Operetta

The American musical was always a mongrel form. *The Black Crook* (1866) was not necessarily America's first musical, but it remains important because it was an amalgam of rip-roaring melodrama and French ballet.[1] Legend has it that the owners of New York's Niblo Garden Theatre took a female French ballet troupe, whose theatre had burned down, and plugged them into a fantasy script featuring much spectacle. The predominately male audience mostly came to ogle at the dancers' scandalously revealed legs, but this nevertheless created a landmark middlebrow event.

Blending divergent elements thus became intrinsic to the musical's format, and two specific elements became standard fodder for such shows. The first element was vaudeville, the fast-paced, glib, grassroots American entertainment phenomenon, with its comedic stereotypes, gag humor, song and dance, and catchy songs. The second element was operetta, invented by French composer Jacques (aka Jacob) Offenbach, itself a popularized, middlebrow take on grand opera.

Vaudeville drew upon largely American-born, Tin Pan Alley composers, whereas operettas came from largely European-born, classically trained composers. The former centered mostly on sales, the latter on "art." Therefore, the vaudeville tradition was democratic, designed to appeal to mass tastes, whereas the operetta mostly implied wealthy European aristocracy, with women in flowing gowns waltzing with immaculately uniformed men, swirling across vast, highly polished palace floors. One reflected America, the other an elite, foreign fantasy world; one spoke to the practical realities of urban American life, the other to a romantic dream world to which one might aspire.

For years a musical entertainment was either a "musical comedy" (which generally meant roots in vaudeville) or an operetta, even if set in the Canadian Rockies.

Lessons and Love

Even though the canon of book musicals often deals with substantial subject matter, the stories are still usually centered on romance. *The King and I* might be about colonialism, or the conflict between tradition and modernity, but the plot itself centers on the growing fondness between Anna and the King. Perhaps it is because America remains essentially a middle-class nation and, therefore, most concerned with domesticity; stories of "boy-meet-girl, boy-loses-girl, boy-gets-girl" remain at the crux of American collective values and hence are a popular staple. There are few if any commercially successful musicals that do not include that central romantic pairing.

Most musicals focus exclusively on how an outside force threatens the central duo's happiness. Sometimes this is a third party, usually a rival lover. Other times the "third party" might be selfish ambition, as in *Annie Get Your Gun*.

The Double Couple Motif

Most of the remaining shows feature more than one romantic couple. There is usually at least a second couple, sometimes even a third. This is most telling. If you look at the evolution of the musical prior to the so-called golden age you can see how the additional couple(s) evolved; in the era of the book musical, this already-established plot device began to be used to express larger societal issues, reflecting both artist and audience concerns.

There are strong advantages to the use of double couples, instead of a primary couple accompanied by a third party. When constructing in threes there is always someone who is the "odd man out," it is always two against one, with the members constantly changing. Threes therefore create chaos and disruption and are, as a result, very effective in either drama or farce, where asymmetry is the rule. But, in the end, two will be happy and the third usually not. However, double couples suggest that there is someone for everyone, with no one left out in the end, even if the final groupings are not to everyone's liking. Double couples are therefore symmetrical, which points toward artifice and traditional comedy. This device can also function as a foil: when the member of one couple loses a partner, their loss is heightened when placed beside the other couple's happy completeness. Consequently, this form can also amplify loss, adding greater dramatic poignancy.

Plots featuring multiple couples can be found in Roman comedy, *commedia dell'arte,* and Shakespeare. It was favored by Gilbert and Sullivan, who greatly influenced the twentieth-century American musical. But American musical theatre did not utilize it with any regularity until the toned-down Kern-Bolton-Wodehouse Princess Theatre musicals of the 1910s. Shows like *Oh, Boy!* and *Very Good Eddie* both relied upon the use of double couples. Perhaps it was due to the limited resources available at the tiny Princess Theatre; with a small cast, the double couple device was an efficient way to create variety and comedic misunderstandings.[2]

Significantly, from that point on librettists increasingly utilized double couples to reflect changes in the composition of their audiences. The primary couple in any given show reflects the societal ideals, not only of behavior, but also in terms of power. The secondary couple served a variety of functions that evolved over time, but they remained subservient to the interests of the primary couple and held lesser sway in the eyes of the audience. Generally speaking, the secondary couple might function in one of four different capacities: (1) they served as an antagonistic function to the primary couples' protagonist function; (2) they served as dramatic foils, highlighting by contrast key dynamics that favored the primary couple; (3) they served a comedic commentary of the primary couple's plight; (4) they spoke to an element of the audience demographically different from those to whom the primary couple addressed.

As the musical evolved from the 1910s up to the 1940s the secondary couple functioned mostly in the first three capacities, with some notable exceptions. But with the book musical firmly established with *Oklahoma!,* in 1943, the fourth element increasingly became a critical dynamic in that secondary couple's use.

Background Evolution of Double Couples

In 1915 Jerome Kern began a five-year run of writing small musicals staged modestly at the Princess Theatre, several blocks from Broadway. Librettist Guy Bolton's Princess Show books, especially those written with P. G. Wodehouse, favored farce, but there was a darker dimension to them. In *Oh, Boy!* (1917), for instance, the primary couple, George and Lou Ellen, are newlyweds but want to keep it a secret. Amongst the various friends who break into their apartment is Jackie Sampson, an actress on the lam from the law. Compared to the virginal protagonist and his bride, Jackie represents another element in society. Where the newlyweds are relatively innocent and somewhat old-fashioned, Jackie is modern and risqué.

In a sense it is no different than that usually found in Shakespeare. There is something for everyone in the audience, from the aristocrat to the groundling; Hamlet is for the politicos and philosophers, speaking in lofty verse, while the gravedigger is there for the groundlings, growling happily in prose. Bolton's script to *Oh, Boy!* appeals to the older generation, the younger generation, the old-fashioned, and the modern. It is smart, witty, lively, and fun. And its range of characters ensures its popularity.

When Bolton and Wodehouse wrote the better-known *Very Good Eddie* (1915), they again returned to the double couple motif, but this time the distinctions functioned differently. Each couple is composed of a dominating spouse and a meek spouse. Circumstances reshuffle the deck, so that the two domineering spouses (Percy and Georgina) end up separated from the two meek spouses (Eddie and Elsie), for whom the audience roots. Eddie and Elsie make do, trying to preserve propriety though instantly attracted to one another. It is clever and cute, with a predictable outcome. And though the configuration lacks the smarter angle of *Oh, Boy!*, it still defines the proper couples as being likable protagonists, with the other the less-likable antagonists. As such they serve as foils to each other, with only a sense that each eventually ends up where they rightfully belong. There is then diversity of characterizations amongst the two couples, but all still belong to the same social milieu.

Guy Bolton returned to the same formula twenty years later when he wrote the book to *Anything Goes* (1934). It resembles *Oh, Boy!* with a relatively innocent romantic pair (Hope and Billy) contending with the brash, worldly, outspoken actress, Reno Sweeney, who in the end winds up with a wimpy British aristocrat, who pales by comparison beside her.

In the Princess Shows, Jerome Kern is seen trying to match his operetta-based music to the American idiom. Though formal in tone to our ears, a song like "Till the Clouds Roll By" was viewed in its own day as revelatory for its quality, freshness, and downright catchiness. This is fitting. The Princess Shows attempted to present whittled down productions depicting average Americans in plausible situations, rather than extravaganzas built on exotic fantasy. Kern's music reflects this. We see him inventing ways to appeal to a popular audience by finding a precise musical expression for the characters and situations found on stage. This represents an important step toward what will become musical dramas, including Kern's own *Show Boat* written a dozen years later.

Kern's experimentation with blending operetta with American popular music was soon matched by Oscar Hammerstein II's books and lyrics. Hammerstein essentially assigned the operetta elements to the romantic,

WASP upper-class characters and assigned vaudevillian elements to the lower-class, increasingly ethnic, who were driven instead by sex. Hammerstein's composer partners matched this dichotomy through their music. Long European musical phrases, usually requiring highly trained voices, found homes in the ballads and romantic duets sung by Golden Age musicals' romantic leads. Secondary characters danced and sang to snappy songs echoing American vaudeville, requiring only limited vocal range.

It all made sense. Broadway composers and lyricists were of immigrant stock as was an increasingly large proportion of their audience. Families with recent roots in Western and Eastern Europe found pleasure in the familiar sounds of European-influenced operettas. Yet, now also Americans, they participated in a modern urban life that thrilled to the clever phrase and catchy refrain of popular songs. Was it commercial? Sure. But so too was the underlying promise of the American Dream. Upward mobility meant increased affluence as much as anything else. Just as they were themselves adjusting to America, becoming half Old World and half Yankee, so too did the evolving Broadway musical reflect a comparable blend. The characters thus matched the music, as the music helped define the characters. It was all so, well, democratic.

Most 1920s musicals did not make use of the double couple scheme. One major exception though is *The Desert Song* (1926), with a book by Otto Harbach and, significantly, Oscar Hammerstein II. The Harbach-Hammerstein team did not use the format for other shows they wrote in the period, most notably *Rose-Marie*. Why they turned to it for *The Desert Song* is unknown, but their use foreshadowed what Hammerstein would construct consistently later in his career.

The Desert Song is set in mythical Morocco and, clearly influenced by the then-popular Rudolph Valentino and Clara Bow films, features the French Foreign Legion, an elusive Robin Hood–inspired Arab hero (the meek Frenchman Pierre in disguise) who sweeps the heroine off of her feet. Margot, the heroine, is engaged to Paul, an overly aggressive French officer; Paul has had a secret romantic liaison with Azuri, a native woman. Also present are Benjamin, a bumbling British correspondent, and Susan, his brass-tacks girlfriend, there mostly for comic relief. It adds up to three couples in all, each with a distinctive persona and function. Margot and Pierre are primary, Paul and Azuri secondary, with the third couple Benjamin and Susan. Harbach-Hammerstein make Margot and Pierre's relationship entirely romantic. Their relationship is in the style of the European-inspired operettas of the day, and their songs are in the operetta vein. They are also supposedly French, though the audience would be encouraged to sympathize with them along American lines. In other words, though ostensibly "French" they are in fact American fantasy characters.

Margot and Paul then also represent the dominant culture and its ideals. There is nothing about them that would indicate they are other than WASP, despite their thinly proscribed "masks" of identity.

The secondary couple is less reputable. Paul is supposed to be heroic, but his zeal reveals him to be cruel, even sadistic. This is no match for Margot! While Pierre is revealed to be the heroic Red Shadow, Paul is similarly revealed to be a brute, and deservedly ends up with the native woman, Azuri. Period audiences would have deemed Azuri sexy, exotic—and essentially base. She dances sensually, is consumed by jealousy to betray our heroes, ruthless and brutal to a degree that matches that of the supposedly civilized Paul. Paul cannot have Margot, perhaps because he does not match her idealized standards, perhaps because he has already slept with Azuri and, therefore, is no longer "pure." So whereas the Margot/Pierre match is defined by romance, the Paul/Azuri match is defined by sex.

Paul/Azuri represent the bottom of the play's society: they are mixed ethnically (where Paul is Christian, Azuri is presumably Islamic); they are defined only in terms of their physicality (sex and violence); the music associated with them echoes Arabian themes, hence foreign to WASP America; and both pose threats to the primary couple. Benjamin and Susan, the third couple, mostly function as comic relief. Benjamin is a comedic of the sort later popularized by Bob Hope—bumbling, fast-talking, object of ridicule, but somehow keeps the girl. Benjamin is cowardly and shy of sex, though not quite effeminate; Susan is strong and assertive and entirely in favor of sex, though not quite masculine. In short, they are comedic, harmless outsiders caught in the middle of a full-blown melodrama, trying to survive relying on silly wit in the face of brute force. They are like clowns that somehow survive the Titanic. As such they are not subject to the moral absolutes that govern the other two couples: they will not be rewarded for operetta-inspired fantasy ideals, nor damned for misbehavior. No one cares if they have sex or not—the two deserve each other and we the audience are happy to have them around to break up the seriousness of the rest.

A few years later Hammerstein used comparable couples in his libretto for *Show Boat* (1927). Again we find the primary couple (Magnolia/Ravenal) who embody the WASP ideal of romantic love leading to marriage and children. They sing "Make Believe" when they first meet, a romantic operetta-style duet; their relationship is entirely serious, even sad. Juxtaposed against them is the secondary couple (Julie/Steve or Julie/Bill). Where Magnolia/Ravenal are WASP, Julie is of mixed blood; where Magnolia/Ravenal result in marriage, Julie is first with Steve, later with the unseen Bill, suggesting sex but not marriage; where Magnolia/Ravenal sing in operetta-like tones, Julie is identified as lower class, known for the minstrel-style "coon song" "Can't Help Lovin' That Man of Mine" and the prosaically wistful, "Bill." There are other couples in *Show Boat* as well, but none can be described as romantic. Ellie and Frank seem mostly concerned with ambition, Queenie and Joe focus on basic survival, and Cap'n Andy and wife Parthy are ever combative. So here the double couples serve as contrasting foils to each other, representing the upper half and the lower half of riverboat society. And since *Show Boat* is so concerned with the implications of racial inequality, it is fitting that both extremes of the caste system be represented through them.

Of Thee I Sing (1931) is one of the few early 1930s shows that is sometimes revived. It featured Gershwin songs and a George S. Kaufman book that made use of double couples in what was beginning to become a familiar configuration. The protagonist-couple is presidential candidate John P. Wintergreen and his girlfriend Mary Turner; the secondary couple is Alexander Throttlebottom and Diana Devereaux. Though a politico, Wintergreen marries for love, which also boosts his presidential campaign. He praises Mary's corn muffins and is later rescued from scandal by her giving birth, again the domestic ideal. Within the context of the play they are serious characters and their love is real. Wintergreen and his bride are both WASP and their campaign song is the closest thing to a ballad in the play, "Of Thee I Sing." In contrast, Throttlebottom is entirely a joke, cut from the same cloth as Benjamin in *The Desert Song*—bumbling, inept, but wins out in the end, and Diana is a conniving sex pot, ruthless and ambitious, akin to Azuri. And though not ethnic per se, she is related to the foreign monarch, Napoleon, a fact that places her outside American values and almost results in war. With Throttlebottom ending up with Devereaux we have another mongrel match, akin to Paul and Azuri, which resolves the plot but does not suggest genuine happiness or love; this duo represent sex, comedy, and outsiders, no longer a threat to the primary couple or to their happiness.

The Throttlebottom/Devereaux alliance is the ying to the Wintergreen/Turner alliance's yang, much as was the case for the Julie/Steve pairing compared to Magnolia/Ravenol. There is room for both pairs in American society, even if one is given clear preference and, along with it, power. After all, Wintergreen/Turner will succeed in their ambitions whereas

Throttlebottom/Devereaux will not, and the same holds mostly true for Magnolia/Ravenol, especially when compared to Julie/Steve. Still, the world of *Of Thee I Sing* and the world of *Show Boat* are enriched by the presence of both sorts of couples; they serve to fill out the communal reality, making the plot and characters seem more three dimensional. Their presence also acknowledges that failure is as possible as success in the world of both plays, and that for those who do not succeed there is a drop in the social order, a downward mobility, perhaps (in the case of Julie) even the hint of alcoholism leading to a not-so-distant death.

Musical Plays Arrive

With *Oklahoma!* (1943) the book musical was firmly established.[3] *Oklahoma!* is credited for its integration of book, music, lyric, dance, character, and theme. But in many ways *Oklahoma!* also was the amalgamation of every musical element that preceded it. On the surface it is a folksy, homespun tale centered on a romance and a picnic dance. Closer inspection shows it to be far more complex and sophisticated. Musically, the show blends operetta ("Many a New Day") with vaudeville ("Kansas City," "It's a Scandal! It's an Outrage!"); even the title number "Oklahoma!" hints at a jazzy blue note accompanying its chorus section. The same range is reflected in the dance numbers, from the Act I's ballet finale to Will Parker's buck-and-wing.

Oklahoma! also builds upon Hammerstein's earlier use of multiple couples. The primary couple, Curly and Laurie, are again romantic, serious, and WASP; the music they sing together are ballads, and Laurie even flirts with operetta, as suggested earlier. Will and Ado Annie, the secondary couple, enjoy a relationship built on sex, are comedic, and also are WASP.

Halfway through the show *Oklahoma!*'s couples reshuffle against type. Ado Annie is tempted by Ali Hakim, a thinly veiled Jewish character: sexual, comedic, and decidedly ethnic. Jud wins a date with Laurie. Jud is lecherous, serious, and, though not ethnic, decidedly an outsider. Curly also flirts with the obnoxiously flirtatious Gertie. In the end, after Jud's death, pairings are restored according to proper type: Curly with Laurie, Will with Ado Annie, and Ali Hakim with Gertie. Jack has found his Jill.

Introducing an Ethnic Twist

Whereas in *Show Boat* Hammerstein overtly asserted black themes, in *Oklahoma!* Hammerstein quietly asserted ethnic themes. Ali Hakim, like

Jud, is an outsider who serves the on-stage community. But where Jud must die, Ali Hakim is allowed greater acceptance by the play's end. Jud's lust threatens to destroy the primary couple; Ali wishes to sleep with Ado Annie, but has no desire for permanence, and hence is not a serious threat to Will and Ado Annie. Besides, it is clear in both "I Caint Say No" and in "All 'Er Nothing" that neither Will nor Ado Annie are particularly faithful to each other. Ado Annie's talk of marriage spooks Ali Hakim and threatens Will, but it is done as comedy. Laurie, in contrast, views love and marriage as serious ideals, even if she kisses Curly with unbridled enthusiasm. Jud's sexuality threatens to destroy Laurie's youthful innocence, and his reappearance on their wedding day actualizes the danger he always posed. Hence Jud must be destroyed, according to the play's value system.

Compared to Jud, Ali Hakim's advances are harmless because he does not disturb the status quo. In "It's a Scandal! It's an Outrage!" Ali complains how nowadays sex must always lead to marriage, articulating his desire to stay away from the finger-wagging forces of civilization. If Ado Annie wants to remain "wild and free," so too does Ali Hakim. In the end he happily surrenders Ado Annie to Will, and, unable to control his urges, winds up with Gertie in a shotgun wedding. No one seems to notice that this is a mixed marriage.[4] Ali is thus tamed, converted to the community's lifestyle and beliefs, like it or not. It is a forced assimilation, yet integrates him into the WASP community. Ali's acceptance is ritually blessed by Curly and Laurie at their own wedding festivities. In the end Ali Hakim must adjust to them, not they to him. This storyline is especially pointed since Ali Hakim was clearly modeled on the Jewish peddlers who roamed the West. Perhaps to tacitly emphasize the point, Rodgers and Hammerstein cast the comic Yiddish actor Joseph Buloff in the role.

Hammerstein repeatedly used double couples in all of his shows with Rodgers, though with telling variations. In *Carousel* (1945) the primary couple (Billy and Julie) are not ethnic, per se, but are decidedly outsiders. The Snows are the secondary couple and are portrayed as slightly comedic and entirely part of the respectable middle class. It is Billy's efforts to gain upward mobility that ultimately doom him and his romantically based love for Julie. But in the end he gains salvation and acceptance in death, singing the pseudoreligious "You'll Never Walk Alone": he is no longer a roustabout but, in death, an angel or prophet, converted to a higher sensibility. His and Julie's love, once almost illicit, is transformed to the spiritual, the sacred, and both are cleansed because of it. As such they trump the affluent, materialist Snows; the "fringe" characters gain prominence.

In *South Pacific* (1949) the primary couple (Emile and Nellie) are juxtaposed against the secondary couple (Cable and Liat). Scholar Andrea Most notes that Liat remains silent, that she is only an ethnic pasteup of a character, two dimensional, and only a plot device.[5] True. But so too is Emile, in a sense. Another angle on the play is that Cable and Nellie are essentially the natural couple: both are Americans (though Cable comes from money and Nellie does not), both stuck in a foreign land, both plagued by the home-style prejudices they carry with them. Moreover, both Cable and Nellie find true love in the South Pacific, and find it amongst the Polynesian locals, not from amongst the American soldiers and nurses. If as Americans they came to Polynesia to convert the natives, in the end it is the natives that convert (and free) them; America seemingly taught them to hate, whereas the Tonkinese taught them to love. For the aristocratic-born Cable, his love for Liat means personal happiness, but fettered by a conservative upbringing he recognizes his love (passion, sex, ethnic mixing) will result in downward mobility in America. For the down-home Nellie, her love for Emile also means personal happiness, but perhaps because she is not as tied to tradition as is Cable, she has the capacity to act with greater personal freedom and learns to accept native ways. However, the suggestion is that she will stay amongst the Tonkinese married to Emile, and will never have to face the folks back home and their prejudices. It also helps that Emile, though once wed to a native woman and possessing mixed children, is French. The continental identity trumps the American in 1940s culture wars. And this dynamic is heightened by the casting of Ezio Pinza, an opera singer, in that role. As a result, Emile is exotic and unorthodox, and an outsider, but entirely acceptable given his highbrow affiliations.

Given the initial template of double couples, then, Emile and Nellie are less ethnically mixed (even with the native but French-singing children) than are Cable and Liat. Emile and Nellie's relationship is romantic and will lead to domesticity (she serves soup at the end); Cable and Liat's relationship is sexually based and is hence doomed. It is not unlike the couple construction found in Hammerstein's earlier work, *Show Boat*. Cable, like Julie before him, is doomed, but his destruction paves the way for Nellie's future happiness (much like Julie does for Magnolia's career); Cable dies, but Nellie finally realizes how deeply she wants Emile to survive that same suicide mission, triggering her final transformation and acceptance of more liberal ways.

Musically, the social distinctions in *South Pacific* are played out mostly between the lovers on one side and the enlisted men on the other, which is to say those who love versus those who fight. The high-toned romantic ballads are all sung on stage in moments of racial mixing: "Bali Hai," "Some Enchanted Evening," and "Younger Than Springtime." The GIs enjoy more carnal, comedic material: "There Is Nothing Like a Dame" and "Honey Bun." Caught in the middle are songs sung by American soldiers, to their copatriots, as they struggle with inner conflicts (inner wars?) caused by love: Nellie's love rant with her nurse friends "I'm Gonna Wash That Man Right Out Of My Hair" and Cable's scathing indictment, "You Have to Be Carefully Taught," again sung amongst fellow soldiers.

Carousel (1945), *The King and I* (1951), *Flower Drum Song* (1958), and *The Sound of Music* (1959), all again feature the double couple configuration. In the first three shows, the double couples represent the clash between traditional and modern ways, with the modern equated with adopting Western ways. Again, the primary couples are more traditional in both shows and their songs are more serious and ballad based, which reflects romantic and domestic values. The secondary couples, by contrast, are more sexual and/or passionate in their intent, as they desire to break with tradition as it threatens their personal happiness. *The Sound of Music* use of double couples is less pronounced, with the secondary couple (Liesl and her boyfriend Rolf) at first innocent ("You Are Sixteen") and later sinister when Rolf becomes a Nazi. But Maria is a stranger who invades the Captain's house (community) and is able to convert the Van Trapp family to her view of life. And just as Maria transforms the family toward that which is conventionally "good," the world outside is being converted to "evil" via the Nazi invasion of Austria. The family must emigrate and flee toward freedom. And as was the case in *Carousel*, the rebellious Maria (like Billy) finds herself through domestic duties and achieves a higher spiritual level, reinforced by another Rodgers pseudoreligious song, "Climb Every Mountain."

The Rodgers and Hammerstein shows established the standard—and formula—that others then followed. Significantly, a number of the most successful also utilized that double couple paradigm, and along with it comparable themes of insiders versus outsiders and implied assimilation. Lerner and Loewe's *Brigadoon* (1947) is a prime example. Two Americans (Tommy and Jeff) travel in Scotland (a foreign country) and come upon Brigadoon, a magically preserved eighteenth-century village, destined to appear only once each century. The two Americans fall for village girls and hence form two of the play's three couples: Tommy and Fiona, Jeff and Meg. But it is also the day of Jean's wedding to Charlie, at the expense of Harry Beaton. In terms of plot construction, the Jean/Charlie wedding represents the communal center of the play: Jean and Charlie represent the perpetuation of the status quo, and their union will no doubt result in children. Harry also exists in this cultural center, but his bitter disappointment with Jean's rejection causes him to try to flee. But if anyone leaves Brigadoon then the magic spell that protects it will break, signaling the town's demise. Harry is denied the right of the émigré, so unable to leave he dies.

The other two romances exist more at the town's fringe. Tommy and Jeff are both clearly outsiders. But Fiona is also marginalized as the older, unwed daughter. Similarly, Meg is marginalized as the promiscuous, comedic character of lower social stock. Consequently, Tommy and Fiona form the romantic duo and the purity of their love enables the town to reappear at the play's end to accommodate Tommy's acceptance. Jeff and Meg, on the other hand, form the secondary couple, comedic in tone and dedicated entirely to sex, incapable of long-term commitment. She is a Scottish Ado Annie, he an American Ali Hakim, a reluctant groom, just passing through. Unlike Charlie and Jean, the other two couples are liminal, operating on the edge between Brigadoon and modernity, and the audience is kept unsure as to which way any will totter.

Jeff is also modern, urbane, and cynical, whereas Tommy is nostalgic, idealistic, and romantic. Jeff fits in with modern-day Manhattan, Tommy does not. His discovery of Fiona rescues him, just as her finding a mate rescues her. But where Harry Beaton was not allowed to emigrate, Tommy can. Perhaps it is because Harry runs due to hate, knowing it will destroy others, whereas Tommy approaches Brigadoon appreciatively, with love, eager to add to the race. Tommy thus gains admission, in essence taking Harry's place, eagerly converting to Brigadoon and its ways, leaving his past identity behind. The idealized dream represented by Brigadoon is a fantasy Tommy happily buys into with its promise of eternal happiness and marital bliss. It is a Scottish version of the American Dream, although the hero ironically flees America to attain it.

Musically, *Brigadoon* relies upon the operetta/vaudeville blend, though written with a Scottish intonation. Tommy and Fiona "speak" through operetta-tinged ballads such as "The Heather On the Hill" and "There But For You Go I"; the comedic Meg is given the boisterously bawdy, "My Mother's Wedding Day" sung to Jeff, a vaudeville number if ever there was one, albeit with a Scottish slant. Cementing the cultural/ethnic differences, Loewe's music reinforces Scottish tradition in the wedding's sword dance. "Come to Me, Bend to Me" works equally well as a romantic ballad and as something sung by an Irish tenor on the vaudeville stage, provided he were dressed in kilt and tam. Perhaps one of the most significant yet subtle moments in the show is when Tommy temporarily returns to America, and is found drunk and depressed in a bar. The orchestra plays the "Brigadoon" theme, but does so in a slow boogie-woogie style, at once mocking old Scottish ways while also satirizing how American popular culture distorts meaningful nostalgia. One wonders if the music is actually being played in the bar or exists solely in Tommy's head to haunt him. I would vote for the latter, as it functions to underscore his disappointment and loss.

Frank Loesser's *Guys and Dolls* (1950) is perhaps the epitome of the double couple format and its assimilative associations. Again we find two couples: Sky and Sarah, on the one hand, and Nathan with Adelaide on the other. Both Sky and Sarah are portrayed as outsiders to the dominant, local gambling community; Sky because he is a loner, Sarah because she is with the Salvation Army. But later we find that Sky's real name is the Biblical-sounding "Obadiah" and that he comes from Midwest farm stock. The name "Sky" points to heaven and he is the proper match for the religious Sarah. Sky brings her down to earth, even as she inspires him upward toward marriage. Their relationship then is romantic and serious, about as operetta-like as Loesser gets as together they sing the gentle ballad "I'll Know."

Nathan and Adelaide, by contrast, are probably Jewish. In "Sue Me" Nathan calls himself by the Yiddishized "nogoodnik" and also asks the Yiddish query, "nu?", that Adelaide clearly understands. They are recognizably New York types. And while there seems to be genuine affection for one another, their relationship centers more on sex than marriage, much to Adelaide's regret. As the secondary couple they fit the mold of being ethnic, sexually based, comedic, and singing songs reminiscent of vaudeville.

In fact, the entire gambling community is a microcosm of ethnic New York culture. Gambling is their religion. They sing "The Oldest Established Permanent Floating Crap Game in New York" as a paean to tradition. The song's final verse ends in reverent chords, in part barbershop, but more akin to liturgical music. The crap game is their sacred ritual. "Prophet" Sky and missionary Sarah get the gamblers to "see the light" and correct the error of their ways. Sky bets on their souls—and they lose. Consequently, all end up in the mission house and join a rousing gospel number, singing their repentance. "Sit Down You're Rocking the Boat" is a conversion scene, where all surrender their former selves (gamblers, ethnic) and embrace the proselytizing Protestantism promoted by Sarah's Salvation Army. Having thus assimilated, marriage is now possible. Sky weds Sarah, and Nathan can finally wed Adelaide.

Cole Porter's *Kiss Me Kate* (1948) plays with the double couple scenario by juxtaposing warring actors Fred and Lilli against their alter egos, Petruchio and Kate. Similarly, secondary couple Lois and her gambling boyfriend Bill also play Shakespeare's secondary couple in *Taming of the Shrew*, Bianca and Lucentio. Fred and Lilli, once wed, will again wed by play's end, demonstrating their fundamental domesticity. Musically they sing "Wunderbar" together, a waltz clearly inspired by Viennese operetta, and also the haunting ballad, "So In Love," which establishes their relationship as romantic, rather than sexual. They are also lead actors in the company, the top of the pecking order, reinforced by their star Shakespearean roles. The "secondary" Lois and Bill are more sexually based and irresponsible, as demonstrated by their song "Why Can't You Behave?" Bill mixes with disreputable gangsters and also dances with several black performers (Paul, Fred's dresser, and two friends) who perform the suggestive, "Too Darn Hot." Bill and Lois are thus comedic and flighty, a lower rung in 1940s WASP America's social ladder.

And yet the message of *Kiss Me Kate* seems to be that while one might dress up in high culture and try to use it for their own advancement, ultimately they cannot disguise their true identity. Though acting the highbrow Shakespeare, Fred and Lilli still behave as unruly, egocentric actors; the singing gangsters argue the merits of using Shakespeare to get girls, but not for romantic (love, marriage) intent but rather for crude (sexual) intent. The outward guise of assimilation, in the end, is a fraud. But since the audience roots for all the abovementioned characters, such behavior is not condemned, merely acknowledged as being an acceptable fact of life.

The last show to consider here is *West Side Story* (1956). Obviously a work designed to portray the destructiveness of prejudice, Arthur Laurents' book also adheres to the double couple format. The primary couple (Tony and Maria) are romantic, sincere, and represent the hope of the future. They sing together in tones akin to classical music ("One Hand, One Heart" and "Tonight"), and though ethnically mixed, suggest domesticity and peace. The secondary couple (Bernardo and Anita) are sexually passionate and entirely ethnic. Since the Puerto Ricans portrayed in the show are newcomers, they do not have the established social clout of the self-styled Americans. They still have one eye on from where they came, rather than solely on America. Yet there is also a balance here as shown musically: if the Puerto Ricans sing the comedic and yet satiric "America," the non-ethnic Jets sing the comparable "Officer Krupke." Musically, each song echoes the distinctive sounds of the two cultures, but lyrically they are both clever list songs, in the same vaudeville tradition as

"Brush Up Your Shakespeare," albeit with a sharp satirical bite. The show suggests that the gangs become more like Tony and Maria, (i.e., mixed), and therefore abandon their ethnic differences. Only then will they have a chance for future success in America. *West Side Story*, paradoxically given its dominant themes of opposing intolerance, is itself intolerant of clinging to one's ethnic identity in the face of assimilation. In the end the survivors sing "There's a Place for Us" ironically over Tony's dead body, a cautionary haunting dirge, akin to Rodgers and Hammerstein's pseudoreligious musical endings, yet written with heartbreaking pathos despite the hopeful lyric.

The Rise of Ethnic Prominence

In the roughly twenty years between *Very Good Eddie* and *Oklahoma!*, a shift occurred in the portrayal of the double couple. At first both the primary and secondary couple were WASP, differing only in personality or lifestyle. But by the time of *Oklahoma!*, perhaps due to Hammerstein's invention, the primary couple embodied romantic love, operetta, sincerity, and basic WASP values, whereas the secondary couple embodied passion, popular culture, the comedic, and were increasingly ethnic. Broadway thus reflected its changing New York City audience, perhaps in reassuring ways. The WASP order was in power, and it was generally welcoming and benevolent. Even though immigration had been short-tailed since the early 1920s, the preexisting ethnic population had gradually gained ground: politically, socially, economically, and culturally. Broadway musicals reflected this: the second couple lacked the primary couple's prestige and had their foibles, but they had increasingly become a welcome, colorful component in the communal whole.

The emergence of the ethnic figure as hero occurred in the dozen years following World War II. Ethnic Marlon Brando and Kirk Douglas now shared top billing with the Clark Gables and Gary Coopers of the world; Marilyn Monroe now partied with the multiethnic/racial/religious Rat Pack. This all culminated with the 1960 election of John F. Kennedy, the first Irish Catholic president. Heroes gave way to antiheroes, the righteous to the cool. Civil Rights legislation further encouraged public ethnicity.

You can trace the evolution of the ethnic hero through their depictions in American musicals. By the late 1950s the ethnic figure, until then relegated to secondary roles, came to the forefront on the musical stage. Note their proclaimed presence in *West Side Story* (1956), in *Most Happy Fella* (1956), *Flower Drum Song* (1958), and in *Fiorello!* (1959): all featured as central characters recent immigrants to America struggling to adjust to American life.

This dynamic became increasingly prominent in the 1960s: Tevye and his village of Anatevka are Jewish. *Cabaret* demonstrates how Nazism (anti-Semitism) threatens Jew and Gentile alike. Other hit shows of the period boast similar concerns. *Man of La Mancha* focused upon a high-minded outsider, fighting for idealism and combating pressures to conform. Don Quixote is also an aristocrat who cavorts with the mongrel lower classes, confusing them with nobility. In the end it is they who prove the truly noble, compared to the base actions of Don Quixote's aristocratically born family. The message is clear: true nobility is gained by merit, not by birth.

Roll Over Beethoven

It is often argued that the rise of rock and roll ended the reign of the book musical. I would go one step further. Because the book musical is directly linked to the aspirations and assimilative experience of the second generation of immigrants, it could not survive once that generation achieved its social and political goals. Unlike their upwardly mobile parents, members of the so-called baby boom generation were born into acceptance and affluence, as part of the Establishment. There was no longer the need to prove oneself, no insecurities about one's rightful place in society. Consequently, the musical, with its function to educate and reassure, did not hold the same meaning, nor did it serve the same critical function for the new generation as it had for their *parents*'.

The pull of rock and roll, along with the emerging Civil Rights Movement, both pointed downward. Affluent kids, assured of their superior place in society, turned their attention to the disadvantaged, not only because of idealism but also because of a sense that there was an authenticity and meaning found amongst the black urban poor that seemed sorely lacking from their own upper–middle class lives. Well-to-do teens felt free to imitate the lower class, assured that they themselves could never fall from their high societal perch. It was perhaps some sort of latent identification with their parents' impoverished roots that drew them there. Regardless, the musical now lacked meaningful appeal, and seemed hollow once robbed of its symbolic importance. The rise of the book musical had reflected their parents' experience: the rise of the second generation (i.e., the children of immigrants), ascending within American society, gaining acceptance and power.[6]

PART TWO: MOVIN' ON UP

Second Generation Jews in Particular

The musical's ascension corresponded to the emergence of New York City's Jewish audience. In America since colonial days, Jews did not publicly assert their ethnicity until the late nineteenth century. They mostly descended from German Jews, highly Westernized, who sought acceptance through a degree of invisibility. The late nineteenth century's mass migration of Eastern European Jews, however, forced change in this public persona. Russian Jews, by contrast, lacked any refinement (embarrassing their German-Jewish brethren), and formed separate enclaves in New York's Lower East Side, included a thriving Yiddish language theatre. As the twentieth century progressed Russian Jews gradually improved their lot. Their children grew assimilated, rejecting Yiddish theatre for nonethnic American entertainments, in fact becoming an increasingly large proportion of New York's theatre-going audience.[7]

Except for a few notable exceptions (Cohan, Herbert, Porter), the creators of musicals were all Jews. It is not surprising, given their religious backgrounds, that they favored works that explored issues of social justice. But it is equally significant that their more personal concerns might find their way into shows as well. More specifically, they were mostly all the children of immigrants. As the second generation, they shared a willingness to assimilate to American life in an effort to gain acceptance and to find economic success, to realize the American Dream. Surrendering one's own cultural identity, to assimilate, seemed part of the bargain. While echoes of Jewish musical traditions occasionally found their way into the music they wrote, for the most part they sought a larger acceptance and adjusted their creativity—and perhaps themselves—accordingly. The Broadway musical stage therefore reflects these artists' attitudes and effort, but also reflects their cultural evolution, from crass vaudeville to slick musical comedy to the more sophisticated book musical, or "musical plays" as they preferred to call them.

More than simply entertain, book musicals embodied the ideals and aspirations of this second generation. When one thinks of the book musicals beginning with *Oklahoma!* one thinks of integration—integration of book, music, and dance. Establishing the book musical prototype, Rodgers and Hammerstein in *Oklahoma!* included a mish-mash of high and low culture, and notoriously wove in a ballet to forward the plot. But in the same breath Rodgers and Hammerstein were exploring societal integration. Hammerstein's libretti established a blueprint for assimilation, a model they religiously followed, as did their imitators throughout the book musical's heyday. With a few exceptions, the most successful of the period's book musicals all offered lessons in acceptable behavior and a model for how Jews might fit into dominant WASP America. They thus instructed their entire audience, Gentile and Jew alike, throughout the 1940s and 1950s.

Their fundamental assumption was that Jews, like any contemporary ethnic group, aspired to rise in American society. Book musicals explored many issues, often centering on social justice. But to a still greater degree they explored the dynamics of being an outsider, trying to gain access to an idealized America community, learning to adjust, in order to gain admission and hence to enjoy the economic benefits that accompany that acceptance.[8] Comedic book musicals usually ended with dreams realized; dramatic book musicals usually ended with dreams shattered. And the "dream" in question can be clearly and consistently equated with the "American Dream" that the authors and composers—and their audience—fought to attain.

Genteel Hegemony and Notions of Refinement

But there was opposition amongst the WASP aristocracy to opening American society to the diverse ethnic populations. Beginning in the mid-nineteenth century, the genteel elite's political power slowly gave way to machine politicians and ward bosses, whose power was based upon the newly arrived immigrant populations. Largely ousted from the political sphere, they instead turned to less materialistic standards by which to measure acceptance into the highest circles. Issues of purity and refinement became the measure by which acceptability would be determined, and many of the old elite took positions as guardians of culture on the boards of art museums, symphony orchestras, libraries, universities—and art theatres. They became standard-bearers for high culture, even as popular entertainments gained considerable ground, as a defense of their values and to protect their vested interests in preserving the societal hierarchy.[9]

Meanwhile, many former immigrants gained wealth. But the standard amongst the elite was no longer simply money, it was refinement. Even as the predominant New York audience flocked to see Ziegfeld's tasteful displays of conspicuous consumption, a form particularly appealing to new money, old money was turning more toward European modernism, thereby raising the cultural bar.[10] In response, the first generation sent their children to colleges, sometimes even Ivy League, and, in imitation of the genteel elite, encouraged mastering European culture through travel abroad. Consequently, many musical theatre luminaries benefited from this trend: Richard Rodgers, Lorenz Hart, and Oscar Hammerstein all attended Columbia University, as did Herbert Fields. And if unable to attend college, the movement toward refinement impacted others as well: note how George Gershwin strove to succeed, not only as a commercial composer, but as a classical one as well.[11]

Theatrically, the emergence of the Little Theatre Movement, and particularly its star playwright Eugene O'Neill, demonstrated American refinement, akin to the efforts of the WASP elite. The organization that promoted O'Neill and produced his work was the Theatre Guild, which was dedicated to placing theatre on a cultural par with the symphony, art museum, and ballet.[12]

It makes sense then that it was the Theatre Guild that provided the idea and agreed to produce what was to become *Oklahoma!*. Just as Eugene O'Neill sought to combat crass melodrama by creating a new, higher-brow American drama, so too did Rodgers and Hammerstein. They combated the tired musical comedy form by creating the artistically integrated book musical. And just as O'Neill modified classical European theatre traditions in forming his innovations, so too did Rodgers and Hammerstein in shaping *Oklahoma!*. The book now mattered. Characters were to be three dimensional. Songs functioned much like Shakespearean soliloquies. The setting was more realistic than was the musical theatre norm. Just as *The Count of Monte Cristo* gave way to *Desire Under the Elms*, so too did *Rose-Marie* give way to *Oklahoma!*.

But there was more. *Oklahoma!* included ballet. Ballet was not new to a Richard Rodgers musical; *On Your Toes* (1936) featured his "Slaughter on Tenth Avenue," choreographed by no less than George Balanchine. But in *On Your Toes* the dance was a dance number, even if operating within the plot. In *Oklahoma!* choreographer Agnes DeMille had characters break into ballet-inspired dance as naturally as they broke into song and did so to forward the plot. Classical ballet was not supposed to be on the musical comedy stage; that venue was for crowd-pleasing jazz or tap. Its inclusion exposes *Oklahoma!* as a deliberate effort to raise the form's status. Having classical dance meant that the music had to live up to classical standards. This was the stuff of high culture, not popular culture. Though situated around a rural picnic dance, *Oklahoma!* was meant as high art.

If the WASP elite had made refinement the *sine qua non* for acceptance into the American establishment, more meaningful than shear wealth, then

Rodgers and Hammerstein, along with their imitators, aimed for admission to the club. Furthermore, if they were in the vanguard, their audience was not far behind. Perhaps attending a book musical was not the same as attending the symphony, opera or ballet, but it was a close second. It makes further sense, then, that the Rodgers and Hammerstein team would again use Agnes DeMille to stage *Carousel*, and that they then created the role of Emile DeBeque for a Metropolitan Opera star, Ezio Pinza. If Rodgers could write for ballet he could also write for opera. And writing material that would be worthy of Pinza coming to the Broadway stage further validated the musical as approaching high culture.[13]

Assimilation and the Rewards of Lost Identity

The only lyric Leonard Bernstein wrote for his sparkling musical mélange *Candide* was entitled "I am Easily Assimilated." In it the Old Lady sings of her remarkable ability to transform herself as she roams the world from nation to nation, culture to culture. Surprisingly, Bernstein's lyric has this Voltaire character improbably born in Ruvno Gubarnya, which is to say a Jewish-Polish shtetl, as she boasts: "My father spoke a High Middle Polish/ In one half hour I'm talking in Spanish/I am so easily assimilated...." It is the song of a Jew, unexpectedly interpolated into an eighteenth-century French satire, prancing around the 1950s Broadway stage to a Latin beat.

This is not to say that audiences attended musicals deliberately to learn the lessons of assimilation; they generally attended to be entertained. But the presence on stage of characters that, even if indirectly, represented their own identities and lives, certainly added to their ability to sympathize and enjoy. Hence, the staged display of ethnicity itself provided powerful validation, legitimizing the societal claims of the seemingly disinherited that they too deserved a piece of the cultural and political pie. The same dynamics still hold true for any minority or disenfranchised group, as seen in the plethora of scholarship on identity politics.[14]

In the case of the musical, both the presence of ethnic characters and the recurrence of themes pertaining to immigrant experience permeate the entire canon of works. Musical plays resonate with issues pertaining to the American Dream with its promise of opportunity, upward mobility and financial reward; they also reverberate with issues of assimilation and conversion as the means to achieve those secular ends. Book musicals therefore serve as symbolic ritual, acting out of the promise of America. On the surface they may seem superficial and frivolous, but when placed within this larger sociohistorical context, one begins to understand that they served a symbolic function and embodied the profound concerns of much of their audience. No wonder musicals reassured, well beyond simple issues of escapism. No wonder the form endures more than almost any other American dramatic or theatrical form. Still, the musical rings hollow without an audience informed by this larger historical context to provide it with symbolic meaning, much as a religion, robbed of belief, is reduced to picturesque myth.

The classic book musical expressed their creative artists' aspirations and lives, as well as those of their immediate New York audiences. But because they addressed what it took to attain the American Dream, the bulk of those shows could effectively speak to audiences well beyond New York and its particular ethnic mix. They are in fact national dramas, addressing the basic American experience, reaffirming our nation's fundamental values. That they also often contain the social and political beliefs of their creators is almost incidental within this larger societal framework.

Transitions

Irving Berlin's first hit was "Marie from Sunny Italy," reflecting his ethnic surroundings; much later in his career he wrote the WASP anthems "White Christmas," "Easter Parade," and "God Bless America." George and Ira Gershwin's first collaboration told modestly of their "cousin in Milwaukee;" Gershwin later parodied highbrow pretence by pointing out "you say tomato and I say tomahto" and mostly wrote of sophisticates, not to mention George's internationally acclaimed classical music efforts. Richard Rodgers and Larry Hart began with "and tell me what street, compares with Mott Street in July?" and a decade later urbanely noted how "the lady is a tramp." Still later Rodgers, with Hammerstein, wrote songs about politics and nature. Upward mobility often meant abandoning one's roots and adopting the concerns and lifestyles of the well born.[15]

In marking the hundredth anniversary of Richard Rodgers' birth, critic John Lahr described the composer as being particularly concerned with appearance, an ambitious social climber, a mass of contradictions. He also notes how *Rodgers'* sought to bury his earlier affiliation with Lorenz Hart after achieving still greater success with Oscar Hammerstein II. Lahr is unsparing in his depiction of a guilt-ridden Rodgers making sure that Hart's estate went to charity instead of to Hart's family. Lahr also notes that it was only in recent years that daughter Mary Rodgers Guittel managed to reassert her father's work with Hart.[16]

When seen from an assimilationist lens one can perhaps begin to understand why Hart might prove a liability to Rodgers and his ambitions. Larry Hart was short, ugly, and miserable; he was also gay, alcoholic, cynical, intellectual, aggressively clever and witty, sexual, and urbane. To some degree, then, Hart embodied the anti-Semitic stereotype of the New York Jew. When the *Oklahoma!* project came along, Rodgers first approached Hart, who refused because it was not his sort of thing and who encouraged Rodgers to work with Hammerstein instead. Oscar Hammerstein took to *Oklahoma!*'s subject matter effortlessly.

Oscar Hammerstein II was everything Hart was not. Hammerstein was straight, a family man, wholesome and optimistic, even corny. His taste favored believable characters and plots, and he used simple imagery inspired by nature in his lyrics. Hammerstein wrote mostly operettas, and favored romantic love and spiritual ideals. Though Hammerstein's father was Jewish, his mother was not. In short, unlike Hart, Hammerstein expressed WASP ideals, even if colored by liberal attitudes toward social justice.[17] Like the musical double couple pairings examined earlier, Rodgers and Hart were much like the secondary couple—ethnic, comedic, sexual, urbane—but ultimately of lesser consequence. Rodgers and Hammerstein resembled the primary couple—WASP, serious, high minded, romantic, ultimately of the heartland. As good a work as *Pal Joey* is, its appeal is limited to urban sophisticates; *Oklahoma!*, by contrast, had far-reaching national appeal.

Working with Hart, Rodgers could never attain the upward mobility he craved; Hart, unable or unwilling to assimilate, proved professionally limiting. Working with Hammerstein, however, Rodgers could mask his ethnicity, complete his assimilation, and gain, not only enormous commercial success, but also a far greater degree of respect and recognition. Lahr tells how Rodgers began to view himself more as a "monument" than as a person: Rodgers had successfully squelched his self to take on a culturally delineated social role. By assimilating, Rodgers achieved the formulaic American Dream, gaining power, prestige, and acceptance within the genteel circles of the nation's cultural establishment. It is damning and ironic that Hart, both Jewish and gay, could not successfully assimilate (i.e., escape his identity) and chose instead to self-destruct, whereas Rodgers proved able to suppress his ethnic identity sufficiently to assimilate and hence flourished.[18]

In 1955 Richard Rodgers and Oscar Hammerstein appeared on the CBS television showcase, *The Ed Sullivan Show*. The event was a celebration of *Oklahoma!*'s twelfth anniversary. Rodgers conducted a small on-stage orchestra and chorus. The orchestra sat behind fluted music stands while Rodgers stood formally before them, baton in hand. The camera lens reveals a series of string instruments (violins, violas, bass), a harp, even a bassoon. Just beyond the orchestra stood a dozen singers, men and women, anonymously in shadow. Under Rodgers, the orchestra began to play the building notes leading up to the rousing, "Oklahoma" number, and suddenly a tuxedoed John Raitt appeared to sing the first verse. Raitt is then joined by Florence Henderson, Barbara Cook, and Celeste Holm. All—including Rodgers, Hammerstein, and Sullivan—are in formalwear, women wearing jewelry. No hint of denim or calico, and so the event seems strangely forced. Here was a tribute to a by-now American classic, the show that started it all for the distinguished composing team, an event staged to affirm their success and high standing. It is clear from the tuxedoed Rodgers vigorously conducting a mini version of a classical orchestra, accompanying the opera-trained Raitt, that we the viewing audience are encouraged to consider *Oklahoma!* a work on par with classical music. Then a bejeweled, elegantly gowned Celeste Holm performs "I Caint Say No": the simplicity of the lyrics and of the Ado Annie character Holm originated strikingly at odds with her rich attire. Nevertheless, the audience reacts to every word, every note. They seem not to notice the incongruities.[19]

Nor is it odd that a weekly variety show, televised from New York City with a coat-hanger-backed Irish-American emcee, assume the prerogatives and trappings of highbrow cultural arbiter. If Sullivan promoted *Oklahoma!* as high art, his show also asserted that Rodgers, Hammerstein, and their down-home characters paradoxically merited being placed upon a pedestal. Rodgers and Hammerstein had "made it" in nationally telecast audience's eyes. But Sullivan's audience related to those on stage personally as well; if Ado Annie can still be herself and yet now dress in pearls, so too, vicariously, could the live audience. To them, *Oklahoma!* deserved such upper-class trappings, and its artistry merited inclusion in America's highest cultural pantheon. But that was in part because the audience felt it too deserved similar rewards. At least for that "brief, shining moment," Richard Rodgers was viewed rightfully as a national icon, associated with our highest cultural standards—and without a trace of any visible ethnicity. No doubt the studio audience (men in 1955 jackets and ties, women in dresses and gloves) shared in the warm, reassuring glow of similar democratic assumptions.

3. The Melting Pot Paradigm of Irving Berlin ❧

Voice of the Immigrant Generations

Songwriter Irving Berlin epitomized the immigrant experience. He was the immigrant who made good, who, in Horatio Alger's terms, made the most of his "luck and pluck" to rise out of poverty and attain riches. He was a self-made man, a shining example of the so-called American Dream. To whatever degree the American musical reflects the immigrant experience, it can be found in Irving Berlin's long and prolific career and the ever-evolving nature of the work he created.

Born Israel Baline, the son of a cantor, one of Berlin's earliest memories is of his house being burned down in a Russian pogrom. His father packed up the family for America and ended up impoverished in New York City's Lower East Side. Ashamed of his small earnings, Izzy went "on the bum." He earned pennies singing on street corners and in saloons. In time, he became a singing waiter at the Bowery's rough-and-tumble Pelham Café, making up dirty lyrics to popular songs. When a competing saloon's waiter published a song, Pelham's boss insisted the still-teenage Berlin and another waiter do the same. "Marie from Sunny Italy" became Izzy's first published song, introducing both a new career and a new name: the sheet music cover read "Lyrics by I. Berlin." By age twenty-four Irving Berlin had become America's most successful songwriter: a career that would last for six decades.

Berlin's rise corresponds with the rise of immigrants in America, particularly in New York City. With barely a grammar school education, and with English as his second language, Berlin wrote lyrics and music that reflected the growing assimilation and increased sophistication of his coreligionists. This was particularly true of second-generation immigrants, eager for acceptance and upward mobility. Berlin's songs expressed their disappointments and joys.

From 1907 on, Berlin demonstrated the uncanny ability not only to recognize and adapt to shifts in popular musical tastes but seemingly to anticipate those shifts. This kept him one step ahead. I would argue that the reason why Berlin could so accurately and consistently do this was because he himself embodied the sensibilities of his audience. His understandings were their understandings.[1]

As a commercial songwriter Berlin eschewed notions that his songs expressed his personal feelings, with the exception of "Till I Lost You," written following his first wife's untimely death. Yet, while this is debated, it is true that, as a commercial songwriter, Berlin deliberately wrote to reflect the shifting demands of the buying public. In this respect Berlin mirrored his times. Since Berlin composed songs literally daily, his work serves as a sort of barometer of changing public concerns. He soaked up New York's diversity and synthesized it into his own brand of popular song. In a famous 1924 letter, composer Jerome Kern characterized Berlin's music, writing that it "perfectly epitomized" the "average United States citizen." He goes on to note that Berlin "...honestly absorbs the vibrations emanating from the people, manners and life of his time, and in turn, gives these impressions back to the world [through his songs]." Kern goes on to conclude, "Irving Berlin has *no* place in American music. HE *IS* AMERICAN MUSIC" [sic].[2]

Berlin's Assimilation to the Jews

To Berlin, and his coreligionists, the American Dream meant upward mobility, most often achieved through assimilation.[3] This attitude, combined with Berlin's seemingly chameleon-like persona, has made him unpopular with those who resent assimilation. He is barely viewed as being a Jew. In the *Encyclopedia Judaica* there is an entry on Berlin, but it is terse and brief; in Irving Howe's *World of Our Fathers* Berlin is mentioned, but not as fully as the range of his achievements would seemingly merit. In her book, *Making Americans: Jews and the Broadway Musical* scholar Andrea Most barely touches on the work of Berlin. In harsher terms, in 2000 critic and Rabbi Marc Gellman wrote that, "....Irving Berlin, a cantor's son who changed his name from Israel Baline, stoked the assimilation legacy with his music. In 1942, when Auschwitz was belching smoke, Irving Berlin was belting out the music for "White Christmas," the most popular Christmas song ever...." Regardless of issues of accuracy or fairness, Berlin's legacy has not been as recognized or acknowledged as his degree of popularity and artistry might dictate. Still, in the past couple of years there has been a new appreciation for the songwriter, which has explored his complex persona; see especially Jody Rosen's book, *White Christmas*, as an example.[4]

And yet, though an agnostic, Berlin did identify himself publicly as a Jew, supported numerous Jewish causes, and was recognized in his own time for his many efforts. Still, his "White Christmas" and "Easter Parade" caused discomfort amongst his own people. For instance, in late 1942 Berlin appeared at a Jewish National Fund benefit dinner in Detroit in order to present a donation check. He offered to sing his latest hit, "White Christmas," but his hosts politely declined, explaining it was inappropriate given the setting, asking him to sing something else instead. Was Berlin then only insensitive, or did he perhaps see himself and his song in other terms, which would make his choice of song entirely appropriate and acceptable?[5]

One answer comes from author Philip Roth, who in *Operation Shylock* writes how, in writing "Easter Parade" and "White Christmas" Berlin wrote songs that secularized religious holidays. Hence, because of Berlin, "…Easter turns into a fashion show and Christmas into a holiday about snow…." But Berlin was not hostile to either holiday, as Roth suggests. Rather, he was bent on viewing America as a land of equal opportunity, and that by neutralizing the exclusive religious associations they too became essentially inclusive national celebrations.[6]

In Shakespeare's *The Taming of the Shrew* husband Petruchio tames wife Kate; but you could also argue that, by play's end, Petruchio has himself been tamed, that husband and wife in essence meet halfway. By the same token, while Irving Berlin adapted himself via assimilation to American culture and life, so too did his work ask that America to adapt to him and those like him. He asked America to make good on its promise of opportunity and religious freedom, to live up to its professed ideals. Berlin did this by painting an America, through song, that did so. If Irving Berlin could assimilate to America, America should in turn assimilate to him, to meet him halfway.

A Songwriter's Career

Irving Berlin began his career as a writer of ragtime music. He was one of the few great writers who composed both music and words. And though English was not his first language, he became an increasingly adept and sophisticated lyricist. His words bounced around in true jazz fashion, complementing the often unpredictable placement of the syncopated beat. He later turned to writing haunting romantic ballads and sophisticated jazz. Later still, he wrote anthems and conventional show tunes. As his music evolved so too did his lyric writing. It is through his words that we can get a glimpse into the man himself, if not personally, certainly in terms of his concerns.[7]

Irving Berlin's songwriting career can be broken down into four major periods. The first (1907–1919) was Berlin's rise to prominence as a Tin Pan Alley songwriter. He wrote songs designed to sell. If he found a song that did sell, he'd write series of songs on the same theme until the trend waned. He wrote "Alexander's Ragtime Band," which made Berlin and his music internationally famous, though not itself a ragtime, and then wrote a slew of knockoffs. He composed songs for Ziegfeld's *Follies*, and for his own revue *Watch Your Step* (1914). This period also includes his first army show, *Yip, Yip, Yahank!*

The second period lasted roughly the decade of the 1920s. It featured mostly peppy jazz numbers and what Berlin called "sob ballads," beautiful melodies with sentimental words. These include romantic ballads, such as "What'll I Do," "Say It Isn't So," "Always," "Remember," and so forth; friend Cole Porter included the "Berlin ballad" as an ideal in his famous list song, "You're the Top."

The third period spanned the 1930s, right up to World War II. The era begins with his two revues written with Moss Hart (*Face the Music* and *As Thousands Cheer*), and includes his original hit Hollywood films written for Fred Astaire (*Top Hat, Follow the Fleet*).

The fourth period extends from World War II through his last hits into the 1960s. These are marked by a decided patriotism. Aside from *Annie Get Your Gun*, the brainchild of Dorothy Fields, Berlin's shows all glorified the American government: *This is the Army, Call Me Madam, Miss Liberty, Mr. President* all celebrated national institutions and the American way of life.

Berlin's Ethnicity: the Crisis of 1924

In 1911, the twenty-three-year-old Berlin had sufficiently "made it" in New York's theatrical world to merit a Friars' Club banquet in his honor, hosted by no less than the flag-waving Irish-American George M. Cohan. Cohan welcomed Berlin with warmth. He introduced Berlin as "a Jew boy that had named himself after an English actor and a German city." Cohan went on to praise Berlin's music, and commented on the songwriter's values, that Berlin "...has become famous and wealthy, without wearing a lot of jewelry and falling for funny clothes. He is uptown, but he is here with the old downtown hardshell." The ethnic references and the concern with appearance underscore the tenor of the times. New York's ethnic mix was a given, a featured element of the city's popular entertainment in a tradition that included minstrel shows, the Irish Harrigan and Hart, and the "Dutch" (aka Jewish) Weber and Fields.[8]

In these years Berlin wrote many ethnic songs, designed to appeal to New York's multicultural mix. As a small boy living on the city's streets he was exposed to the full range of nationalities, their cultures, and their music. Remember, his first songwriting effort was a pseudo-Italian number. Berlin then wrote of Germans and Irish, Italians and Jews. He wrote coon songs. And it was not just Berlin; this so-called Melting Pot music was the popular norm of the day. Interestingly, years later Berlin wrote Groucho Marx asking him not to perform any of his old ethnic songs; that, taken out of context, they would be misconstrued.[9]

What stopped the rage for ethnic songs was World War I. A wave of nativism swept the nation; people and businesses with German-sounding names were attacked. The nativism continued after the war. Fear of Bolshevism triggered a Red Scare in America. Those preaching socialism or pacifism were persecuted, some even expelled. Songs that featured foreign-sounding accents and melodies fell into disfavor. In such times one didn't want to appear "different," especially not "un-American."

In this context, 1924 proved a pivotal year for Berlin. That summer he attended the Democratic National Convention held in Madison Square Garden. He witnessed the long struggle to select a nominee to run against then-president Calvin Coolidge. Berlin favored Alfred E. Smith, and even composed a campaign song for him. But the Convention proved a battle ground over the direction and makeup of the Democratic Party. Disturbingly, Smith's main rival, William McAdoo, enjoyed vociferous support from the Ku Klux Klan. In the end both Smith and McAdoo lost, but nativist intolerance prevailed. Shortly after gaining reelection, the Coolidge administration engineered passage of the Immigration Act of 1924, which significantly restricted immigration specifically from both southern and eastern Europe: Italian Catholics and Russian Jews.[10]

Leading up to this same period Berlin teamed with producer Sam Harris to build The Music Box, designed to showcase Berlin's music. From 1920 to 1924, Irving Berlin single-handedly wrote the songs for four successive *Music Box Revues*. But it was not until the 1924 *Revue* that Berlin introduced any Jewish songs, and he seemingly did so to showcase that edition's star, Fanny Brice (though she identified as Jewish, Brice learned her Yiddish accent to please New York audiences[11]). In the spirit of his earlier "Yiddle On Your Fiddle (Play Some Ragtime)," Berlin wrote "Yiddisha Eskimo" and also "Don't Send Me Back to Petrograd" for Brice to sing.[12]

While the Eskimo song is comedic, "Don't Send Me Back to Petrograd" was essentially not, despite its raucously vaudevillian melody. Through the lyrics we can hear Berlin respond to current events, revealing his own concerns. The song is a serious plea cloaked in the guise of laughing jazz, as the lyrics beg not to be sent back to his Russian roots, but adding that, "The very best people you know/were foreigners not so long ago" and later adding in a note of desperation that he will "promise to work the best I can/I'll even wash sheets for the Ku Klux Klan" as long as he can stay in America.[13]

It was the last ethnic song Berlin ever wrote, a clear rejoinder to the Immigration Act of 1924 and American intolerance. But a close inspection also shows the author's anxieties. That assimilation is not just an ideal but also a self-protective strategy is seen in the lyric that "the very best people that you know/Were foreigners not so long ago." She then asks for the same "chance," that he too can assimilate, lose his apparently objectionable ethnic traits, and hence warrant remaining in America. She then refers to his "cousins and their uncles and their aunts" that echoes Gilbert and Sullivan's *H. M. S. Pinafore's* lyrics, implying even Anglo-Saxons had immigrant roots. The singer then goes on: she will even debase herself— and here Berlin names the specific enemy—"I'll even wash sheets for the Ku Klux Klan." And yet the message is especially clear: even an intolerant America is preferable to Russia's horrors, echoing Berlin's own early memories of Russia's anti-Semitic pogroms.

On another front, also in 1924, Berlin's friend Alexander Woollcott, theatre critic and celebrity, wrote a biography of the songwriter. This is odd. Of the few books Woollcott wrote in his lifetime, the bulk of which are collections of his articles and reviews; the Berlin book is his only real biography.[14] Woollcott himself noted it peculiar to write a biography for someone still only in his thirties, with creative years ahead of him. *The Story of Irving Berlin* paints Berlin as a Jewish immigrant who has contributed mightily to America, and also as living proof of Horatio Alger's rags to riches myth. In florid prose, Woollcott portrays Berlin as a self-made man, admires his use of Jewish melodic tradition, and presents him as one who best reflects then-modern-day America. The book ends with a flourish, returning to Berlin's modest beginnings, with a reference both to

Berlin's father and to his long-ago Pelham Café boss: "I am not free to put in words how deeply I honor the true and gentle American who was carried out of Russia by the refugee Rabbi and who served for a time the drinks and the songs at Nigger Mike's."[15]

Apparently, Woollcott enlisted Berlin's help with the book. But still, why write it? Berlin regularly used public opportunities to promote his work, but he consistently shied away from discussing his personal life. Given the timing, perhaps the biography was a response to the rising tide of anti-Semitic nativism. Woollcott wrote his book in 1924, the same year as the Klan publicly pressed the Democratic convention, the same year Congress enacted immigration restrictions, in the same year Berlin's song begged, "Don't Send Me Back to Petrograd." Woollcott's prominence and prestige, particularly since identified with the WASP status quo, lent credibility to Berlin's legitimacy as an American. Moreover, Woollcott's book argued that Berlin's triumph symbolized the immigrants' possibilities; Woollcott's Berlin example provided a stirring defense of open-door policies.

It was also in 1924 that Irving Berlin met his future wife, the well-heeled society debutante, Ellin Mackay. Theirs was truly a love match, one her father vehemently opposed. Their forbidden courtship remained big news through to their 1926 elopement; their high society mixed marriage was front-page news even in *The New York Times*. By wedding Berlin, Ellin was dropped by some of her former set; by wedding Ellin, Berlin gained access to upper echelons of high society. The poor immigrant boy had truly made it. His place in America was that much more secure.[16]

Ostensibly, Berlin stopped writing ethnic songs. But in fact he utilized their sensibilities under more acceptable guises. They took several forms, coexisting with all the other songs Berlin wrote during the late 1920s and early 1930s. This is seen in Berlin's first forays into film. *Puttin' On the Ritz* (1930), starring Harry Richman, and *Mammy* (1930), starring Al Jolson. Berlin's ethnic concerns percolated beneath the surface in each. For example, for *Mammy* he wrote "Let Me Sing and I'm Happy." Presented as a Jolson minstrel number, the song shows the post-1924 Berlin beating a hasty retreat from politics, debasing himself almost as much as the girl who offered to wash the KKK's sheets. He sang,

> What care I who makes the laws of a nation;
> Let those who will take care of its rights and wrongs.
> What care I who cares
> For the world's affairs
> As long as I can sing its popular songs.[17]

By the song's end he says that all he cares about is being allowed to sing, satisfied with just being "happy," preferably in blackface and down on his knees! It asserts no higher aspirations. The music itself is upbeat minstrelsy. Blackface again offers the immigrant a nonthreatening, culturally acceptable disguise, deferentially occupying the lowest rung of American life. It is the safety found in playing the fool.

Neither film did well. Frustrated with the results Berlin returned to New York and wrote two highly successful revues with Moss Hart, *Face the Music* (1931) and *As Thousands Cheer* (1933). Both are lighthearted satires of early 1930s America. *Face the Music* (1931) presented the formerly well-to-do now commiserating in a luncheonette, the entire show a droll look at the Great Depression; *As Thousands Cheer* (1933) was a living newspaper, with songs and skits illuminating each section.

Berlin surprised many when he brought African American singer Ethel Waters from Harlem and featured her in the latter, and he shocked many when he wrote "Supper Time" for her, a bluesy indictment of lynching. But Berlin's choice is not surprising if one considers it as being residual from 1924, since the song hearkened back to the same nativist prejudices that resulted in the immigration restrictions. Showing his true colors, Berlin insisted the white cast members take their bow with Waters, despite their fierce objections.

Blackface/Whiteface

Buoyed by the revue's success, Berlin returned to Hollywood in the mid-1930s to again write songs for films, this time regularly featuring Fred Astaire. This marks an important transition. From roughly 1910 to 1930 the primary entertainer to sing a Berlin song was Al Jolson. But from 1930 on the two men most often identified with performing Berlin were Fred Astaire and then Bing Crosby.

In the 1910s and 1920s Jolson was the preeminent star of vaudeville and of recordings. His professional stature was built on live performance, mostly in New York City. Neil Gabler has argued that the casting of Jolson for the first talking film, *The Jazz Singer*, rather than George Jessel who originated the role on Broadway, was based primarily on issues of ethnicity. In the original, the protagonist, Jack Robins (aka Robinowitz), abandons his show business aspirations and instead returns to the traditional Judaism of his father, becoming a cantor. But Gabler points out that the film version has Robins make the opposite choice. He goes on to say that

Jolson was the better choice for the role because he was perceived as being a more assimilated Jew than Jessel. That Jolson closely identified with Jack Robins, and also threw in his own brand of blackface minstrelsy, only heightened his assimilationist aspirations.[18]

But Jolson did not enjoy the same level of success in films as he had on stage and through sound recordings. He was not a strong enough actor to make the leap, despite numerous attempts. Even a film like *Mammy*, written with him in mind and featuring a strong score by Berlin, did not prove particularly successful.

When Berlin returned to write for the screen, times and tastes had changed. The Depression was in full force and the nation favored escapist entertainment in its films, which echoed the affluent good times of the 1920s. The hits most often took the form of screwball comedies or Americanized operettas; the films of Fred Astaire and Ginger Rogers served to combine both.

Berlin wrote songs for a number of Astaire films of the period: *Top Hat, Follow the Fleet, On the Avenue, Carefree*. The two men became close personal friends for the rest of their lives. But the choice of Astaire as a Hollywood leading man is, at first glance, puzzling. Certainly, he was an extraordinary dancer, and songwriters appreciated his accuracy and clarity when singing their songs, even if his voice was reedy and thin. But a leading man?

Essentially, Astaire epitomized what Berlin and other Jews strove to achieve. He was debonair, polished, sophisticated. His screen persona was that of a raffish, outspoken fellow, not obviously attractive, whose audacity and romanticism and wit in the end won out. It didn't hurt that he could dance. But even his dance—so smooth and elegant—was done mostly to jazz. Unlike a Gene Kelly, who was athletic, handsome, and sexy, Astaire got by on style. Kelly was American whereas Astaire was continental. In short, Astaire was someone the immigrant might himself become. It was almost like Astaire was himself Jewish beneath the relaxed urbanity. In a film like *Top Hat* he is audacious, rude, clever, funny, and articulate, relying mostly on good intentions and charm to win over the girl—and the audience. He is the antithesis of a Clark Gable or a Gary Cooper; Astaire is all clever and chatty, balding, small, and thin. No rugged individualist he. And yet his romantic nature and persistence win all.

Astaire only got on his knees to execute a dazzling dance move, never as an act of submission. His characters were largely wealthy, self-assured, and worldly. He danced with sophistication and class. In his famous pairings with Ginger Rogers, the primary dance numbers had the couple dressed to the nines, swirling on equally polished floors to the strains of deeply moving romantic ballads.

In short, Astaire was everything Al Jolson was not. Where Jolson was clearly ethnic, Astaire appeared a WASP; where Jolson was all unpredictable, high-voltage energy, and bombast, Astaire was quietly smooth; where Jolson was loud and pushy, Astaire was subtle and clever. Where Jolson was excessively sentimental, Astaire was coolly detached even when voicing passion. But there is more. Where Jolson was urban, Astaire was urbane; where Jolson showed lower-class roots, Astaire suggested an affluent upbringing. Where Jolson represented Eastern European peasant stock, Astaire represented continental café society polish, albeit an American version given his underlying wholesomeness.[19]

In a sense Berlin himself can be found in both Jolson and Astaire. If Jolson sang Irving Berlin's songs in blackface, then Fred Astaire essentially sang the next generation of Berlin songs in "whiteface." If Jolson displayed Berlin's ethnic past, Astaire displayed Berlin's assimilated, successful present and hoped-for future. Jolson's appeal was mostly an extension of his New York City stage success, as well as his faceless recordings. He fit in in New York much like Berlin's own music had, reflecting local audience interests and tastes. But when Berlin wanted to expand his audience, the context and presentation of his work had to change with it. What worked well in New York did not necessary enjoy comparable nationwide appeal.

Astaire too was different, with his fast talk and innovative jazz dancing. But unlike Jolson he was not ethnic. Astaire represented social aspirations to which the average American moviegoer could more readily relate. If anything, Astaire was clearly an American born who mimicked English taste and who danced spectacularly. Astaire was the vehicle through which Berlin and his coreligionist colleagues could gain a visible acceptance. His face became their public face. It was an acceptable, more dignified "whiteface" mask behind which a Berlin could now hide.

Berlin's Ritzy Put-On

The history of the song "Puttin' On the Ritz" illustrates the complex ethnicity of Irving Berlin's post-1924 music and life. Berlin wrote the song in 1927 for the film of the same name. The movie starred the wooden Harry Richman, who sang the now-familiar song in tie and tails accompanied by a multiracial chorus of tap-dancing showgirls. Though a lively jazz number, the opening verse depicted New York City's contemporary African Americans as spendthrifts, strutting down Harlem's Lenox Avenue, noses snobbishly raised, "Spending ev'ry dime/For a wonderful time...." The song's chorus then mocked the incongruity of blacks parading as affluent whites:

> Spangled gowns upon a bevy
> Of high browns from down the levee,
> All misfits
> Puttin' on the Ritz.[20]

Berlin was not a racist. Only six years later, it was Berlin who forced his *As Thousands Cheer* cast to treat Ethel Waters with respect. And fifteen years later, the cast of Berlin's *This Is the Army* became the first integrated unit in the U. S. army.[21]

Given Berlin's own understanding of how financial success leads to upward mobility, "Puttin' On the Ritz"'s criticism of African American profligacy can be seen as more than insensitive parody. Berlin lived well, but never flaunted it and was generally careful with money. Since the song was written in 1927, however, with Berlin still perhaps reeling from the events of 1924, one suspects that there is more to it. As we have seen, 1927 was the same year Berlin wrote "Let Me Sing and I'm Happy" with its use of blackface to mask immigrant angst. Might there be a link between this dynamic and the negative portrayal of black culture depicted in "Puttin' On the Ritz"?

In one sense this picture of Harlem could be seen as a reflection of the Jazz Age, with its freedoms and excess. Certainly Harlem's culture influenced the rest of the New York arts scene through its music, dance, art, and poetry. Berlin repeatedly attended the black hit revue *Shuffle Along* and was friendly with its composer, Eubie Blake. No doubt this music, like so much else, influenced Berlin's own songwriting.

Perhaps Berlin was simply trying to capture an aspect of America, like a reflecting mirror, with no ironic intent; perhaps he was just trying to fit in. Or perhaps Berlin, feeling the 1924 pinch of threatening haters, sought to put down African Americans, so as to make the immigrants look good by comparison. Musically, "Puttin' On the Ritz" actually celebrates black culture, jazzy and joyous. It is sung by a white man (a Jew) in the film, but, unlike Jolson, Richman does not appear in blackface. He is seen as a white amongst blacks, but careful to differentiate himself.

Returning to the lyrics, we hear the singer (Richman/Berlin) invite us to accompany him to Harlem. This suggests that "we" are not ourselves native to Harlem, and most likely are of the same society as is Richman.

And since he is dressed so well, and that he is inviting us essentially to go slumming, are we not better off than those whom we will observe once there? Perhaps the "we" then are amongst the wealthy, with their history of slumming. Or perhaps the "we" are the same average New Yorkers who Berlin later invited, in a role reversal, to go uptown and scrutinize the rich in his 1937 song "Let's Go Slumming." But, either way the listeners are promised a good time by looking down their noses, watching the foolish behavior of the Harlemites.

The 1946 Revision

Berlin later revised "Puttin' On the Ritz," giving it a strikingly different social cast, for the 1946 film, *Blue Skies*. Berlin moved the action from Harlem to the tonier Park Avenue; his poor blacks masquerading as rich whites were now replaced by rich whites who could afford to spend, now strolling up toney Park Avenue instead of the previous Lenox:[22] Much of the rest of the song is then a description of their posh, fashionable attire. It is ironic that the wealthy are shown dressing in imitation of movie stars ("Dressed up like a million-dollar trouper/Trying hard to look like Gary Cooper, Super duper.") But it is the new ending that is most telling:

> Come let's mix where Rockefellers
> Walk with sticks or umbrellas
> In their mitts
> Puttin' on the Ritz.[23]

Gone is any trace of the earlier version's cynicism. The rich are on formal public display, much like in "Easter Parade," noses still raised but now justifiably. The song remains an invitation, but contains a different sort of message. The listener is told that, if he or she will dress up properly, then they too can now "mingle" with the most prominent and affluent (e.g. the "Rockefellers").

Interestingly, the music itself expresses Berlin's ethnic issues. Beneath the syncopated beat, the minor key melody of "Puttin' On the Ritz" is Jewish, all sentimental and sad. But this melody is itself "dressed up" in the latest musical fashion of jazz: bouncy, lively, sophisticated. This suggests that Berlin aimed the song—music and words—directly at a Jewish audience, the one living "downtown," as opposed to "uptown." Thus, Berlin's invitation to dress up can be equated with becoming assimilated, and mingling with "Rockefellers" means upward mobility is now possible.

Another take on the song might be that of Berlin himself enjoying his newfound respectability. Since the wealthy seem to be taking their cues on how to dress from "million dollar troupers" such as "Gary Cooper," why not also take their cues from another successful entertainer, Irving Berlin? It is happily ironic then that the poor Jewish boy who seemingly dreamt of gaining access to the celestial rich, and took great pains to imitate the WASP establishment's ways in order to do so, should now himself be the object of their envious imitation.

If melodically the 1927 version was also directed at Lower East Side Jews, then its critical tone and its invitation to go slumming suggested solace through social superiority. Despite threats from Southern nativists, here in New York, one could feel reasonably safe, albeit at Harlem's expense. But by 1946, because of Jewish acceptance caused by World War II, there was no longer reason for competition or alarm. Jews were far more secure, and upward mobility could be found only a few blocks up a New York City street.

Berlin at War

In 1924, Irving Berlin seems to have withdrawn from American politics; in 1942 he returned with a vengeance. Much as he had done in the Great War, Berlin offered to organize a soldier show. He had been drafted into the army for World War I; he volunteered at age fifty-four to help aid the war effort. Berlin created *This Is the Army* and he supervised a troupe of soldiers who constituted the production company: writers, performers, musicians, stagehands. Occasionally, Berlin himself would perform his standard written for the previous war, "Oh, How I Hate to Get Up in the Morning," as part of the new show.

The production first toured America before heading overseas. In Washington, DC, they performed for the president and Mrs. Roosevelt, and afterwards partied with Eleanor at the White House, well into the evening. In Europe, they performed in England before heading to Italy and performed steadily near the front. After a hiatus back in the United States, they then traveled to the South Pacific from island to island, carrying equipment (both guns and instruments and stage equipment) up and down rope netting of ships, down to waiting boats, before setting up makeshift stages and performing for that group of GIs before setting off again. It was a grueling three-and-a-half years and earned Berlin a special Medal of Honor for his contribution and sacrifice.[24]

While abroad Berlin made it a habit of writing songs promoting friendship. *This Is the Army* was essentially intended to entertain the troops, yet Berlin and his men also entertained the locals wherever they went. In England, for instance, Berlin wrote "My English Buddy." He apparently wrote comparable ditties for natives when in Italy, and so forth. On the surface this seems both fitting and ironic. Remember that Berlin began his career while still a small immigrant boy absorbing the sounds of New York City's different ethnic groups later to utilize them to write songs in various ethnic styles. He wrote songs that mimicked Yiddish, Irish, Italian, German, and black musical idioms, ultimately blending them together to form his own style of American song.

The music in *This Is the Army* would best be characterized as being "American" in tone and style, but it was in terms that Berlin himself had originated and popularized. By blending the forms together, Berlin was acting out the melting pot via his music. It was hence uniquely democratic from the start. Remember Jerome Kern's quote, that Berlin "IS American music." His ability to mimic the sounds of other nationalities was what scholar Eric Lott termed "love and theft."[25] That Berlin did so effectively is demonstrated by the great popular appeal of his songs with each of those same ethnic groups. There is no record of any group outraged because someone outside their ethnicity had composed music in their nationalist style. Quite the contrary, music sales soared suggesting that the songs were entirely acceptable to their listeners, regardless of the composer's lineage.

So some twenty-five years after the Red Scare helped erase the American appeal for ethnic songs, Berlin has the opportunity to return to them. He can write songs in native musical idioms in order to create goodwill amongst the locals for the American troops. Only that's not what happened.

Berlin did occasionally perform Italian songs, but they were not the ones he wrote. Quite the contrary, what he sang were authentic Italian songs he learned in his youth on New York City's streets. So in that respect, the fact of America as a haven for immigrants did pay off. But apparently the songs Berlin himself wrote were standard Berlin songs, which is to say his own peculiar melting pot amalgam that became definitively "American."

It was all so ironic. Here come soldiers from the New World, an army heavily composed of the children of former immigrants, rushing to the rescue of the Old World from which many of their families originally fled. Here are Irving Berlin's performing soldiers, integrated and assimilated much like himself, performing scenes and songs that reflected their own assimilated American lives. Here is Irving Berlin himself, writing songs for the sake of promoting international goodwill. Here was American showbiz itself being exported as an ambassador to promote an open culture of optimism, of democracy, of American Dreams.

And leading them is Irving Berlin, the living embodiment of that same American Dream. He is the talented former immigrant who, through Horatio Alger-style pluck and luck rose from the tenements to achieve unprecedented affluence and acceptance. Berlin was living proof of American possibilities in their best sense. He was bright, energetic, accomplished, possessing an unprepossessing charm as he himself performed on stage, not as the world-famous songwriter, but as the everyday GI *schmo*, whining happily about killing the bugler. No son of kings here; this was a self-made man who gained prominence thanks to hard work and talent.

By exporting *This Is the Army*, America was exporting Irving Berlin himself and all that he represented and had become. And for American forces fighting to defeat malevolent Axis oppressors, what better way to define America as being the "good guys" than to display Berlin. Just as Berlin had shed his Russian Jewish beginnings to achieve all that America had to offer, so too could the peoples of Europe and of the Pacific Rim shed their unhealthy past in favor of a fresh, Americanized future.

Changing Times, Changing Context

In his analysis of Berlin's song "Blue Skies" Jeffrey Magee notes that the song appeared in two separate Hollywood films: *The Jazz Singer* (1927) and *Blue Skies* (1946). He goes on to describe how changes in cultural attitudes between the two periods altering the context in which each film presented the same song, thereby changing its meaning. He writes:

> In 1927 Al Jolson's performance of 'Blue Skies' signaled disruption, ethnic class and blend, and even change itself, both cultural and technological. In 1946 Bing Crosby's rendition intoned reassurance, white ethnic homogeneity, and the restoration of order and stability. The movie *Blue Skies* strips away all of the song's original Jewish resonance at a time when Jews themselves were increasingly viewed as homogenized 'Caucasians'....

Much like his song, Berlin's own 1946 image was similarly transformed:

> Far from the 'Ragtime King' of the 1910s and the "jazz composer" of the 1920s, Berlin now stood as a national hero who had written sturdy all-American anthems like "God Bless America" and secular holiday ballads like 'White Christmas.'[26]

Note the similarities of timing between the two versions of "Blue Skies" and the two versions of "Puttin On the Ritz." Berlin wrote both songs in 1927, and both reappeared in 1946. In the case of both songs, the earlier version was ethnically charged and aggressive in tone, whereas the later versions proved milder, responding to an America no longer hostile, but rather, welcoming.

In postwar America the immigrants found greater acceptance. Berlin still occasionally wrote songs depicting the road from downtown to uptown, but they tended to be less highly charged. "A Couple of Swells" comically depicts two hobos aiming to join the elite, but who, lacking the funds to ride, are forced to walk. It echoes "Puttin' On the Ritz" thematically, but lacks its bite. And the entire score of *Annie Get Your Gun* romanticizes a hillbilly's climb to success through show business. It could be a deethnicized portrait of Berlin himself.

The last chapter of Irving Berlin's professional career celebrated America. It was the gratitude of a former immigrant for enabling him, not only to succeed, but to find acceptance in a new land. He had climbed the ladder to the top, gaining recognition from a series of presidents, and was clearly welcomed and appreciated. Berlin responded not only with unchecked patriotism, but also his newfound view from the top. His final three shows reflected his lofty status: *Call Me Madam*, *Miss Liberty*, and *Mr. President*, all set amidst the America's government and institutions. But despite his perch, Berlin seemed never to forget his immigrant roots. Fittingly, he felt particularly proud of his music setting for Emma Lazarus' poem "The New Colossus," found on the Statue of Liberty, written for *Miss Liberty*.

This change was also marked in Berlin's politics. The onetime devotee of FDR became an Eisenhower Republican. If Berlin wrote a 1924 campaign song for Al Smith, he crossed over to write Republican campaign songs in both 1952 and 1954 with the catchy phrase, "I like Ike." In part this was an issue of personalities. Berlin appreciated Eisenhower, and, had Eisenhower accepted the Democratic Party's offer to run as a Democrat, one suspects that Berlin would have remained a Democrat. After all, the "I like Ike" idea was written for *Call Me Madam*, before Eisenhower declared his political party preferences. But this transformation more deeply reflects Berlin's desire to identify with the status quo; since he had "made it" and was now identified with the powers-that-be, his political metamorphosis naturally followed.

In His Seventies in the 1960s

Berlin complained that he lost touch with the baby boom generation, that this master of adjustment could not understand the appeal of rock and roll music, nor could he write in this vein. He decided instead to fold up his tent and retire. Now a conservative Republican, Berlin last appeared publicly at an event hosted by then-president Richard Nixon; Berlin fervently sang his "God Bless America." He supported the war in Vietnam, apparently at odds with his own daughters (Barrett), and could not fathom what he saw as their unpatriotic opposition. "What care I who makes the laws of the nation... as long as I can write her popular songs." In the last thirty years of his Methusalah-like long life, Berlin continued to write lyrics and songs, but refused to share them with the world, hoping some day for a comeback.

Berlin could not relate to this the younger generation. To some degree. it was simply due to his own old age, that he had lost touch, that the changes in lifestyle and values were too wide a river for him to cross. When he was a young man, Berlin too wrote songs that featured a radical new beat, with lyrics often scandalously sexual. The young Berlin was also influenced by black music, first as found via minstrelsy and later that written by composers like Eubie Blake. But by the 1960s Berlin had grown old and stodgy, conservative and sentimental. His worldview now radically differed from that of baby boomers and their increasingly blues-based rock and roll musical tastes.

But if we follow the issue of immigrant assimilation we find another cause for Berlin's inability to relate to the younger generation. As stated before, Berlin himself epitomized the immigrant experience, with its desperate battle to gain acceptance, affluence, and security in the New World. Just as Alexander Woollcott had long ago portrayed him, Berlin did paradigmatically represent precisely this dynamic. His appeal, beyond the sheer quality of his compositions, also had to do with his ability to voice the experience of a certain generation. This was mostly the second generation of immigrants, namely those who grew up in America and assimilated in order to achieve upward mobility.

The rock-and-roll generation included their children; the baby boomers included a vast number of the third-generation descendants of immigrants. Unlike their parents, this generation was born into a 1950s America, where they were largely accepted and led relatively affluent lives. Lacking the need to win favor, many turned instead to helping others in need, using their lofty position within the society to do this. Linked to this was a sense that the 1950s American culture was somehow artificial and suffocating in its conformity and emphasis on propriety. The appeal of black culture thus held many rewards. The civil rights movement gave this new generation a moral center, later heightened by the antiwar movement. This righteous attitude though reflected interest in helping others as they themselves (as former immigrants) were perhaps not helped. This was reinforced by rock and roll, both because of its driving sexual beat and honest directness, and because it was also drawn from the romanticized black culture supported by the civil rights movement. The music's raw simplicity seemed honest and true compared to the homogenized culture of their parents.

But it was that very homogenous artificiality that had enabled their parents to gain acceptance in the first place. If one "played the role" then one could fit in, regardless of whatever the conflicting reality was underneath. Assimilation did in fact result in a certain degree of social acceptance. Whether or not that guaranteed happy or content lives is another issue entirely. But the music and sensibilities of an Irving Berlin had preached a gospel of assimilation leading to just this very acceptance. If, once achieved, it was now time for a change, then Berlin could not then, by definition, be a part of it.

Berlin: Ever On Stage

Several Berlin songs center on fashion. The list would include "Top Hat, White Tie and Tail," "Easter Parade," and "Puttin' on the Ritz." Getting dressed up meant a special occasion. But in Berlinese it also meant playing the part right. Scholar Laurence Bergreen saw Berlin as a politician; I think Berlin was essentially an actor. To him "show business" meant literally that, the business of putting on a show, on stage and off. Berlin could reshape himself to reflect his times, play the part, so as to gain acceptance and stability. His own experience taught him the value of adapting to one's environment; by assimilating he found fame and fortune. Irving Berlin really did embody the American Dream, and his consequent patriotism reflected sincere appreciation. After all, back in Russia a man was measured by birth, not by ability; in America Israel Beline could reinvent himself, become "Irving Berlin" and rise as high as his talent and ambition could take him. Irving Berlin believed you had to put on the Ritz in order to achieve the ritz.

In Mel Brooks' 1974 film comedy *The Young Frankenstein*, Gene Wilder's Dr. Frankenstein becomes convinced that he can transform his "monster" into a socially acceptable citizen. In a scene reminiscent of both *King Kong* and *Top Hat*, Wilder and the remade monster make their stage debut wearing white ties and tails, top hats and canes, and attempt a Fred Astaire-inspired song and dance to "Puttin' On the Ritz." At first all goes well, but it soon dissolves into disaster, despite Wilder's efforts. But it is doomed from the start. The sophisticated attire does not disguise the monster's vulgar origins, and his bestiality is accented by his inability to do more than grunt the song. Yet the suave Wilder, by comparison, appears to fit in, despite his decidedly non-WASP physical appearance.[27]

Much like the Gene Wilder's Dr. Frankenstein, Berlin believed he could tame the ethnic "monster" simply by dressing it up and teaching it a few good steps. And Wilder learned his dance steps from Irving Berlin.

4. How to Succeed ⌘

As the twentieth century progressed, the overall work situation for immigrants and their children changed. Many of those who arrived in the mass migrations between the 1880s and mid-1920s settled in New York's Lower East Side. Theirs was a hardscrabble life, packed into densely populated tenements, scrambling to make a living, hoping to educate their children so that they could move up and out.

While each person's experience differed, Jews of each consecutive generation sought ways to advance, to improve their lot. This was reflected in a number of significant Broadway musicals, which, perhaps unwittingly, chronicled each new phase. Though the characters and situations depicted in this succession of shows were rarely ethnic, they consistently preached assimilation as a conditional step toward achieving fiscal success and personal happiness.[1] These shows thus proclaimed the concerns of Broadway's predominantly Jewish composers, lyricists, librettists, producers, directors and corresponded to those of their New York audience.

An examination of business-themed musicals reveals the obstacles and travails experienced by Jews and others as the century progressed. They chart how outsiders gradually made their way, revealing the variety of strategies used in order to get ahead. Each show demonstrates up close issues of risk and reward, the negotiation between outsiders and insiders, the relative rewards and cost of assimilation. Together they collectively present the shifting definition of what constituted American success.

This chapter is organized chronologically, not so much play by play, but rather according to shifts in occupations and attitudes. Shows from the first quarter of the century celebrate street smarts as key to success. Shows later depicted how the pressures to assimilate manifested itself in a variety of improving work settings, reflecting the gradual rise and integration of ethnic peoples (whether defined as "ethnic" or simply as "outsiders") into mainstream America's work life. Ultimately the Dream was largely realized, but at what cost?

PART ONE: BETTING ON A DREAM

Luck Be a Lady: Romanticized Gamblers

There are many paths to achieving the American Dream. To immigrants, the conventional path lay through assimilation, or at least that is how things are portrayed via musicals. However, another path was also apparent, one that ran contrary to conformist norms. It is the path of the gambler. I would suggest that gambling was deliberately proscribed as the alternative to assimilation and hence merits close consideration here.

Early Twentieth Century: From Ravenal to Arnstein

Both *Show Boat* (1927) and *Funny Girl* (1964) portray the romantic and professional life of an early twentieth century star entertainer: Magnolia in the former and Fanny in the later. *Show Boat* is fiction whereas *Funny Girl* is built upon fact (i.e., the life of Fanny Brice). *Funny Girl* features a Jewish protagonist and her Jewish lover; *Show Boat*'s romantic leads are both WASPs. However, *Show Boat*, based on Jewish author Edna Ferber's novel, includes numerous references to multiculturalism, ranging from the African-American Joe and Queenie, the mixed-blood Julie, the Puritanical Parthy, and the Catholic convent where daughter Kim is schooled. So though *Show Boat* has no Jewish characters per se, it is imbued with Jewish sensibilities, heightened by the contributions of Oscar Hammerstein II and Jerome Kern. Hence, it is a portrait of a diverse America as conceived by Jews.[2]

In *Funny Girl*, Fanny's ethnicity is first seen as a deterrent: she is unlike other girls from her over-the-top personality to her ethnic sized nose. However, Fanny's being different propels her to stardom. This happens in the number "His Love Makes Me Beautiful." Uncomfortable with Ziegfeld's inclusion of her amidst a bevy of beauties dressed in wedding dresses, feeling by contrast ugly and out of place, Fanny stuffs a pillow under her dress to appear pregnant. This causes the audience to laugh, but with her rather than at her. Hence, by highlighting her difference Fanny stands out, becoming a star. The real Fanny Brice clowned and sang her way to the top, and her repertoire always included numbers designed to accentuate her ethnicity, a balance replicated throughout *Funny Girl*.

In *Show Boat* Magnolia finds stardom by portraying ethnicity. The first time she sings "Can't Help Lovin' That Man of Mine" the black cook Queenie comments that that is a coon song, usually unknown to "white folk." Magnolia learned it from Julie and it is her favorite song. Much later in the show, when now down-and-out Magnolia auditions for the Trocadero night club, she gets the job both because Julie steps aside allowing Magnolia to sing that same song. It gets Magnolia the job and is the first step toward launching her highly successful career. We also learn that Magnolia is adept at performing black face. Much like Fanny, Magnolia is beholding to ethnicity as a stepping stone to stardom.

Both *Funny Girl* and *Show Boat* also take pains to show their heroines' modest roots. We see Magnolia performing in bad plays with bad actors on the Cotton Blossom show boat and are fully aware of the modest but loving family from which she sprang. Similarly, we see Fanny start out in low-class vaudeville and witness her modest Henry Street roots, where her mother runs a neighborhood saloon.

Much more compelling parallels lie in the story of each heroine's love life. Both wed for love, both wed professional gamblers, and both are ultimately abandoned by their loving but unreliable spouses. Magnolia falls in love with Gaylord Ravenal, a Mississippi gambler; Fanny falls for Nicky Arnstein, a New York gambler.[3] To the relatively innocent eyes of Magnolia and Fanny, each man is handsome, suave and sophisticated, living exotic lives far beyond the two women's sheltered upbringings. Magnolia's mother Parthy objected to the match, but her father Cap'n Andy helped it along; we know little about Fanny's mother's attitude toward her marrying Nick.

Each couple marries for love. Once wed, each moves away to live the high life elsewhere. Magnolia and Gaylord move to Chicago where they have their daughter Kim. Though we don't see them, we hear reports that they party amongst the city's elite, living opulent lives. Similarly, once wed, Fanny and Nicky enjoy a life of fine restaurants, champagne, and jewels. They revel in materialistic splendor, reflecting each husband's good luck at the gaming tables. This point is especially hit home by Nicky's refusal to wed Fanny unless he makes a bundle, not wanting to be beholden to Fanny's bank account. Their "glitter and be gay" worlds eventually unravel, however, as the gamblers' luck turns. Eventually Gaylord abandons Magnolia and Nicky leaves Fanny. Gaylord leaves Magnolia flat, forcing her return to the stage for a livelihood. By contrast, because Fanny is already a star her pain at abandonment is not economically devastating, though certainly as emotionally crushing as Magnolia's.

Not only do both abandoned wives carry on, both make still-bigger names for themselves professionally. Unlike the Cinderella musicals, both *Show Boat* and *Funny Girl* center primarily upon romance, rather than social acceptance. Magnolia and Fanny fall head over heels for their respective beaux, seemingly oblivious to their men being gamblers and hence rather disreputable ne'er-do-wells. Consequently, both Fanny and Magnolia attain public renown but privately suffer.

So why wed gamblers? This choice is both intriguing and complex. Certainly, the American Dream is tied to capitalism, to notions of materialistic attainment. American business is closely linked to risk and reward and is itself a form of gambling. Even poker and craps are games that ape business practice and skill.

Magnolia and Fanny wed gambles because they themselves are risk takers. Magnolia is a risk taker by marrying for love, despite her mother's stern warning that Mississippi gamblers do not make suitable husbands. Fanny, by contrast, is from the start intent on a show business career. Talent, ambition, and good luck fueled her success. Once successful, along came Nicky. However, the sensible choice for a woman would not have been to consider a life on stage at all, but rather concentrate on hearth and home.

Why are professional gamblers seen as romantic?[4] Perhaps gamesters are appealing because they are the antithesis of everyday businessmen who lead comparatively quiet lives. Gamblers are exciting. They are spontaneous rather than plodding, wild and free rather than Puritanical, and live in the moment, not shut away counting pennies. In addition, in both *Show Boat* and *Funny Girl* the two gamblers are also willing to take a chance on their respective leading ladies. In essence, Gaylord and Nicky are "betting" that Magnolia and Fanny will make perfect mates.[5]

In Jewish cultural terms, perhaps gamblers represent the opposite of *yeshiva buchers*, the traditional Talmudic school boys. By definition gamblers are more Americanized and perhaps more manly. Gamblers are akin to aggressive businessmen, who tend to be realistic and ruthless, direct and opportunistic, somewhat immoral and certainly materialistic. If a girl wanted to be rich then better to hang her hat on such a man rather than on a distracted scholar. In addition, since the businessman tends to be more hands-on, compared to the introverted and cerebral student, there is also the implication of having a better love life as well.

Ravenal and Arnstein are more worldly than the two heroines, at least at the start of their respective relationships. Magnolia and Fanny are virginal where the men are experienced, adding to each man's commanding mystique. Ravenal and Arnstein also display life experience. Each heroine is in essence asking the older, mature man to help her become a full-blown woman, to help her become a sexually active adult.

Nicky Arnstein was played in the original production of *Funny Girl* by Syd Chaplin and in the film by Omar Sharif. Both actors were known for their polished appearance and debonair manners: nothing rough or crude about either one. Each was elegant and continental, and each would trump even upper-class America's genteel ideal.[6] And where Gaylord Ravenal was fictional, Nicky Arnstein was both actual and still alive at the time of the show's debut. In *Funny Girl*, he is portrayed as gallant, not wanting to live off of Fanny's money, a man of principle and pride. In truth the real Nicky Arnstein gambled away a great deal of Fanny's money and proved less than honorable. However, what is real is not as important here as what was shaped on stage. The Nicky Arnstein of *Funny Girl* was an entirely assimilated Jew, could pass as high society, the glittering living embodiment of a fantasy American Dream. He fit in nicely amongst the well-heeled, yet, as a gambler, lived entirely by his wits, beholden to no one—as long as he kept winning.

It is implausible that an Italian or Jewish (or Egyptian) immigrant, sans education or polish or wherewithal, would ever be allowed near the high stakes gaming tables of New York, Chicago, or Atlantic City, let alone those of Monte Carlo, London or Paris. Assimilation was part of the price of admission.

The problem for our heroines was that the external appeal quickly collapsed once the winnings stopped. After living in the finest Chicago hotels and socializing with the city's elite, Magnolia's fortunes deteriorate. She is forced to surrender even her shoddy apartment when she learns of her husband's abandonment. Magnolia's pretty fantasies of a handsome husband and enjoying the good life all melt away; she must finally face the grim realities that lay beneath the glittering surface. She is rescued by reconnecting with her roots via the reemergence of Frank and Ellie, of Julie and Cap'n Andy, which collectively engineer her successful return to the stage.

Similarly, in *Funny Girl*, Nicky Arnstein's polished exterior belied his shaky moral underpinnings; there is nothing truly substantial beneath this gambler's flashy exterior. The thrill of an exciting life with Nicky is quickly replaced by Fanny's terror and despair. Still, Nicky was a male version of what Fanny wanted to become: sophisticated and successful on her own terms, thanks to her unique talents, living the high life above the *hoi polloi*, free from having to compromise or fit in.

Both the fictional Magnolia and the actual Fanny represent the highly successful woman in our society—and I say, "represent" because they were public celebrities that others would model themselves upon. Yet, despite their material fame and fortune, each privately grieved over a failed marriage. They may have "made it" as career women, but neither fame nor fortune protected them from broken hearts. There is a reassurance here for the average playgoer: despite succeeding in business, each woman ultimately remained governed by her heart, thus preserving her essential domestic femininity.

Dreams, or Fantasies? Pluck, or Luck?

The American Dream promises materialistic success; but how to achieve it? Horatio Alger's heroes rose from rags to riches through pluck and luck. Pluck suggests honest ingenuity, persistence and a ready opportunism. If luck is indeed where preparation and opportunity meet, then Alger's formula also suggests careful planning and self-improvement. This in turn requires intelligence, learning, patience, and keeping to one's goals. Alger advises one climb up the ladder of success one rung at a time. Judgment, clean living, and perseverance will ultimately be rewarded with economic security if not actual "riches."[7]

In America, issues of identity, color or faith should not prevent someone from full participation in the nation's economic system. It remains a fantasy, but is plausible, one that might be had with sufficient, well, pluck and luck. However, like most fantasies, ideals are exciting precisely because they seem unattainable. Dreams are often more a projection of individual desires rather than three-dimensional reality. Besides, with riches come income taxes; with fame a loss of privacy; that pretty girl or boy might prove objectionable. Fantasies may help make everyday life more palatable, or may motivate ambition, but are themselves empty castles in the air.

Better to plan ahead. Better to master that knowledge and those skills. Better to save one's pennies, work hard and long to build a good reputation for oneself. Though bland, a middle-class life can provide safety and security. A married couple wants the stability of a roof above and food on the table, a protected nest in which to nurture children and instill civilizing beliefs.

That may be all well and good if you are accepted into the respectable middle-class. But what if you are not? What if you are ethnic or poor? What if you are at the bottom of the societal ladder, scrambling to survive, dreaming of getting ahead? What if you have few genuine options? What if, even if you do work, you simply do not earn enough to see much improvement in your life?

And even if you subscribe to Horatio Alger as the path toward a better life, is that all there is? And how long must one wait to get there? Will it be in this lifetime?

Assimilation versus Freedom

The real fantasy of the American Dream is its implied promise of freedom. Not freedom from want but rather the freedoms of excess and autonomy: freedom to exist outside of conventional constraints; freedom from money worries or from what other people think; freedom to find love and acceptance as oneself or the freedom to reinvent oneself according to one's own terms.

Assimilation is a means to fit into "the system." It is part of a larger strategy where one studies the norms and then adjusts themselves accordingly. This usually meant altering one's outward appearance and behaviors; some went further in a concerted effort to change even their inner workings, to erase every vestige that could be construed as "foreign." This is a daunting task. Furthermore, it suggests that, fundamentally, one is not acceptable as is.

Due to prejudice, ethnic people were often not allowed to "fit in" to WASP institutional settings, whether educational or corporate. "Irish need not apply" was later echoed in restrictions against Italians and Jews. Even if one did assimilate there was no guarantee they would gain admission or acceptance.

Prior to the mid-1950s, restrictive prejudice was rife in America. So if denied accepted into schools or hired for jobs, then better to go off on ones' own. It is no coincidence that many well-educated second-generation Jews turned to the professions instead of corporate America; as doctors, lawyers or accountants they were not as susceptible to glass ceilings or gentlemen's agreements, enabling them to flourish and succeed more on their own terms. Better this than needing to disguise themselves in order to fit into a regimented, perhaps even tacitly hostile, work environment.

The Promised Land was filled with traps, even in American Dream America. There was the trap of poverty, the trap of assimilation, the trap of drudgery, the trap of middle-class respectability—so many cages, so many hurdles to overcome in order to gain wealth and freedom at the other end. Better to gamble. Better to sidestep the whole system if possible, to circumvent the conventional in the hopes of leapfrogging the entire ethos and system.

Gambling is a short cut to achieving the Dream. Get-rich-quick schemes, patents on products in the hope of hitting it big, playing the lottery or the horses or the stock market are all part of the American landscape. Ignore the Protestant Work Ethic and bet at casinos instead. Never mind that the odds are always with the house, and that most who bet are those in greatest need who can ill-afford the costs, let along shoulder the losses. Still, a dream of freedom through risk and reward still tantalizes better playing one-armed bandits than tending to grindstones.

Leap Frogs

Part of the gambler's attraction is that he functions outside the norms of constricting society. He is not concerned with respectability or other such rules of conventional behavior. He flourishes on the fringe, an itinerant outsider, sidestepping the laws. He appears confident and cool, sometimes even sophisticated. He lives for the moment, relying entirely on his abilities and luck. If he loses a fortune he will certainly make another tomorrow. He is clever and opportunistic, savvy, and somehow wise. And because he is indifferent to respectability, his freedom and assurance have an exciting appeal.

But excessive gambling is disreputable because it threatens hearth and home. *The Music Man*'s showstopper is a fundamentalist-gospel-style song condemning a local pool hall's opening on the grounds it challenges family values. *Guys and Dolls* is built upon the opposition of a gambler's life to living a respectable domestic life guided by religion. *My Fair Lady* is built upon a bet made between Higgins and Pickering that Higgins could make a lady out of Eliza Doolittle. Significantly, Higgins first exhibits the rebuilt Eliza at the Ascot horserace. There, amidst the upper crust, fashionable gamesters, Eliza's enthusiasm caused her to revert back to her Cockney roots, as she screams on her horse of choice. Gambling is the purview of both the rich and the poor, and Eliza's naturalness is refreshing in its honesty and spontaneity, in contrast to the Ascot crowd's stiff affectation, which is what first attracts Higgins' rival Freddie to her. But Eliza is a fraud, even if an engaging one, as she too tries to leap frog middle-class life. Ironically, it is precisely the chains of bourgeois respectability that eventually trap her previously amoral—and happily free—father.

Beating the Odds

Scholar Michael Alexander examined the early twentieth-century Jews' attraction to Jewish gamblers when he explored the life and career of notorious bookmaker Arnold Rothstein. Alexander argues that because Jews traditionally functioned as outsiders living Diaspora lives, they tended to romanticize Rothstein and his ilk.[8]

Besides, stories of people like Rothstein were exciting, especially compared to the daily humdrum. They were much like the Old West outlaws mythologized by nineteenth-century dime novels. Look at Jewish gangster Bugsy Siegel, who built up Las Vegas as a Mecca for gamblers. Or consider Myron Lansky, brainy bagman of the Lucky Luciano mob. Over time Jews became less identified with violence and increasingly with crimes of fraud. Perhaps this was tied to the life of the mind, the pleasure at working out ideas, playing with words and numbers; perhaps it had to do with a collective history of trying to beat the odds in order to survive, as if the ability to outsmart the other guy was a competitive sport that fed macho pride.[9]

In the first half of the twentieth century Jewish gangs thrived in America's cities, including individuals like Dutch Schultz and groups like Detroit's Purple Gang. But by mid-century Jewish gangs had mostly disappeared, though individual Jewish gangsters still made news. So why did this change? Perhaps it was because American institutions increasingly opened up opportunities to the rapidly rising Jewish middle class. Just as you saw fewer Jewish boxers and basketball players, so too did you see fewer Jewish gamblers. In the 1920s Jews increasingly became shop owners rather than employees, and from the 1930s on their children increasingly attended college with many joining the ranks of professionals. As America's doors slowly opened, the need to operate outside the system diminished, and with it a decline in illicit activities. Mobsters also cleaned up their public image. Following World War II, newspapermen like Damon Runyon and Walter Winchell regularly reported on hoodlums as colorful celebrities, spotted at hotspot nightclubs like The Stork Club and Toots Shor's, hobnobbing with star entertainers and athletes.

The portrayal of gamblers in 1940s and 1950s Broadway musicals reflected this shift. *Show Boat* and *Funny Girl* portrayed an earlier era's gamblers as troubling ne'er-do-wells. Witness the change evident in *Guys and Dolls* (1950), a show built from Runyon stories. *Guys and Dolls* portrayed gamblers as cartoons, loveable and quaint and ultimately ready to settle down. By 1950 the Siegels and Lanskys were approaching middle age. So it is fitting that an aging professional gambler like Nathan Detroit see the error of his way via the Salvation Army mission and finally weds Adelaide; we presume he will no longer "get off the train at Saratoga" ever again. Now husband and wife, Nathan and Adelaide will leave their low-class ways behind in favor of plump middle-class domestic bliss.

Where the gamblers in *Show Boat* and in *Funny Girl* are portrayed as flawed romantic leads, in 1946's *Kiss Me, Kate* they are now viewed as vaguely shady threats. The *Taming of the Shrew* stars, Fred and Lilli, squabble, but are both seen as being otherwise respectable. Bill, on the other hand, is the one with a gambling problem. Fittingly, he is a member of the secondary couple (the other being Lois), suggesting lower status as would befit such behavior. The plot has Bill sign an IOU for a sizeable gambling loss in Fred's name, so that the gangland enforcers chase after Fred instead. It is all rather sordid back-stage antics, in sharp contrast to the high-brow Shakespeare being performed on stage. Gamblers are no longer suave romantic leads but rather low-class, brass knuckle instigators. Whereas the classical actor Fred struggles to regain Lilli, restoring their marriage, the gangster characters are relegated to being funny at best, troublesome at worst, reduced to singing vaudeville clowns, pandering to entertain, safely removed from the average theatre-goer's life.

Significantly, in both *Show Boat* and *Funny Girl*, the romantic relationships are portrayed as complex, the stories as realistic and serious, the characters reasonably dimensional, and the stakes high. Similarly, the music at the end of each show is wrenching and heartbreaking, as Gaylord sings a sad reprise of "You Are Love" even as Fanny sings the authentic Brice torch song, "My Man." In contrast, *Guys and Dolls* features characters far less realistic and music that is catchy and frivolous, befitting a two-dimensional comedy, with a reprise of "Guys and Dolls." But if we peek beneath the plot's surface we find more in keeping with assimilation and the American Dream. In *Show Boat* and *Funny Girl* both Gay and Nicky prove failures. Neither finds a way to fit in to societal norms, to find an alternate method of making a living. Hence, each abandons wife and family. On the other hand, in the case of *Guys and Dolls* both Sky and Nathan are converted by taking a religious bet and, thus transformed, are ready to fit in sufficiently to take on the new role of loving husband. As a sunny comedy, no one wonders whether they will be able to sustain this role over time.

Bewitched, Bothered, Bewildering

A troubling variation in our assimilation and the American Dream motif is Rodgers and Hart's *Pal Joey* (1939). Critic Brooks Atkinson respected the show but disliked it, famously asking how one can draw "sweet water from a foul well?" Written near the end of the musical comedy decade of the 1930s, *Pal Joey* defied the typical sunny optimism and collective innocence then prevalent. Joey is neither a gambler nor gangster, though he would rub shoulders with them à la a Toots Shor. Joey is a cad and the show is strikingly sardonic and archly world-weary, even if it contains perhaps Rodgers and Hart's finest musical score.

Pal Joey is cynical about heroes and love. Joey is a romantic heel, entirely self-serving and insensitive to others. He is a seedy night club singer who falls in love with Vera Simpson, a rich man's wife who makes Joey her gigolo. Vera dresses him up and finances his club but in the end dumps him. Learning nothing from the experience, Joey goes on with his dissolute ways.

While both Joey and Vera's behavior is despicable, what makes the show particularly malodorous is that it perverts the American Dream. Joey starts out at the bottom. He sees high society Vera as a means to get ahead. With Vera's guidance Joey improves his appearance and manners, both necessary to his professional advancement. He gains success running his own club. On the surface, so far, this fits in with notions of assimilate for success. That he achieves this through unsavory means is, in this respect, besides the point. The larger pattern is thus far in keeping with our paradigm.

However, if we take a few steps back and look from a distance we see that *Pal Joey* is a bitter repudiation of the American Dream. That Vera dumps him shows his success is short-lived and entirely dependent upon her good graces—or whims. Joey may think he has progressed in this world and that he has gained some measure of autonomy, but that is a sham. Joey is in fact disenfranchised as Vera holds all the power.

As a decidedly unsympathetic antihero, we are not unhappy with Joey's demise. But this too is troubling. The show seems to say that Joey starts out as scum, rises in the world because of his ability to please the well-to-do, is dressed up to look successful, but in the end gets what he always deserved, returning to the bottom, again only scum. It is written from Vera's point of view, not Joey's. She uses him and then discards him, much like an empty champagne bottle, or, in this case, a cheap bottle of beer. No matter how someone may dress up or behave, scum is still scum. If Joey had written it, would we see Vera as scum? Probably not since she has what he wanted and never gets.

If one argues that Joey is incapable of change and is therefore somehow admirable, then his poor behavior still damns him in our eyes. If he is simply incapable of self-improvement, then he is again stuck where he belongs, amidst society's dregs. Joey may dress up but that never changes our opinion of him. Vera deigned to step down from her high society perch in order to slum, but really just to find a bed mate. If she embodies the upper class, then that class is disreputable as it is riddled with avarice and greed.

She and Joey are a fit pair who meet in society's middle. She dips down as he rises up and, for a time, "horizontally speaking," the relationship works as long as it benefits each party. This Titania sleeps with this ass Bottom, but it changes nothing. The love drug here is booze, but that is an excuse, not an explanation for Vera's behavior. In the end she returns to her world just as he returns to his. *Pal Joey* accuses the American Dream of being a fraud and challenges the notion that assimilation truly serves as a path toward respectability and success.

Pal Joey premiered in 1939, the eve of World War II. It was one of the last shows written by Rodgers and Hart. Rodgers would soon shift away from the urban and urbane toward the folksy optimism of *Oklahoma!*, a change that also meant his turning away from the increasingly depressed and unreliable Hart. Rodgers would soon team up with the wholesome Oscar Hammerstein II, and shortly after *Oklahoma!*'s boffo debut Hart would end up dead. Perhaps the appeal of *Pal Joey* to Rodgers and Hart had something to do with their own deteriorating relationship and to Hart's profound personal despair and disappointment, despite achieving such great renown. To Hart the Dream proved bankrupt.

PART TWO: UNIONS

Love of Labor and Labors of Love

Pins and Needles and *The Pajama Game* form musical bookends. The former, first presented in 1936, embodied 1930s Depression, liberal sensibilities; whereas the latter, first presented in 1954, embodied that era's conservative attitudes. *Pins and Needles* was a revue featuring a nonprofessional cast of unknowns; *The Pajama Game* was a standard book musical, which featured veteran performers, legendary director George Abbott, and rising choreographer Bob Fosse. Still, one suspects that the 1930s show somehow laid the groundwork for the 1950s show as its antecedent. If so, America had grown complacent and tame over those eighteen years, not unlike the New Deal politics of FDR in comparison to the suppressed affluence of the Eisenhower years.

Both shows present workers in the clothing industry threatening to strike, and that is about all they have in common. Unlike *The Pajama Game*, *Pins and Needles* could not be considered a standard musical, even though it enjoyed a long Broadway run of over 1,100 performances. It is an anomaly, the product of an actual labor union, featuring an amateur cast of union members. The show was a revue that throughout its three-year run regularly introduced new scenes and songs to reflect recent social and political events. The primary composer was newcomer Harold Rome, who later went on to write a number of Broadway shows. In addition to Rome, the show's large creative team most notably included composer Mark Blitzstein and lyricist John LaTouche. *Pins and Needles* thus featured a group of nonprofessional clothing workers putting on a show, whereas *The Pajama Game* featured professional theatre people pretending to be clothing workers.

Pins and Needles appeared the same year as Blitzstein's infamous *The Cradle Will Rock*, a Bertolt Brecht–inspired opera produced by the Federal Theatre Project, that satirized industrial America's injustice, and that was famously banned by the Federal Government because it threatened to make waves. Unlike the Blitzstein work, *Pins and Needles* used humorous vignettes to depict the everyday lives and concerns of American workers. It was decidedly left wing, highly critical of totalitarianism abroad and *uber-*conservative traditionalists at home. It was a period piece, a product of the Great Depression, anticipating the war to come. Furthermore, as a product of the International Ladies Garment Workers Union, whose members were predominantly Jewish, most of its artists and cast were themselves New York Jews, giving the show a decidedly ethnic flavor.

The Pajama Game also depicts workers who come close to a strike. It is based upon the novel *7 ½ Cents* by Richard Bissell, a native of Iowa, who drew upon his own experiences working in a clothing factory. Whereas *Pins and Needles* is set in multiethnic New York City, *The Pajama Game* is set in Cedar Rapids, Iowa and its characters are largely homogenous, working-class WASPs. Where *Pins and Needles* was satiric and political, *The Pajama Game* is folksy and, except for their demands for a raise, presents a work force largely content with its lot. *The Pajama Game*, unlike its predecessor, has only sympathetic characters who, even if they thieve, blame communists for the labor strife, and present their strike goals only in terms of individual materialistic rewards. In short, *Pins and Needles* tends to criticize America from a largely socialist position, whereas *The Pajama Game* is decidedly nonpolitical and capitalistic in intent. Lastly, whereas *Pins and Needles* centers on the actual problems and fears of the men and women in its cast, *The Pajama Game* ultimately centers on a fictional romance, not on any larger societal ill. The earlier show looks outward; the later show inward.

Because *Pins and Needles* is such an anomaly, and because it is not a book musical, and because it has never enjoyed a Broadway revival (perhaps because its material is so historically specific), it falls beyond the parameters of this study. However, it is important to us in one respect: it depicts predominantly Jewish characters who are members of the working class. It also portrays the labor union as a desirable means to improve workers' lives, a path that enabled many to join America's middle class during the 1950s. The characters in *Pins and Needles* struggle and sacrifice believing in the American Dream, as opposed to the American "fantasy." Rather than circumvent the system they have tried to fit in to it. In both shows, despite the talk of strikes, characters speak from the position of being honest, hardworking Americans, who have upheld their end of the social bargain, who now expect management and society to uphold their end in kind.

Tops and Bottoms

The Pajama Game is about business, but it is not about getting ahead in business. Factory workers at the Sleeptite Pajama Company threaten to go out on strike unless granted a 7 ½ cent raise. Mr. Hasler, the boss, bitterly and comically blames foreign agitators and communists for causing the fuss. Our hero Sid is the newly hired factory superintendent who sports the foreign-sounding last name of Sorokin. His labor counterpart, head of the worker grievance committee, is the American-sounding Katherine "Babe" Williams. The two fall in love, but their love is threatened because he is management and she labor. The secondary couple is quirky and comedic: Gladys Hotchkiss—Mr. Hasler's flirty assistant—and her jealous boyfriend, Vernon "Hinesie" Hines, who drinks too much and enjoys throwing knives.

We know little about Sid; he is in many ways a mystery. We later find that he came recently from far-away big-city Chicago, where he was a factory worker. Locally unknown, Sid talked his way into the Sleeptite supervisor job, even though he actually lacked the credentials. In this regard *The Pajama Game* resembles *How To Succeed in Business Without Really Trying* in the protagonist's use of deceit to get an opportunity that would not otherwise be available to him. Sid is a liminal figure because he is management yet has a background that also makes him sympathetic to labor. Unlike J. Pierrepont Finch, protagonist of *How To Succeed in Business Without Really Trying*, Sid has real hands-on know how of the business and is not afraid to work. He is seen several times with his sleeves rolled up, elbow deep busy repairing broken machinery. If Sid succeeds it is because he really is trying and really cares about the welfare of the Sleeptite company.

The 1957 film version features many from the original Broadway cast. The character types here are a wonderfully mongrel mix, not defined so much by ethnicity (sans Sid) as according to contrasting age and odd body types, giving the show an exaggerated caricatured look. This casting gives the plant employees a working-class authenticity, not usually found in the average Broadway musical of the time.

The Pajama Game portrays mid-1950s Middle America, suggesting that it represents the norm. The eleven o'clock number in the show is "Seven and a Half Cents" in which factory labor leaders tally up what that raise would amount to over time and the material objects they could afford as a result. It is charming and funny, especially given the modesty of their dreams, which makes them endearing since they ask for so little. The show's finale soon follows: a fashion show for the average Joe. Instead of sleek models wearing the latest Paris fashions, here each lead parades dressed in various types of pajamas that badly echo high society events. After all, they work for Sleeptite, not Dior. It is all lighthearted fun, but still a proclamation of pride in being everyday Americans, playfully thumbing their nose at the well-to-do, happy that they can again play together having weathered the earlier strife. Even once-raging Mr. Hasler takes part in the fun, signaling an absence of residual malice or resentment or any sign of class difference amongst them. They are at root all friends, past differences quickly forgotten.

Is this socialism? More likely not, as it takes place in the plant and celebrates American business. It also asserts a pride in traditional American values. Unlike the big national chain with whom they compete, Sleeptite survives by providing quality goods at a fair price. The competing national chain is mentioned briefly and has a Jewish-sounding name, implying that that outside threat is somehow foreign and does not feature the same degree of quality in material or manufacture. So the plant's nationalism does teeter on the edge of nativism as contrasting business practices suggest contrasting cultural values.

It is odd that *The Pajama Game* proved a success on Broadway, given its subject matter, setting, and values. New York City had long been home to the nation's clothing trade and was almost entirely Jewish, owned and operated throughout most of the twentieth century. It was often familiarly referred to as the *schmatta* trade from the Yiddish word for rags. Despite this potential link, the show is not set in New York City but rather in Cedar Rapids, Iowa. To a New York audience this might as well be the other side of the moon. It is the same white bread WASP Midwest as portrayed in *The Music Man*, though portraying a much later era. But whereas *The Music Man* portrays River City as a solidly middle-class world, *The Pajama Game* instead favors the working-class side of town. Still, a pajama factory certainly would have suggested a Jewish industry to the 1950s New York City audience. Perhaps they attended anticipating an updated version of *Pins and Needles*, especially since the plot centered on a labor dispute. What then was its commercial appeal, besides the romance and snappy numbers?

Victorian Secrets

Note that in the picnic number characters mention that this is the only day they have off all year! It is their "Once-a-Year Day," which further accentuates the modesty of their demands, as well as the sense that even on their one day off they party together. This show is intent on showing wholesome American workers, largely happy with their everyday lot, though still filled with dreams. And it is a group that is honest and fair. When a worker failed to help Sid by handing him a screwdriver, Sid shoved him aside, whereupon the worker ran off to complain. But the grievance committee found his complaints unjust and decided against him, knowing he was a malingerer. These are honest, hardworking people, respectful of their chores, and intolerant of shirkers. They represent the best in the American worker. So when they then consider going out on strike we the audience know that their demands are just and, sure enough, it is the blowhard, intransigent boss who proves to be at fault and only relents when pressured by Sid.

Unlike most melodramatic shows, in *The Pajama Game* secrets are kept. Sid is able to coerce Hasler because he found out by examining the company books that for six months Hasler had pocketed funds earmarked for the employees. Sid confronts Hasler privately and alone, forcing the boss to relent. In other shows such a revelation might well be made in public, to the horror and admonishment of the crowd. Not here. In fact, Sid never tells anyone about Hasler's criminality, enabling Hasler to keep his job and maintain his place in the factory community. Other secrets also abound. The file room key would enable Sid to read the company books, but Hasler's secretary Gladys wears the file room key on a chain around her neck, beneath her blouse. She tempts Sid suggesting that if he wants the key he will have to seduce her. He would need to "uncover" Gladys in order to uncover company secrets. Similarly, when we first see Hinesie, he appears only a middle-aged factory foreman, responsible and demanding. We later discover Hinesie drinks and that his hobby is knife-throwing, that when drunk he is insanely jealous of Gladys to the point of throwing those knives. By play's end Gladys' indiscriminant flirtations are forgiven, Hinesie's fit of violence is forgiven, Hasler's theft is forgiven. It is as if the final scene's pajama tops and bottoms capably cover up any sign of deviance or sin.

The company is also rife with sexual improprieties. In addition to Gladys' promiscuity, the in-house labor leader Prez apparently has hit on every female employee before finally settling, perhaps surprisingly, on the oversized Mae. The song "Once-a-Year Day" catalogues all the hanky-panky going on amongst the workers as they frolic at the company picnic. And speaking of hidden improprieties, both Sid and Babe keep their office romance a secret. No wonder Bob Fosse could justify making "Steam Heat," a dance of labor unrest, into one of his signature pelvis-grinding routines.

But the show's biggest secret is Sid himself. Babe openly reveals her true self. When first introduced she calls herself "Babe," but we soon learn her given name is Katherine. Once Babe and Sid begin to date, we are introduced to her modest home and to her aging father, who still works for the railroad, and who keeps a collection of stamps. No mention is made of her mother, which, given Babe's closeness to her father, suggests she is deceased rather than having run off. By contrast, it is telling that there is almost no mention of Sid's personal life or past. He remains a sort of sphinx. Yet Sid is eager to fit in with Babe and her father, taking an interest in the things that interest them. And he and Babe are downright playful about their sexual feelings for each other, as witnessed by the song, "There Once Was a Man."

So why does Sid not share more about himself given his intimacy with the Williams family? We do find out that he is hiding his roots as a factory worker; we know he is from Chicago; we know that he feigned his background in order to get this job and that this job is very important to him.

Sid's name suggests immigrant ancestry. In Richard Bissell's novel, *7 ½ Cents*, the source for the musical, we learn that Sid is second-generation Russian, born and raised in the Gary, Indiana, steel town, amidst mostly fellow Slavs and Jews. Like many immigrant children he has worked his way up, determined to learn and make something of himself.[10]

Given the Red hunting fever of the early 1950s, it seems odd to have a musical's protagonist with a Russian sounding last name, though that might also provide Sid with a reason to hide his past. Sid's hiring is especially peculiar given that Mr. Hasler blusters against communists throughout, aligning himself with the McCarthy right. If Sid had previously worked in a Chicago factory as part of the labor force, then perhaps, in addition to wanting to hide his lack of experience in management, he also does not want to be aligned with labor or with those who go out on strike. Sid's promotion to management signaled not only his professional advancement, but also his abandonment of any past associations with unionism or with the Left. In the Sleeptite culture portrayed in *The Pajama Game* it is certainly rare to find anyone of a different ethnic slant, let alone one representing management. This would be a real wrinkle in the factory's cultural fabric.

Whether Sid was Russian or not, he was certainly an outsider. Being an outsider he would work hard to fit in to the culture, to gain acceptance and camaraderie and, in this case, even romance. Sid wants to end his isolation. Yet ultimately it is because he is an outsider that he is able to rescue the factory and its community of workers. Both Babe and Mr. Hasler literally raise their fists in defiance of each other; Mr. Hasler is alternatively combative and condescending. Both sides stay stubbornly intransigent. A strike seems inevitable.

The first schism occurs when Babe leads the other workers in trying to sabotage the plant's output by slowing down their individual productivity. This challenges Sid's authority. When Sid calls Babe out in public he is forced to fire her, making their personal relationship the first casualty of this disagreement. Later, when confronting Mr. Hasler about his wrongdoing, Sid explains his own motives by saying that he did not want to see the factory go under, that he wanted to keep his job. But he might as well have also explained that he wanted to keep the ship afloat because it had welcomed him. The onetime outsider had found himself an identity and a home.

Sid was once labor but is now management; Sid is now management but was once labor. He belongs to both worlds, he belongs to neither. Because he is not invested as fully in either he can see beyond the narrow demands, can maintain a certain objectivity and clarity others lack. Perhaps if he only was solely management then he would probably just roll up his sleeves again, this time to fight. But Sid sees the dangers in just such a confrontation. So he goes undercover. Because he is not the boss Sid is denied access to the company books, but because he is management he is allowed access to Gladys. Because he is management he knows how to read the ledgers, and when he realizes the truth he sides neither with labor nor management but rather with the truth. Perhaps that is why he does not blow the whistle on Hasler, because he simply wants to make the place function regardless of legality. Besides, with so many factory workers having relatively shady pasts, including himself, who is he to moralize. This is a company composed of scamps, all finding happiness together. No need to moralize; just be thankful for it, warts and all. The business is rightfully called "Sleeptite." Beyond selling pajamas, the name is a statement of reassurance, much as a parent comforts a child at bedtime, that all those who subscribe will find peace and safety, that all will indeed sleep tight, not having to worry about having the bed bugs bite. The company is far away from the House Un-American Activities Committee and its targets, safely nestled in small-town Iowa, a haven that perhaps protects the poor, the tired, the huddled masses seeking to breathe free within its four walls, an idealized microcosm of America itself, equally accessible to all seeking asylum and employment.

Much like Harold Hill in *The Music Man*, Sid is the outsider who, because he is an outsider, is able to mediate the locals' problems and introduce solutions that resolve their seemingly impossible differences. He is a healer. Though lacking any real political clout, he is a sort of *deus ex machina*, bringing everything and everyone into a nice, neat resolution. And perhaps one of the reasons the outsider is the one to resolve differences is because he himself is different. Within the given community, whether it is the Sleeptite factory or the town of River City, a certain homogenous norm is expected, thus making any other point of view inacceptable because it becomes a power struggle between inhabitants over what constitutes their lone identity. But since the outsider does not hail from these parts, he sees them all as parts of a single whole, even if they themselves are ready to come to blows. To Sid the Sleeptite factory community includes both labor and management and relies upon both; this inspires him to seek means of reconciliation.

The song "7 ½ Cents" suggests trust in the Protestant Work Ethic rather than circumventing the system. The workers are intent on keeping their jobs and putting in those forty-hour weeks over a period of years in order to reap their fantasy rewards. They are also cognizant that they would have to save that money in order to realize their fantasy wishes. There is no sense of finagling or finessing anyone here, no sense that one needs to change their external appearance in order to get ahead. Each person is shown literally at work, even Sid who we see fixing two different machines by hand, as well as "fixing" the impending labor strike. Hinesie, aside from his disturbing knife-throwing tricks and occasional drunkenness, is seen at work as the efficiency expert, and sexy Gladys wears the company file room key around her neck as a pendant, where other girls might don bobbles instead. And though the dialogue occasionally shifts to gossip amongst the girls and hints of romances beyond the central love story of Sid and Babe, almost the entire rest of the script is composed literally of shop talk.

In addition, as a community that works together, parties together, sings, and socializes together, there is no sense of anyone being perceived as an outsider. Even the new supervisor with the ethnic-sounding name (Sid) is included in all of their festivities, as well as in sharing their professed aspirations, à la the song "7 ½ Cents." It is telling that the song culminates with Babe's dream of saving up so much money that she can eventually buy her own pajama factory and thus supplant Hasler as boss. The dream of upward mobility angle is ever present, even if it takes twenty years of saving to achieve it.

PART THREE: OUTSIDERS

From the Other Side of the Tracks

The Pajama Game opened in 1954, whereas *The Music Man* opened only three years later. Both are set in Iowa, in a Midwest town far apart from New York City and the usual Broadway sensibilities. The cultures of Cedar Rapids and of River City are Middle-American homogenous, with a healthy skepticism toward outsiders. And while neither Sid Sorokov nor Professor Harold Hill is overtly ethnic, local xenophobia would naturally make either of them suspect. Both shows portray communities on the brink of civil unrest, one due to a pending strike and the other due to rebellious children, and neither seems to be sufficiently capable of a happy resolution. It took an outsider to solve the problems of each, one who wished to fit in and yet also brought alternative ways of thinking and being. Even though ethnicity is not a part of either show's setting, the patterns of assimilation remain, and both protagonists are essentially immigrant newcomers, who, as included outsiders, find ways to achieve a peaceful resolution and preserve their host community.

Though the two shows enjoy similarities, they also contrast sharply. *The Pajama Game* is contemporary, set in the 1950s, whereas *The Music Man* is set nostalgically in the 1910s; the former concerns factory life amongst the working class, whereas *The Music Man* centers on the respectable middle class. And where *The Pajama Game* centers only on a factory's workers' conflict with their boss, *The Music Man* involves an entire town and its mayor, taking on various civic concerns. Where *The Pajama Game* is about preserving collective happiness through monetary gain, and even tolerates aberrant behaviors amongst its individual members, *The Music Man* is about fighting over a community's ethos, how the status quo is suspicious of any sort of what it deems questionable behaviors (such as playing pool), rigidly demanding conformity to middle-class respectability from all. So whereas working-class *The Pajama Game* is narrow in setting its characters are relatively open minded, *The Music Man* portrays a broader variety of settings peopled by the narrow of mind.

Marian the Librarian

Nothing about Meredith Willson was Jewish, aside from his showbiz affiliations as a radio bandleader. He wrote *The Music Man* based upon his own Iowa childhood and went through scores of rewrites and many rejections before his show was finally produced. Still, *The Music Man* reflects concerns and solutions comparable to many other shows we are examining here. The characters and setting might not be ethnic, but the action follows the same patterns as if they were, no doubt contributing to the story's resonance with the 1950s New York audience.

There is the show's heroine. Let us start right there with the catchy take on her name: "Marian, the Librarian." The character's actual name is Marion Paroo, but because her name rhymes felicitously with her occupation she becomes subject to a memorable song in the show. Marian is *The Music Man's* female lead. Her character is painted as a progressive in otherwise conservative River City, Iowa. She is also rapidly becoming a spinster because she so differs from the norm, hence the reliance on her job rather than upon a husband. Marian is different.

Also in town is Marcellus, a onetime con man who has gone straight and is living in happy obscurity until his former partner in crime, Professor Harold Hill, arrives in town. Hill persuades Marcellus to revert to his old ways in order to aid Hill with his schemes. Hill's con is relatively harmless, a threat only to the locals' notoriously tight purse strings: he wants to sell them on starting a boy's band. When Hill arrives he is fleeing from previous towns where he likewise attempted to sell this scam. Therefore, Hill is an itinerant grifter, a salesman par excellence with a shady reputation, the ultimate outsider, and a seller of dreams.

America has always loved con men. They are half showmen and half businessmen who entertain thanks to their flamboyance and gall. It is a long tradition reaching back to the ever pragmatic Benjamin Franklin, generations of sharp Yankee traders, and includes the legendary hokum of P. T. Barnum. It also spills into those fundamentalist preachers who yearned for celebrity, like Billy Sunday or Aimee Semple McPherson. Harold Hill is their happy disciple, full of marvelous humbug and outrageous toe-tapping charm as he spreads the Good (albeit secular) Word.

Ultimately Hill meets Marian and the two, both bent on selling culture to narrow-minded locals, quickly hit it off. Along with Marcellus they conspire together. In the end they succeed, not only in getting the town to buy instruments and uniforms, but in getting them to appreciate their young and in helping the youngsters find self-esteem. It is as if Hill were bringing a newfangled American Dream oasis to this skeptical Midwest cultural desert, and, by getting them to buy in, they find meaning in their lives, despite the ebbing protests of the Mayor and his wife. Unlike the previous "victims" of Hill's shenanigans, River City opts to welcome him rather than prosecute him.

Though featuring no ethnic characters, *The Music Man* still concerns itself with outsiders, with the progressive in conflict with the traditional, making the case for an evolving, rather than static, America. The big "con" here is Hill's clever redefinition of American life, sold via theatrics. Hill uses stump speeches and salesman spiels, and in arguing for the underdog he reveals his own fundamental humanity—in spite of himself.

Unlike the other Iowa towns, River City, despite its faults, is somehow a hotbed of sublimated culture and a place that can welcome change. After all, though she is miserable, Marian does have an accepted role in this town. Similarly, another outsider, Marcellus, has found a home here. Can Hill—the professional salesman, the professional con man—also find his Eden here? If so, then why? He has travelled around the region trying to persuade others that they have a need for his products, but in River City he finds a place really is in need of what Hill sells. Here Hill genuinely has a place, and thus a place where he can stay.

Then there is his discovery of Marian. Hill hoped to put some city-slicker moves on small-town Marian, but in the end it is he who is trapped by her. Unlike our con man protagonist, Marian is not a gold-digger but pure of heart. This is crucial to the show, for without her presence, Hill would be seen only as a self-serving, deceitful scoundrel. Her love makes him human, encouraging us the audience to view him as more than charming. And since he reciprocates her affection we (and he) realize there something genuine to him, beneath the razzmatazz. Marian thus redeems Hill.

In addition, Hill's mentoring of both Tommy and Winthrop also demonstrates his possibilities. He becomes a beneficial Pied Piper to River City's children, who are either rebellious or suffer poor self-esteem. Hill works his magic to instill them with self-worth. The children respond to his dreams, most notably Marian's lisping little brother Winthrop, who so eagerly awaits the Wells Fargo Wagon bringing musical instruments, that he forgets his painful self-consciousness and sings joyfully in celebration. If this man can achieve such miracles then there is unexpected worth to his spiel.

Hill could not fit into River City had the town not first accepted his marching band. Other towns apparently only saw the expense of the uniforms and the musical instruments, but River City bought into the larger fantasy he painted for them. On the surface he preaches the gospel of music, the sales pitch of culture and self-improvement for the young. But in a deeper sense Hill promotes respect and opportunity and is thus a prophet of American dreams, well beyond the average salesman's gospel of profit. Hill successfully converts the town to his vision when they accepted the marching band into their lives. River City thus becomes a place where Hill has a role, a town inclusive of him and his values. Hill proves more effective than even Marian the librarian in introducing cultural ideals, and this couple, once assigned to the town's fringe, become pivotal to its newly expanded worldview. Hill essentially enacts Marian's Enlightenment.

Just as "Professor" Harold Hill unexpectedly becomes a civic leader, he also becomes domesticated, tamed. He will wed Marian. And just as Marian resisted matrimony in the form of the formerly narrow-minded insiders, she will wed Harold. Together they will redefine the community's mores. Nineteenth century definitions give way to modernity: the huckster is reformed into a husband and the librarian can also be a wife. And the town can expand itself to accommodate culture and humanism beyond the purely skeptical and practical. Thus the fake professor proves a real teacher; the charlatan is transformed into the legitimate. Making himself integral to the ongoing well-being of River City, the onetime outsider becomes welcomed into their midst.

Postwar Musical Careerwomen: Ambition or Love?

Exhibit A: *Annie Get Your Gun*

Can a woman can make it on her own, in American musical terms? Most often women in musicals accomplish the American Dream by marrying a successful man. Even *Hello, Dolly!*'s autonomous and strong-willed title character concerns herself primarily with luring Horace Vandergelder into marriage. And since musicals tend to center more on women and romance, this is a comfortably familiar expectation.

Annie Get Your Gun offers a different perspective. It debuted in 1946 and was unusual in that it depicted a woman who first proves herself a success in show business, who achieves financial freedom and worldwide acclaim before finally relenting to win her man. Her competitive streak and ambition prevent her from giving in to Frank Butler for almost the entire duration of the show even though she is clearly smitten with him. As originally staged, whenever Annie runs into Frank all she can do is just gape at him, although their subsequent conversation inevitably soon leads to who is the better shot. This comic business is crucial to the play's effectiveness, especially with 1940s audiences, as it made it clear that, despite her masculine-like drive, Annie is entirely feminine and will be domesticated.

The script shows Annie as driven to succeed because of her poor and illiterate beginnings. Her rise to the top is as much about her learning how to fit into a more cosmopolitan world as it is about her winning acclaim for her talents and skill. In this regard she is no different than Fanny Brice as portrayed in *Funny Girl*. We see her climb each successive rung of the ladder of success, gaining understanding of societal rules and gaining professional polish along the way. Like *Funny Girl*, *Annie Get Your Gun* is a stage biography, which perhaps colors its impact as well. But this Annie Oakley is not as true to life as the Fanny Brice painted by *Funny Girl*. In the theatrically capable hands of Herbert Fields, sister Dorothy Fields and songwriter Irving Berlin, Annie becomes as rustic and foreign to American ways as, well, Berlin himself, even though she was a WASP and he a Jew. So Oakley's triumph reflects the Jewish creative team's own assimilation concerns.

Oakley starts out as a rube but steadily gains her peers' respect. Professional success is never a problem for her: she is confident and brilliant at her craft, and producer Buffalo Bill Cody is quick to recognize and reward his rising star. Cody's function here is comparable to how Ziegfeld made a star of Brice in *Funny Girl* and a star of the title character in *Sally*. But here Cody is shown to become also a friend to his star. Annie lacks conventional feminine polish and is seen almost exclusively in the company of men, with whom she has more in common. What she lacks is the romantic savvy to know how to win Frank. This she eventually gets from an unexpected source: her friend Chief Sitting Bull.

The choice of Sitting Bull to provide this key knowledge aligns the show further with assimilation themes. Like Annie, Sitting Bull is an outsider, also from what was ironically an alien culture, one who similarly performs in the Wild West Show. He too has had to change himself to gain acceptance and find professional reward; though this legendary warrior now pleases others for a living he does thrive. Without Sitting Bull's words of wisdom Annie would never seen the errors of her combative ways and would have continued on with her life without Frank, unwed.

And what was that advice? Deliberately lose the sharpshooting context to Frank. Annie sacrifices her pride in order to appease Frank's ego. Annie thus playacts the traditional female role in order to accommodate Frank's traditional male role. Though she is autonomous, Annie will pretend that Frank is the dominant provider, will defer to him and thus seemingly lose her autonomy along the way. Because she does this deliberately, we the audience know it to be a pack of lies, which preserves Oakley's integrity in our eyes even as succumbs in good romantic happy-ending fashion. No need for business success to interfere with achieving the traditional female benefits of the American Dream: hearth, home and family. Annie initially outwardly assimilated to gain professional renown; she then internally assimilates in order to gain a husband.

Exhibit B: *Gypsy*

A dozen or so years after *Annie Get Your Gun*, *Gypsy* premiered. Like *Annie Get Your Gun*, *Gypsy* is about a woman trying to make it in show business. But by 1959 the times had changed and that is reflected in the show.

Even though the title points to famous stripper Gypsy Rose Lee, and is loosely based upon her memoirs, the musical ultimately centers on her domineering stage mother, Rose. We see Rose drive her two daughters, the talented Baby June and the shy Louise, going town to town, intent on achieving vaudeville success. Along the path Rose is romanced by Herbie, but he sours on her ruthless ambition and walks out. Rose similarly drives away her hope, Baby June, and is left only with the talentless Louise. Rose and Louise sink lower and lower. It becomes clear that Rose loves her fantasies of success more than her daughters, and nowhere is that more clear than when Rose pushes Louise to perform a strip tease at a seedy burlesque house. Sweet, endearing Louise thus loses her professional innocence at her own mother's insistence.

Louise takes to the work and transforms herself into the legendary Gypsy Rose Lee, with a bevy of beaux and earning top dollar for her craft. Once she achieves success, though, the now- adult daughter has no place for her mother. The show ends sadly—or perhaps cruelly—with Mama Rose singing "Rose's Turn." It is her turn in the spotlight, having dedicated herself to her daughters. The number is also a wrenching soliloquy, with musical twists and turns which chart her emotional breakdown, a retrospective of the show and of her life. Rose claims to possess as much talent as her daughters, perhaps more, and that she, not Louise, should be a star. It is angry, spiteful and resentful, a solo burlesque, an emotional striptease, with Rose shimmying and bumping and grinding, determined to outdo her ungrateful daughter. We see Rose stuck in a tragic fantasy world in which all her sacrifices pay off, in which she is appreciated. She almost wins us over before we recall her ruthless manipulation of her children, sacrificing them on the altar of success, of how Rose narcissistically sought to live her life through theirs. Rose is no heroine, despite the glitzy finale. Mama Rose used the American Dream to justify her selfish behavior. Like Brecht's Mother Courage, who, despite her name proves neither maternal nor courageous, Mama Rose's heart-stirring, *tour de force* appeal to the audience's heart strings is ultimately self-serving. We ought to know better: Rose alone is responsible for her own demise.

Gypsy removes her clothing but shields her heart; Rose's strip reveals her troubled emotional state. This suggests that, up until that point both women remained covered. To assimilate is to cover up one's true self, to outwardly don an acceptable facade in order to move forward. It might be motivated by ambition, or could be governed by fear. How striking that both mother and daughter strip bare at the musical's end after a lifetime of cover-ups, and how striking that that act makes a star of the daughter but signals the mother's collapse.

Gypsy Rose Lee and sister June Havoc remained stars the rest of their lives. Perhaps they succeeded because Mama Rose paid the price for their success, but none of the three come off sympathetically in *Gypsy*. Even though we understand their reasons, it is nevertheless true that June selfishly abandoned the family and Louise cruelly discarded her mother upon achieving stardom.

Gypsy offers a far more matter of fact worldview than anything found in *Annie Get Your Gun*. *Gypsy*'s characters are complex and often contradictory; the only time they pander to the audience is when they perform, be it vaudeville or burlesque; the possibility of romantic love for Mama Rose appears early but quickly dissolves. The show depicts show business as an unforgiving struggle, with more days spent with rejection than reward.

Ultimately, *Gypsy* cynically substitutes sex for love, business for domesticity. This is fitting since it is the story of a stripper. The show argues the necessity of being cold and businesslike, especially for a woman trying to make it. Mama Rose chose business over love, ill-treating both Herbie and her daughters. Perhaps Rose was so driven that she confused the two, thinking that to push her daughters was somehow itself an act of love. But love devolves into a commodity in the show. This is highlighted when the other strippers instruct Louise that "You Gotta Get a Gimmick." Their stripper routines are so over the top that they burlesque sex itself, making it and them comic rather than erotic. There is nothing Feminist to what they say: the girls are simply swapping trade secrets. What they do and how they are viewed is a given; their primary goal is to stand out, which is the real secret to stardom. Clever Louise listens closely and learns the tricks of the trade. It is sort of a reversal of Annie taking advice from Sitting Bull. Annie already enjoyed stardom and economic autonomy, but sought help in order to get her man. Here Louise learns how to attract men's attention in order to achieve stardom and its rewards.

"You Gotta Get a Gimmick" is assimilation advice. No one will make it just by relying upon what God gave them. Something more needs to be added, something with special appeal: one sports a bugle, the second "twinkling" lights, the third, though refined, still bumps and grinds. Each is a strategy designed to gain acceptance, win applause, and succeed.

Gypsy is a cynical show. It is cynical about family, about relationships, about women's chances of success beyond making the most of their physical attributes. It argues that a woman makes it in show business by pointing out in no uncertain terms that she is in fact a woman. And what better way to do that than to strip?

Louise finds a "special" man. We never see her find love, hearth, or home. Unlike other shows we have covered, where female stars obsess over their mates, Louise ends up essentially alone. She even rejects her mother. As a star stripper she enjoys having plenty of men without needing to please just one. Love was never part of the equation between her and Rose, and her father was absent, so why should it suddenly matter now? *Gypsy* frankly demonstrates that for some women the American Dream means only business.

The show's titled *Gypsy* obviously refers to Gypsy Rose Lee. "Gypsies" are also the singer/dancers who people the casts of Broadway shows, who move from show to show, making the most of the life as long as possible. It also points to the stereotypical Gypsy woman, a reference Gypsy Rose Lee certainly intended for her stage persona. Such women are exotic and erotic. They move from place to place, never belonging anywhere, living perpetually outside accepted societal norms without any apparent attachments. They are often seen as immoral, even criminal, as apt to thieve as make love. They are strong and independent and not ever to be trusted as they are ultimately out for only themselves, which only adds to their allure. Gypsies never fit in, jealous of their freedom.

There is little sentimentality found in *Gypsy*, little feeling for others or desire for anything other than the materialistic. Louise creates an alter ego for herself, one in which she no longer needs to be under her mother's thumb, one in which she uses men rather than have men use her. Louise becomes Gypsy Rose Lee, but she also starts to resemble her mother. Mama Rose is correct in the end: it was she who was always the real star. Rose rejected assimilating to a conventional life, rejected keeping house, insisting that driving her daughters through vaudeville was itself a form of domestic love. But it was a sham. That proved to be Mama Rose's "gimmick." In the end the stripper is forced to remove her gimmicky costume and shed her props in order to reveal herself for who she actually is underneath. They are left with no glittering distractions, no razzle dazzle, only the unforgiving glare of the lights and the spectator's increasingly clinical, troubled gaze.

PART FOUR: FROM OUTSIDER TO INSIDER

Succeeding in the 1960s: Outside to Inside, Bottom to Top

Frank Loesser's *How to Succeed in Business Without Really Trying* won the 1962 Pulitzer Prize for its satire of corporate America. It is also an exemplar of how notions of assimilation played during the time when Eisenhower gave way to Kennedy. Old warhorse Ike and his banged, dowdy Mamie were replaced by the glamorously young Jackie and Jack; a self-made Midwest Protestant ceded the Oval Office to an Irish Catholic Boston scion. Puritanism gave way to hedonism, black-and-white to color. Ethnic outsiders now governed America's mainstream. Fairy tales can come true/ it can happen to you/if you're young at heart, or so Sinatra sang.

Much like *The Pajama Game*, *How To Succeed in Business Without Really Trying* was based upon a book from the early 1950s. By 1960 the corporate world it portrayed had blossomed into junior executive fruition. Where *The Pajama Game* was set in a small Midwest clothing factory, *How to Succeed* is set in the high rise New York corporate headquarters of the World Wide Wicket Company. *The Pajama Game* portrayed working life from labor's point of view, a community of garment workers who preferred to get along and fret about the need for a divisive strike. *How to Succeed* shows modern corporate life as a giant shark tank, as suited executives conspire to discredit their rivals in order to get ahead, no love lost, every man for himself.

How to Succeed's hero is the impish J. Pierrepont Finch, a window washer who assiduously follows a self-help book to get ahead in business, hence the show's title. The window washer, accustomed to being on the outside looking in, adjusting ropes and pulleys from the top floors down, takes the big leap and enters the World Wide Wicket building from the ground floor doors where he then systematically climbs back to the top in a span of only a few days.

Finch is an empty cipher, a fraud. We know almost nothing about him, only what he seems to lack. Finch has no identity beyond the book. But by adhering to the book's instructions, he circumvents the fact that he has no background, training, or experience. He gets by mostly on ingratiating charm, dodging and darting to seize opportunities and avoid pitfalls. Finch's path resembles an arcade game, with us the audience cheering him on and keeping score. His role as protagonist encourages us to root for him, otherwise we would probably not do so. He may be the cutest shark in the tank, but he is still a shark.

Early in the show Finch meets his love interest, the secretary Rosemary, who goes after him. After some delays the two finally go out on a date where she sings Finch (or Ponty as she likes to call him) a song to him intended as both a love ballad and a business pep talk, "I Believe in You":

> You have the cool, clear eyes of a seeker of wisdom and truth,
> Yet there's that upturned chin and the grin of impetuous youth,
> Oh, I believe in you, I believe in you....

The one dissonant line is her description of him is the first. It is entirely misplaced; there is nothing about Ponty that merits that description, underscoring the fact that she is projecting onto him qualities that he simply does not possess. Since Finch is an empty vessel, this seems to work. Rosemary thinks she seems something in him and it strengthens the audience's reasons to root for him. Finch is inspired by her portrait, later drawing upon it to gird himself before a corporate battle. Rosemary thus invents her lovable "Ponty" for us, and he subsequently embraces her flattering description to buoy himself against his scheming rivals.

But is there truth to Rosemary's description? Finch's entire *modus operandi* is to appear as others wish to see him, so that, as their reflection, he can garner their support for his advancement. It makes sense that the romantic Rosemary should fall into this as well. To Finch attributes as wisdom and truth might set him apart in a largely impersonal corporate system. Finch is different, he does stand out, both as hero and target. His opponents appear avaricious by comparison, even though his intentions are really no different than theirs.

Paradoxically, because his rivals grew up within the privileged corporate system, there is a candor about them that Finch lacks. But their "honesty" is not admirable. They are all born schemers with nothing more to them, whereas at least Finch is sufficiently unversed as to require a guide book. So he becomes oddly sympathetic amidst this pack of wolves. And because our former window washer is an outsider accustomed to observing from without, his rivals' true natures are evident to him and to us.

If Finch ever did do a speck of work he would be immediately found out; but the message of the show is that external image matters far more than substance or know-how. So Finch manages to leap frog over everyone, one at a time. We root for him because he is isolated, because his actions are transparent to us, because he differs from his rival, the hyena-like Bud Frump who, in addition to being whiny and infantile, is the spoiled beneficiary of nepotism. Since Frump is more despicable than Finch, we favor Finch as a sympathetically attractive foil.

A Secretary is Not a Toy

How To Succeed in Business has a lot to do with women. We are told in song that "a secretary is not a toy" and yet that is exactly what they seem to be in the show. While the business world is portrayed as entirely male, the building is teeming with tempting females. One of the show's early numbers is an instrumental where the almost-identical secretaries—lined up in identical desks and chairs and typewriters—begin their day's work: elaborately preening themselves before handheld mirrors. Their business appears to be sex, not secretarial chores.

Rosemary falls for Finch at first sight. One would presume he does so for her as well, but he is so hell-bent on success that he seems oblivious. Rosemary immediately volunteers to help get him a job, so she searches out her gal pal Smitty to help. But before she returns Finch has already won the good graces of the personnel chief by dropping the boss's name. But the point here is the secretary's surprise that he is able to accomplish this alone. In this business at least, it is the women who actually run everything.

This dynamic is clearly seen in the company president, Mr. Biggley. He is so important that he is caught between three women: his mistress, his wife, and his secretary. Hedy is Biggley's curvaceous, squeaky-voiced, perpetual-wiggle of a bimbo mistress and she uses her kewpie-doll, tight-sweater sexuality to demand a job of him. She later complains when no one will take her on as their personal secretary. Why? Because others learn of Hedy's link to the big boss and see nothing but trouble. Finch takes on Hedy and uses her as a tool to aid in his own advancement. Still, she remains a walking time bomb. Later, as the televised Treasure Girl, Hedy spills the beans both about her liaison with Biggley and about the location of the hidden treasure, which almost ruins the company. She eventually winds up with the Chairman of the Board, causing his retirement and making way for Finch to take his job.

Biggley's wife is also a source of trouble for Biggley. She nags him to promote her nephew, the obnoxious Bud Frump. Biggley dislikes Frump and resists, but Frump blackmails Biggley into cooperating. How? Again it is because of women. Frump discovers his uncle with Hedy and threatens to spill the beans to his aunt, Biggley's wife.

Biggley's third Achilles' tendon is his secretary, Miss Jones. Unlike the other secretaries, Miss Jones is older and powerful. She is the queen bee, protective of her boss in a way that suggests she is unwed. Yet it is through Jones that Finch gains access to the top. She takes a liking to him, promises to keep his name in mind, and hence oils the way for his advancement.

There is another dimension to Biggley that Finch capitalizes upon. Finch discovers the "old man" likes to knit, so Finch does so too to win approval. Yet this is as domestically female a task as there is and a behavior entirely unexpected for a conservative alpha male. It is not a question of sexual identity as Biggley has Hedy on the side. But it does suggest his attraction to women and women's roles. After all, he even knits caps for his golf clubs.

The most important woman in the show is Rosemary. She wants to be Mrs. Finch. Finch is at first oblivious and only gives into her gradually. They do go out together, but it is only when he sees she has been reading business magazines that he is really sold on her, saying she is not like the usual woman. In the song "Been a Long Day" Rosemary freely admits that she intends to trap her beloved Ponty by means of her feminine wiles. It is Rosemary who gives Finch the pep talk confidence to succeed, and it is she who in the end demands that he resort to honesty in order to exonerate himself, much against the advice of his trusted guidebook. In many respects, Rosemary is a feminine version of Finch, working within the guidelines of her own sex in order to set her sights on the right man, do what she can to allure and encourage him, and end up as his partner and wife, taking part in his success. And it is also telling that, when Finch finally does attain the topmost office, he suddenly realizes that it means nothing without having Rosemary beside him. So at precisely the moment of business success, once again it is domesticity that triumphs. Despite its 1960 edginess, *How to Succeed in Business Without Really Trying* still affirms faith in the traditional view of the American Dream.

I Believe in Me

One could argue that what Finch does is no different from what the secretaries do at the show's start. Just as they primp before mirrors hoping to make the most of their individual attributes to get a man, so too does Finch in order to get promoted. Finch charms and flatters, imitates and ingratiates, all in an effort to garner favor and advancement. With each promotion he also dresses better, knowing that image is an important part of the game.

Once appointed head of advertising, Finch is to present his advertising campaign plan to the Board. This is a pivotal scene in the show. Thus far, as stated, Finch has done no real work, accomplishing nothing beyond self promotion. He is about to face his judgment day with no place to hide. Finch stole "his" plan from the scheming Bud, unaware that Biggley has already nixed. Bud's plan is thus a trap designed to blow up in Finch's face. Ponty does not know this, but the audience does.

The scene is the executive washroom. The other executives enter first, badmouthing the young upstart. Then Finch enters and tries to counter the hostile tension with charm. But he is amidst jealous rivals, all conspiring against him. The close intimate quarters accentuates their uneasy coexistence. Safety will only come when and if he is promoted, and that in turn depends upon his ability to sell the board on this advertising campaign. The stakes are high. His colleagues are as eager to drag him down as he is to rise above.

Significantly, rather than spend time on polishing his presentation, Loesser has Finch polishing his appearance in front of the washroom mirrors. Perhaps image can trump substance. Wanting to look his best, Finch even proceeds to shave. The whirring of the electric razor creates a masculine musical accompaniment to the ensuring song.

His rival executives sing "Gonna Get That Man" as the oblivious Finch sings, in counterpoint, a reprise of "I Believe in You" which seems to counter their collective hex. It is one against the many. Ponty oddly sings to his own mirrored reflection. Here is the song earlier sung to him by Rosemary. The audience might presume it a romantic reprise. Traditional musicals would have the hero hearken back to fond, loving thoughts of his love and of their relationship. But Finch instead sings it directly to himself in the mirror. Is it then only a paean to narcissism? No. It is clearly intended as a pep talk. Besides, his enemies are many and he has only himself; perhaps mirror images can serve as his own army, provide reinforcements? Ultimately, Finch sings it for the same reasons he works on his "look" in the mirror. Hers was a song of praise, a song that assigned special, admirable qualities to him that he probably does not possess, attributes she wants in her love, wishing them to be the case. Finch knows how to appear corporate and accomplished, but his strongest suit is his ability to win over others, not acumen. This is the moment of truth for him and he is not up to it. So if substance fails, be prepared to play one's strength. It was Finch's ability to mimic others, his ability to assimilate, which enabled this outsider to climb so high so quickly.

We the audience are likewise taken in by him. When Finch sings "I Believe in You" into the mirror we are charmed by his charm, not considering his *chutzpah*, his gall. Rather than being offended by his sacrilegious use of Rosemary's love song, we are engaged by it, wanting to believe that he is thinking of her, even if the evidence of his flirting at his own reflection belies that sentiment. So while Finch indulges in self-serving ambition, all we can see are personalities and relationships. The inherent theatricality of the piece is its metatheatrical: *How To Succeed In Business Without Really Trying* is ultimately about someone being an actor, pretending to have attributes he in fact lacks, overcoming his deficiencies through likeability rather than merit. And since this is a theatrical show, we the audience want to be flattered as well. We also want the good guy to beat the less-likeable guys and we also hope eventually gets the girl. Oh, and we also want him to succeed in business without really trying. After all, isn't that also one of our secret desires?

What exactly is it about this guy that merits our approval and support? Yes, the audience identifies with him. It also has to do with the rise of 1950s corporate culture that required workers to become largely interchangeable parts. But the show's success is due to more to it than being another example of modern industrial alienation. It appeals to the average audience member's sense of feeling like an outsider dying to get in and not exactly sure how to do so. The great American upper-class is an exclusive club that denies most of us admission. Much like Finch we are only occasionally allowed to peak into such rooftop nests, but only in order to wash the corporate windows, not to dine with the native-born gods.

Yet if Finch follows the how-to book, why can't we? Surely we have potential comparable to Finch. Like him perhaps it is only a matter of wearing the right clothes, saying the right things at the right times to the right people. Surely we can be as charming and loveable and hence deserving as is he. Perhaps is not about superior knowledge or ability, skills or credentials. We suspect that it is the luck of birth, of having attended the right schools, gained membership in the right clubs, had the chance to meet and get to know the right people. So do like

Finch: learn to imitate and remember to check your look in the mirror. And, doing thus, we too will—much like the window washer—rise to the top, but no longer as outsiders, rather as those who occupy the penthouse office, partaking as equals amidst the American business world. Finch has such a book to show him the ropes; we have the musical version to do the same.[11]

Grand Old Ivies

Finch finds out that Biggley attended Grand Old Ivy and then sells the boss that he too is an alumnus of the same college. He uses innuendo and the careful display of Groundhog colors. The notion that Finch attended any college, let alone an Ivy one, is certainly in doubt. As Biggley reenacts college fight songs and rituals, Finch mimics his lead, learning as he goes. We see it is a sham, but Biggley is too engrossed to notice and so buys it: another point in Finch's favor. Besides, according to the boss college is not about education or knowledge but rather rah-rah clubbiness. All that is missing is the secret handshake. Again, appearance matters more than substance.

The message here is not whether Finch attended college but that real credentials are not meaningfully valued in this system. It is not what Finch does or does not know; it is his pedigree that matters. Biggley later fires one of Finch's rivals for being an enemy Chipmunk, suggesting a still-more exclusive club governs the system. Beginning as a window washer it is unlikely Finch attended any college, again damning him as an outsider, perhaps even as lower class, perhaps lacking the funds, perhaps being kept out due to a quota. Finch puts on just the right show, and it is because the corporate system at World Wide Wickets is so corrupt that he is able to succeed.

Corporate Chutes and Ladders

Near the end of the show we are introduced to Wally Womper, Chairman of the World Wide Wicket Company. Outraged by the Treasure Hunt fiasco, Womper instructs Finch to take the blame. Just as Finch is about to sign his letter of resignation, he mentions that he will have to return to being a window washer. Womper hears this and absolves Finch. It turns out Wompers also started out as a window washer and that he too rose up the ranks thanks to a book. However, Wompers' book chronicled betting records, meaning he used blackmail to get promoted.

Finch, along his nefarious path, exploited the sins of many, but none was gambling. Womper is an older man, old enough to retire yet still frisky enough to appreciate marrying Hedy. He is of an earlier generation than that of Finch. The sins of the current employees are primarily carnal. Gambling is noticeably absent here; as noted earlier, it belonged to the previous generation's way of life.

To the older Womper the notion of a book was not in any way literary. His was a book of numbers, a book of transactions. It is a mathematically expressed record of illicit behavior. The younger Finch's book, in contrast, is composed of words, not numbers. The irony is that it purports to be instructive, supposedly in the tradition of an Increase Mather or Benjamin Franklin, but is instead merely a mechanistic guidebook. No self-improvement is necessary; just follow the easy step-by-step directions, much like assembling a model airplane. It is no more literary than that of Womper's. It is the same get-rich-quick notion adjusted to the changed conditions of a new generation, one that requires more interpersonal deception than street smarts to implement. Womper practiced coercion whereas Finch practiced innuendo. The tough street hustle has given way to corporate finesse.

Finch is thus the professional descendent of Womper and hence rightful heir to the World Wide Wicket throne. It echoes George Bernard Shaw's *Major Barbara* in which arms dealer Andrew Undershaft passes over his ineffective birth son as his successor in favor of the unlikely classics scholar Cusins, because he too was a foundling. So too do Womper and Finch share roots, and so too does Finch prove the "natural" inheritor of the business (as opposed to Frump, who mistakenly bets on his birth right instead).

I Want to Believe in You...

It is 1961 and a new generation is taking over, college-educated, increasingly professional. The era celebrates postwar American affluence and effective assimilation as the children of immigrants have largely found acceptance, provided they still imitate America's status quo.

Librettist Abe Burrows and composer/lyricist Frank Loesser reshaped Shepherd Mead's original book into a musical fit the New York stage. It was they who added romance to the original plot, who sharpened its satire, and who updated the tale to fit the New Frontier.

Though there are a slew of wonderful songs in the show, including "The Company Way" and "The Brotherhood of Man," let us first return once more to "I Believe in You:"

> You have the cool, clear eyes of a seeker of wisdom and truth,
> Yet there's that upturned chin and the grin of impetuous youth,
> Oh, I believe in you, I believe in you.[12]

Robert Morse was cast as the cocky, ambitious Finch. Morse sported an endearing smirk, the stride, the boyish charm, and hair combed forward over his brow. I have no evidence but think the song awfully reminiscent of then-newly elected President John F. Kennedy. Kennedy was ambitious and aggressive, Harvard-educated but still a bit of a scamp. Kennedy brought inspirational vision along with swagger and style to the White House. No doubt some hoped he brought not only image but content as well. Perhaps those hopers hoped so hard that they repeated over and over, "I believe in you," as if hoping would make it so. And let us not also forget that Kennedy's father Joe made his fortune in part from bootlegging. He had strong ties to gangsters and made the rest of his fortune betting on the stock market. JFK was his polished son, untarnished by the father's indiscretions. But the 1960s were no longer the 1920s, and where Irish once need not apply, now one sat in the White House. And where the father used unscrupulous means to force entry into a hostile WASP world, the son was a Harvard graduate and war hero. Though pals with the ring-a-ding-ding Sinatra rat pack and chasing skirts on the side, JFK was able to keep his public image squeaky clean during his time in office. Dad may have been a gambler, but the son smacked of youthful exuberance and refreshing optimism. "I want to believe in you, I want to believe in you...."[13]

The last big production number in the show is "The Brotherhood of Man." It takes place in the corporate board room, just as Finch is rescued *deus ex machina* style by his unexpected link to Womper. The song is a gospel celebration, musically topped off by Miss Jones holding a high note above the chorus of male voices. It echoes Loesser's the ending for *Guys and Dolls*. "Sit Down You're Rocking the Boat" similarly featured a chorus of illicit "businessmen" who suddenly find religion after a lifetime of competition. Just as the gamblers are now replaced by businessmen, *Guys and Dolls* has given way to *How to Succeed in Business Without Really Trying*. The very title of the latter, however, also points to capitalism as a thing of chance, rather than as something one pursues persistently, ala the Protestant Work Ethic. After all, much like throwing craps, Finch finds success thanks far more to ingenuity than any sustained preparation, commitment, or effort.

As for the two songs, it is interesting that the earlier *Guys and Dolls'* eleven o'clock number echoed a religious revival meeting number as the many sinners sing to repent whereas the *How to Succeed in Business* counterpart number, written only ten years later, now expressed a more secular ethical humanism. In the former, all had to convert to American Protestantism; in the latter, the song proclaims that the American Dream is now inclusive of difference. My! how times had changed.

PART FIVE: BABY BOOMS

Sondheim's 1970s and 1980s Stage Business

Use of the musical as a setting to explore the relationship of assimilation to business took a turn especially in the 1970s musicals of Stephen Sondheim. While not set in conventional work settings, several of his shows are concerned with issues of professional success. Sondheim treats success as a luxury item, unlike comparable shows written in earlier decades. To Sondheim open opportunity seems to be a given, the American Dream attained. Rather than focusing on striving to gain acceptance, as earlier shows had consistently done, Sondheim's characters' crises center more on issues of personal freedom and happiness. His musicals thus reflect upon the ultimate promise of the American Dream, whether is the pot is gold at the end of the business success rainbow.

Many of Sondheim's musicals explore the individual in relationship to the group. For example, *Company*, though not about business, studies Bobby in relationship to his group of married friends. In an assimilation variation, Bobby struggles over whether he can wed without replicating their unhappy norms. Bobby is torn. He is disheartened by their misery and yet is tired of living alone. This dilemma is never resolved by show's end. It fits in with some other musicals we have seen in that our protagonist is an outsider trying to negotiate his community of friends. However, unlike earlier shows, our hero is accepted by the group even though he does not/will not/ cannot alter his own behaviors (i.e., wed) in order to become like them. The twist is that, while he is jealous of them, it turns out they are jealous of him. By play's end, there is no resolution, Bobby never does make up his mind or take any definitive action, thus remaining in unwed limbo as a seemingly permanent outsider—or liminal insider.

Though *Company* is not about business, its pattern of estrangement from the welcoming group remains a theme that is repeated in the few shows Sondheim wrote which do include work settings. It is as if the same kinds of stories are being told, but from a radically different point of view. Remember, this is the same Sondheim who worked on *Gypsy*, the Sondheim whose sensibilities best reflected those of 1960s through 1980s America.

Ultimately, two works distill Sondheim's attitudes towards acculturation and business: *Follies* (1971) and *Merrily We Roll Along* (1981). The two share many similarities. Both are constructed around the lives of friends once closely tied to the entertainment business; both consider issues of relative success; both show the ravages of time upon youth, youthful expectations, and dreams. Both shows ultimately consider what constitutes genuine economic success and whether love and relationships can still then endure.

In other words, *Follies* and *Merrily We Roll Along* both celebrate and question the American Dream. Both shows are deeply concerned with making it to the top, but also show those who fail and those left behind. But they go one step beyond even that: they also show reveal one who succeeds to be essentially unhappy, disappointed with their lives, or coldly indifferent mannequins of their former selves. Success may win fortune and success may win plaudits, but each show explores at what cost: how hollow their lives have become.

Sondheim accentuates their empty shells by giving us glimpses of their spirited youthful selves, so we can appreciate the sad transformations by comparison. In *Follies* we see the two couples (Ben, Phyllis, Buddy, and Sally), not only in their present state, but also when young. We thus witness the innocence, energy, hope, and excitement of first opportunities: first jobs, first loves. But with their older selves ever present, ever watchful, we are saddened by their innocence, aware of the pain to come. We know that their hopes will grow jaded, that small disappointments will only escalate, that minor infractions will haunt them the rest of their lives. In another author's hands, one of a more sentimental bent, we might see the older selves viewing the young wistfully, like Hammerstein's warm lyric about a couple who lovingly grow old together as a "Darby and Joan." Instead Sondheim presents a once-loving, long-spurned wife raging at her arrogant husband in "Leave You," bragging cruelly of her infidelities and threatening divorce. They may be successful in the eyes of the outside world, but suffer within.

Merrily We Roll Along also reveals a long history of betrayals and regret, though this time done in reverse. The story is told backwards, with hit songwriter Franklin Shepard returning to his alma mater to receive an honorary award, and thus forced to confront the ghost victims of his selfishness. In the end we see him as he once was, again alongside his college friends, dreaming of making it together in show business. But, since the show unfolds backwards, we (and he) are fully cognizant of their youthful innocence and how all those promises and ties will be abandoned over time, slain on the altar of his own ego and ambition. Success and relationships do not mix in Sondheim's worldview.

Both shows drip with irony. Sondheim does not encourage us to applaud these jaded souls. Each musical is written with regret. Characters may grow older and supposedly wiser, but regardless of their middle-aged skepticism, each mourns the loss of youth, innocence, and wide-eyed idealism. You may say the younger selves are fools who are blissfully unaware of what lies ahead. You could argue that they do not appreciate the larger resonances of offhand indiscretions, understandings that can only come with age. Yet, unlike their older, all-knowing alter egos on stage in each show, the younger selves possess verve and sparkle sadly lacking in the old. As characters that only exist in the past, the younger selves may be onstage ghosts, but they are remarkably spirited and full of vitality in ways their "real" older selves are not. Much has been lost along life's path.

Each character in both plays has made choices; what they do or do not have now in life is a direct result of those choices. At each crossroad the character was forced to decide between heart and head, between thinking of others and only thinking of they themselves. Making it professionally is thus equated with betrayals and abandonments. Their lives are littered with loss and regret.

These two Sondheim shows consider the relationship between illusion and disillusion, not so much illusion versus reality. Illusion versus reality is about learning, about finally acknowledging the truth. It also implies that the characters' initial illusions are somehow ill-considered or downright wrong, hence in need of correction. From that point of view, illusions are potentially harmful. However, in *Follies* and in *Merrily We Roll Along* the characters suffer from disillusion. To be disillusioned means that one is still in the grip of initial illusions, ideals in which they still want or need to believe, but which have been discredited. It is the opposite of hope, the antithesis to belief, and without cure. What remains is not objective reality but rather only blithe cynicism. It is a strategy for survival more than an approach to living.

Both shows demonstrate Sondheim's take on the relative promise of the American Dream. Though a decade older than the baby boomers, Sondheim shares that younger generation's skepticism, their questioning and doubt. But because both musicals also show youthful possibilities, and despair at their loss, we know that once upon a time there was perhaps a deep seated desire to believe in that national ideal. Once upon a time the Ziegfeld girls did personify American beauty, the girl next door, with famous chorines who strutted across the various follies' stage and who wed millionaire husbands. And once upon a time college friends agreed to stay together and work their way to the top as a team, making it while still preserving their close-knit relationship.

Follies and *Merrily We Roll Along* are shows that silently weep over the loss of identity and fidelity. Yes, in both the adult selves have betrayed their younger selves, doing so as the necessary cost of doing business. But understand that those "younger selves" were also far closer to who each person actually was, closer to their true identity. Their journey toward success was also a journey of assimilation and compromise. They transformed themselves systematically, step-by-step, conflict by conflict, decision by decision, discarding the old, adapting the new. But in their case, abandoned were their original fundamental values and beliefs. The two shows' respective protagonists Ben Stone and Franklin Shepard have become great successes, but, because success came by having their "real selves" chipped away, they are no longer who they once were. No wonder none of their youthful relationships still survive, even with their wives. Ben Stone is no longer Ben Stone, and Franklin Shepard is no longer Franklin Shepard. They have become different men. Ambition has robbed them of their original selves. It is almost Faustian, where each has sold their identity soul to the devil success. Sondheim thus charts in painful detail the gradual corruption of identity. He paints the actual process of assimilation as a series of systematic compromises that forces one to eliminate self in order to achieve the success of the dominant cultural "other." Yes you have made it; no, you are no longer the same person. Or perhaps it is simply the natural loss of innocence, the inherent corruption that occurs when becoming an adult. But the other characters, also now adult, do not seem to experience that same loss. From what we see on stage, the adult versions of Stone and Shepard are clearly far less happy than their younger selves; it is thus apparent that, as deracinated adults, they have lost themselves and, consequently, lost their way.

Unlike shows of the previous decades, like *Annie Get Your Gun* or even *How To Succeed in Business Without Really Trying*, Sondheim's winners do not win it all. They are forced to make choices, doomed to have one but not the other: happiness or success. Maybe they more closely resemble *Show Boat* or *Funny Girl* in that they end unhappily. Yet *Show Boat* and *Funny*

Girl are designed to leave the audience in tears as our heroine romantically sings her final sad lament. Not the case in *Follies* or in *Merrily We Roll Along* where we do not particularly like the one who succeeds. In fact, in this respect we the audience are robbed of our own desire to see the winner sympathetically. No heroes here. Perhaps the most heroic in both shows is Carlotta, who sings "I'm Still Here," an ode to simple survival as success. Significantly, the song is a litany to the actor's ability to adapt to ever-evolving popular trends—to assimilate—over fifty years of societal upheaval and change.

And yet there is sweet water in the seemingly foul well of Sondheim's two shows. We have already noted the fondness with which he portrays the two youthful couples, so that is a plus. We can also applaud the composer's heart for showing the complex feelings and relationships, courageously creating antiheroes who ring true, even if we wish them to be otherwise.

Sondheim, unlike his predecessors, came from a position of inclusivity. He was wellborn and well-educated. His upbringing more closely resembles that of those Jews coming of age in the early 1960s, with their assumption of upper middle-class acceptance with fewer experiences of discrimination than their parents. This is not to say that his was a happy experience: his parents divorced, his mother was thoughtlessly narcissistic, and Sondheim was himself a Jewish gay man living in a mostly homogenous, homophobic 1950s world. Much like Bobby in *Company*, Sondheim lived between worlds, not fitting in to standard conventional norms though finding acceptance amongst his audience and peers. Sondheim's work reflects his times, how the issue of assimilation as a prerequisite for professional success had eased. His work has 1970s Jews finally secure enough to be able to question the American Dream. Is it all that it was cracked up to be? Does achieving economic success guarantee fulfillment and happiness? Such questions are luxuries, options available only to those who feel an enfranchised part of America's whole.

A 2005 Postscript: Looking Through Purple-Colored Glasses

A generation after Sondheim's heyday we find slightly different answers in *The Color Purple*. A 1910s black woman living in the Deep South is abused first by her father and then later by her husband. She begins to find escape through the love of another woman, eventually freeing her from her marital bind. But it is not until she begins her own business making pants that she gains the economic wherewithal to achieve independence and autonomy. Her gay relationship gives her the courage and determination to build her business; her business gives her a status and respect that transcends both her color and her sexuality. To the rising middle-class black audience of the 2000s the message is clear: with pluck and luck you can go from rags to riches; the American Dream still works.

5. Cinderellas

PART ONE: WELCOME IRENE, SALLY, NELLIE, AND FANNY—ACCULTURATION AND THE CINDERELLA MUSICAL

In 1957, CBS broadcast a made-for-television Rodgers and Hammerstein musical, *Cinderella*. The production was a straightforward, musical adaptation created specifically to star Julie Andrews, who had just won recognition for her work in *My Fair Lady*, and featured book and lyrics by Hammerstein with music by Rodgers. Performed live, it was viewed by over 100 million Americans, or 60 percent of the population. In 1997, Walt Disney Productions similarly aired a revival of the same show, this time produced by Whitney Houston and featuring a racially mixed cast headed by the African American pop singing star Brandy in the title role. Seen by over 60 million viewers, it was "the highest rated television musical of a generation."[1] Clearly, this reception indicates a welcoming of diversity, at least in the portrayal of a familiar fairy tale. Yet it is important to note that the mixed casting does change the way in which an audience might view the story; the all-white 1957 version allows one to focus on this modern-day operetta entirely as a fairytale, operating entirely in a self-contained world apart from our own. The 1997 version, because of its mixed cast, reminds us more of the world in which we ourselves inhabit, situating the familiar story in contemporary America as we self-consciously point out that it does in fact still work, despite the then-unorthodox casting. What had been "just" a musical adaptation of a fairy tale, with seemingly little meaning beyond that, had become an inadvertent statement about how far America had come on issues of homogeneity and race, in addition to what we will accept as theatrical convention.

It is also interesting to note the enormous popular success of the *Cinderella* broadcasts (including the 1965 Lesley Ann Warren version). American audiences responded enthusiastically even though the show itself is not regarded as amongst Rodgers and Hammerstein's better work.[2]

There seems to be a certain resonance between the Cinderella story and the cultural ethos of America itself to which this story speaks, perhaps explaining its popular appeal. On one hand, many a young women see themselves as a misunderstood, put-upon drudge, waiting to be rescued by a still-unknown Prince Charming. Musicals regularly count on such feminine romanticism to sell tickets. But there are many romantic stories; why the particular appeal of this one?

The original folk story is distinctively European. It requires formal social class distinctions governed by an aristocracy. Furthermore, because its roots are feudal, class distinctions are fixed. Traditionally, it would be culturally taboo for classes to mix, let alone marry. Consequently, one is locked into the class to which he or she was born. In such a world, a Cinderella would be entirely a fantasy, practically unattainable. But in America, where the aristocracy is defined primarily through money, and where class distinctions supposedly do not exist, fluidity of social standing is possible and potentially open to any and all. To a European Cinderella is a nice story; to an American, it reaffirms the implicit promise of upward mobility.

Significantly, few Broadway musicals recreate the actual Cinderella story, though many are built upon it. The most prominent are probably the Rodgers and Hammerstein mentioned above, and Stephen Sondheim and James Lapine's postmodern take on it within their *Into the Woods*. For the most part, it is not the story itself but rather its use as a model that Cinderella has made its greatest and most meaningful mark. Rarely do they include characters named "Cinderella" or "Prince Charming"; most feature distinctively American characters and settings.

The Cinderella story, when thus used as a model, itself becomes what I will term a "paradigmatic script" rather than a story unto itself. For those watching a musical modeled on Cinderella we are often made aware that it is not the fairy-tale original, is less "realistic," and hence more contrived. It is more self-consciously theatrical. We are usually familiar with the original story. Since many paradigmatic script versions include variations, we may notice the ways in which the new treatment corresponds to the original story, as well as the points at which it veers off in other directions. When the Cinderella paradigm is applied to material that has an ethnic component, either overtly or covertly, it begins to include another dimension: it points to the degree to which one's ethnicity is either affirmed or denied.

Cinderella as Paradigm

A simple description of the Cinderella story reveals the links between self-transformation and upward mobility. Cinderella begins as disadvantaged working-class girl, enduring prejudice and mistreatment. She surreptitiously transforms her outward appearance in order to attend the ball, portraying herself as an affluent and refined woman. The Prince, seeing her thus, falls in love with her. She must leave, loses her shoe. Using the shoe, the Prince wanders in his kingdom until finding its match in Cinderella. He weds her, thus bestowing both love and nobility, an inversion of her original condition. Happy ending.

At first blush, this is a tale of upward mobility, suggesting personal growth. Cinderella rises from poverty and oppression to achieve a position of affluence and power. She first endures abuse and scorn but later finds love and respect. At first a rather sexless girl she eventually realizes beauty and maturity. Her goodness is confirmed by an absence of spite, her charm built upon innocence and a dreamy passivity. In *Into the Woods*, she simply sighs, "I wish."

Yet the path to upward mobility is constructed upon assimilation. Our heroine would not have won the Prince if she had not transformed her outward self for the ball; it is by emulating the aristocracy that she gains access to the Prince, which in turn leads to her ultimate triumph. While true when our Cinderella is WASP, the paradigm takes on further meaning when our Cinderella is Irish, Jewish, or black

The Craze

Historically, "Cinderella Musicals" pertain to a series of Broadway shows written and produced between 1919 and 1924, which were all the rage. It began with *Irene* and included roughly a dozen shows in all. They included works by George M. Cohan, Jerome Kern, and Rudolph Friml. The African American team of Sissle and Blake, fresh off their groundbreaking all-black revue *Shuffle Along*, offered up *Elsie*, an unsuccessful show that ironically featured an all-white cast. And the comedy team of George Kaufman and Marc Connolly even did a mildly successful send-up with their *Helen of Troy, New York* (1924). It was the success of *Irene* that started the wave of copycat shows.[3]

While there are many variations amongst these dozen or so shows, they all centered on the trials and tribulations of a female protagonist (usually Irish American) trying to make her way. Most have low-paying jobs, most become romantically involved with a wealthy man (usually WASP) with whom they eventually wed. Significantly, though, most also have a career by play's end, either with their newfound mate or independent of him.

Cinderella shows reflect the new age of urban, working women. After World War I, "modern" women flooded major urban centers. Tin Pan

Alley songwriters responded with songs deliberately aimed at this wave of women. Shop girls and secretaries formed a big part of their audience and market, and songs like Irving Berlin's "All Alone" and George Gershwin's "The Man I Love" spoke to their lovelorn urban isolation and became hits.[4] The heroines of the initial Cinderella shows spoke to the same audience, reflecting the conditions under which they lived and worked, expressing their hopes and dreams. But despite romantic longings, such working women were largely independent and self-sufficient and this too is reflected in the fabric of the Cinderella musicals.

Another argument describes such shows as nostalgic and fluffy, providing meaningless escapism for those who just survived the trauma of the recently completed Great War. Yet there is too much substance to the shows in terms of their portrayal of young women negotiating for a respect and independence with potential future mates for this to hold true. Yes, we are not quite yet at the seriousness of *Show Boat*, but neither are they entirely frivolous in the stakes of what they portray. They are more than about love; they are also about woman fighting for autonomy. Add the further ingredient of many being the now-adult children of immigrants, and their ethnicity raises the stakes still higher.

First Irene

Let us first focus on three Cinderella musicals of the era: *Irene* (1919), *Sally* (1920), and *Little Nellie Kelly* (1922). As the show that ignited the Cinderella rage, *Irene* has special interest here. It featured music by Harry Tierney, lyrics by Joseph McCarthy, and a book adapted by James Montgomery from his original novel, *Irene O'Dare*.

Irene is a poor Irish shop girl who, while tuning a piano at a high society Long Island mansion, meets the wealthy scion Donald and the two promptly fall in love. Donald's cousin persuades the comely Irene and her friends to model a fashion shop's gowns, and then Irene successfully introduces the gowns at a society ball as "the Countessa Irena O'Dari." Donald asks her to remain the Countessa for business reasons, but Irene refuses saying she will not live a lie. Eventually the two reconcile as Donald makes it clear he is marrying Irene O'Dare, not a false contessa. Irene takes over the fashion shop, thus rewarded with both love and her own business.

The Cinderella elements are clearly evident in *Irene*. She and her mother struggle to survive oppressive tenement lives. There is a ball, a disguise, a triumph followed by a retreat. There is a prince who must confront and accept her modest roots, followed by marriage that will result in both affluence and social mobility.

Yet also prominent in *Irene* is that the heroine's Irish identity is itself central to the plot; it is not hidden nor is there any apologies given. The show was noted for its lifelike tenement sets as the action shifted back and forth between the poor Irish world and the homes of wealthy WASPs. And though Irene transforms herself convincingly to play the role of a continental sophisticate, she ultimately demands to be accepted as her modest Irish self. *Irene* is indeed a fairy tale, and it is built upon the skeleton of the Cinderella story, but its real fantasy is its assertion that ethnic and class differences can be overcome. Their mixed marriage reflects a societal ideal promoted by its authors and, given its success, applauded by Broadway audiences.

Then Sally

The following year, Florenz Ziegfeld built upon the success of *Irene* by offering his own Cinderella show, *Sally*. Written as a star vehicle for Marilynn Miller ironically by the "Princess" musical team of Jerome Kern, Guy Bolton (sans P. G. Wodehouse), and ballet music by Victor Herbert, *Sally* proved the biggest commercial success of all the Cinderella shows.

Sally begins with a society matron bringing a group of poor girls to work at a Greenwich Village restaurant. Sally becomes a dishwasher and befriends a former Russian Duke, now called "Connie." When the wealthy Blair Farquar visits the restaurant to arrange a society party there, he becomes enchanted by Sally and urges her in song to cheer up. She dances for joy and impresses Blair, Connie and a visiting theatrical agent, Hooper. When the ballerina for that event's entertainment backs out, Hooper has Sally pretend to be her and dance in her place. Thinking the disguised Sally is the ballerina, Blair berates her, but Hooper announces saying Sally has won a spot in the *Ziegfeld Follies*. Elated, Sally dances up a storm at the party before she and Blair reconcile and go off to wed.

Again, we see the Cinderella musical elements: the poor girl dreaming of a better life, the chance encounter with a man of wealth leading to romance, the ball scene in which the disguised heroine makes a splash, the career opportunity while she also gets her millionaire man. And yet *Sally* differs sharply from *Irene* largely because it is an Anglicized version of the form. The only ethnic presence in Sally is her friend Connie, and he is a down-on-his-luck, expatriate aristocrat. Yet Connie works in the kitchen alongside Sally, the once mighty now fallen, and played by comic Leon

Errol, known for slapstick, not snobbery. Connie's ethnicity is used only for inversion: it shows that in America the aristocrat rubs elbows with the intrepid Sally as she scrubs pots. This democratized aristocrat is loveable and approachable. And Sally, since she keeps such company, thus contains the possibility of aristocracy within herself. In America, just as the formerly upper crust may end up as kitchen help, so too might a scullery maid ascend to princess.

Ziegfeld's did all to promote both Marilynn Miller and *Sally* well beyond the norm. In addition to his particular affection for Miller, it also shows his belief that the production had particular commercial appeal.[5] This *Cinderella* show resembled the highly successful *Irene*, but without the ethnic baggage. Sally is simply poor, not ethnic. Every and all Americans could root for her, and none need worry about associating her with encroaching immigrants threatening for a piece of the American pie. Nor need they worry about the dilemma of a mixed marriage. *Sally* was safely sanitized, rid of any trace of difference, palatable for all. It could be enjoyed by ethnic audiences, as well as nonethnic, Middle America. The American Dream was painted in neutral tones, vaguely available for all comers. Compared to *Irene*, though, the equally charming *Sally* is banal and bland, relying solely on fantasy, Marilynn Miller's star power, a memorable Kern score, and the great showman Ziegfeld to put it across. Given how big a hit it was, perhaps this explains why it was quickly forgotten and has enjoyed few if any revivals.

And Then Came Nellie

Little Nellie Kelly (1922) is our third example of an early *Cinderella* show. Featuring a book, music, lyrics, and direction by the indomitable George M. Cohan, we see another attempt to capitalize on the Cinderella boom.

The poor Irish girl Nellie works in a department store. Wealthy WASP Jack Lloyd falls for her. Seeking to win her, he throws a party at his aunt's mansion. Jerry Conroy, like Nellie both Irish and from the Bronx, crashes the party to woo her himself. When the aunt's jewels disappear, Jack is falsely accused. Nellie decides to wed Jerry instead of Jack, and remain amongst the Irish working class rather than lead an affluent life of WASP ease.

Again present are the now-familiar *Cinderella* musical elements. Unlike *Sally*, here is a return to a strong ethnic presence. Unlike *Irene*, *Little Nellie Kelly* advocates sticking to one's own kind, that ethnic solidarity mattered more than achieving the American Dream, and that those two concepts were irreconcilable. It is a staunchly conservative stance, more reflecting old ways, rather than modern trends.

Gerald Boardman tried to explain this conservative dynamic as found in the Cinderella plays of both Cohan and comic Eddie Dowling, commented, "Writing, as both Irishmen were, for heavily Irish or working-class audiences, they were undoubtedly responding to some hard-nosed inner reality these playgoers retained."[6] *Sally*, with all of its Ziegfeld associations, would have spoken to a more affluent, perhaps better educated audience, than that for *Little Nellie Kelly*. And *Irene* with its sympathy for transcending the old neighborhood and finding virtue elsewhere would find no sympathy from *Little Nellie Kelly's* parochial crowd.

Unlike *Little Nellie Kelly*, *Irene* displayed lifelike Irish tenements on stage. How shocking! Escapist musical comedy is not supposed to portray unpleasant city blights. Irene thus "innocently" forced audiences to address the socio/economic stakes lying beneath the surface romance. *Irene's* success is thus doubly remarkable and attests to its importance, beyond introducing Cinderella shows into the mix. Cohan's *Little Nellie Kelly* backed off from gritty realistic depictions, instead opting to romanticize the poor in order to achieve a more palatable outcome. For a show like *Little Nellie Kelly*, it was easier for the heroine to reject her wealthy WASP suitor in favor of her impoverished Irish sweetheart if one did not have to picture the loving couple subsequently living in squalor.

Closing the Doors

If there were differences in values amongst the audiences respectively for *Irene*, *Sally*, and *Little Nellie Kelly*, it was because the nation itself was at odds about how to come to terms with the huge increase in immigrant population and their rising presence in American life.

The Cinderella musicals' bookend years of 1919 and 1924 are telling because they correspond to a growing national shift away from ethnicity. The Cinderella craze began in 1919, the same year as the Red Scare, where those with foreign-sounding names and radical views were persecuted, jailed, or even exiled. This impacted the entertainment industry: for example, the long-standing market for ethnic songs dissolved by 1919. It was also an era that saw the rise of the Ku Klux Klan, which came shockingly close to taking over the Democratic Convention in 1924. Nativism was on the rise and 1924 also saw the enactment of laws that closed America's doors to mass immigration, particularly those from Eastern and Southern Europe. By 1924 Cinderella musicals had run their course. Is this a coincidence?

Perhaps. Audiences no doubt grew tired of repeated iterations of the form, a succession of poor, usually Irish, heroines valiantly striving to attain their dreams: with *Mary, That O'Brien Girl, The Gingham Girl, Sally, Irene and Mary, Elsie, Cinders* and *Helen of Troy, New York*, one after another. Yet it was the Cinderella musical that managed to maintain an attractive, non-threatening ethnic presence on the Broadway stage during years when ethnicity itself came under sharp attack.

With the closing of America's doors a chapter ended on Broadway, both musically and ethnically. That same year, 1924, marked the debut of George and Ira Gershwin, accompanied by Adele and Fred Astaire, in *Lady, Be Good*, a new musical comedy form built upon affluent escapism and that new jazz music. The year afterwards marked the first success of the writing team of Richard Rodgers and Lorenz Hart, and Broadway audiences discovered another Jewish writing team delighting in the ultra-contemporary sophistication of the Jazz Age. Perhaps the Cinderella shows were only placeholders, waiting patiently for the older Irish audience to give way to the new, aggressively upwardly mobile, college educated Jewish audience that would increasingly come to dominate Broadway in the decades to come.

This is not to say that ethnicity disappeared from the New York stage. Perhaps encouraged by the success of *Irene*, in 1922 came Anne Nichols' hit comedy, *Abie's Irish Rose*, about the marriage between a Jewish boy and an Irish Catholic girl. Then in 1925 came a show no doubt inspired by the Nichols play, this time a musical alarmingly titled *Kosher Kitty Kelly*. Perhaps the "KKK" title was also a nod toward the threatening Klan. Though a flop, this show similarly retreated from mix marriage by having the Irish lass eventually wed an Irish lad, while the Jewish boy ends up with a Jewish girl. But Nichols' show was not a musical, let alone a Cinderella musical, nor was its author of ethnic origins. And while ethnicity was in the air, the *KKK* musical seemingly sidestepped portraying Jewish Cinderellas who marry rich *goys*.[7]

Cartoon Ethnicity…

In 1922 Noble Sissle and Eubie Blake made history with their black revue, *Shuffle Along*. In addition to its lively jazz score, *Shuffle Along* is also credited with introducing romantic love between black characters; earlier musical comedies always burlesqued such moments, insisting blacks incapable of such lofty feelings. It seems a comparable dynamic may have been at work in *Irene*, though applied to immigrants in general, Irish in particular.

New York City's diverse ethnic population had been presented on musical stages before: in the 1880s, the shows of Harrigan and Hart thrived on ethnic portrayals, but they were cartoon images, slapstick figures culminating in knockdown melees. Similarly, a decade later the Jewish Weber and Fields' shows did much the same. And ethnic communities seemed foreign and exotic to mainstream Broadway audiences; affluent WASPs took adventurous larks to Chinatown, not unlike visiting Toyland or Oz. But *Irene*, much like *Shuffle Along*, dared to portray an Irish woman with beauty, brains, and spunk, who insists on being accepted as she is and a beau who grants her both respect and romantic love. It was revolutionary for the musical stage, and though perhaps not quite as radical as the Sissle-Blake effort that followed two years afterwards, functioned along similar cultural lines.

...Or Invisibility?

So where were the Jewish Cinderellas? All these Cinderella shows are peopled by Irish and WASPs. Theatrical magnate Abe Erlinger favored old-fashioned entertainments right up to his 1924 end; perhaps that is part of the story. The Shuberts too were Jewish. Tin Pan Alley was similarly heavily Jewish. By 1919, Florenz Ziegfeld had included Eddie Cantor, Fanny Brice, and Bert Williams in his *Follies* for almost a decade, though the performed largely as stereotypes designed to draw laughs. Jewish entertainers had proven adept at adapting American entertainment forms and using them to for their own purposes: both the Weber and Fields' burlesque revues and the Al Jolson/Eddie Cantor blackface routines took standard American entertain forms and used them to express Jewish sensibilities and sentiments.[8] The Cinderella musical was similarly ripe for the taking, but no one took.

Encoding Ethnic Mixtures

John Bush Jones wrote that, "...the "Irishness" of most of these female protagonists suggests that the Cinderella musicals let recent immigrants see that they too could make it in America."[9] If Jones is correct, then other groups identified with the plight of the Irish heroines, viewing them as all-encompassing ethnic standard-bearers beyond being simply "Irish." If so, then they would understand the Irenes, Nellies, and Sallys of the stage as representing any and all ethnic groups, whether Jews or Italians or Greek. Or perhaps that era's nativism of those years drove ethnicity underground, so that Irish heroines became an encoded representation for other, less "acceptable" types. Through much of the twentieth century, Jewish producers shied away from portraying Jewish characters, whether on stage, film, radio, or television. Besides, a mixed marriage between an Irish girl and a WASP man would be far more palatable than a marriage between a Jew and a WASP; at least they are both Celtic and Christian. Remember that when society darling Ellin Mackay eloped with Irving Berlin in 1924 the scandal made headlines nationwide.

Consequently, when applied to ethnicity, particularly religious mixing, the Cinderella paradigm proved provocative. Though outwardly an innocent fairy tale, when seen in societal terms the Cinderella tale pointed out economic inequities and promoted social mobility. Add to that issues of ethnicity and religion and this concoction proves threatening indeed to societies bent on conservative homogeneity. It might be acceptable for Catholics to wed Protestants, but portrayals of mixed races or faiths seemingly proved too volatile, especially for Broadway's commercially-based musical stages. On the rare occasion when it was presented—most notably in Rodgers and Hammerstein's *South Pacific* and also *The King and I*—the male lover is safely killed off by the end, insuring such thorny issues remain safely away in distant Samoa or Siam. But even those are musical plays, not light Cinderella musical comedies that relied on an outward naiveté.

It was not until the mid-1960s that a Jewish Cinderella musical found a home on the Broadway stage, fully forty years after the initial wave of Cinderella shows had subsided. The year 1964's *Funny Girl* was the first musical hit written along Cinderella paradigmatic lines to feature an overtly Jewish heroine. In some ways *Funny Girl* resembles the melting pot *Irene*, in other respect the ethnically conservative *Little Nellie Kelly*, and in still other ways closely resembles the deracinated *Sally*.

Fanny and Irene...and Nellie...and Sally

Funny Girl resembles *Irene* in that it stubbornly insists upon its protagonist's ethnic roots. Like Irene, Fanny is portrayed as a hardworking Jewish girl from the slums who works her way up the showbiz ladder. She becomes a star because she recognizes that she does not fit into the beautified American girl chorus dressed as brides and stuffs a pillow under her dress as if pregnant. That caused the audience to laugh with her, not at her. She then embarks on making the most of her Jewishness and unconventional looks.

Though from a different angle, Fanny's insistence on being her ethnic self closely resembles Irene's demands not to continue her charade as the contessa and be accepted for who she is. Furthermore, just as Irene ends up owning her own business, so too does Fanny gain financial success because of her stardom. The construction of the two shows also stresses ghetto roots: *Irene* zigzags between 9th Avenue and Long Island while *Funny Girl* careens between Henry Street and Broadway; both show the heroine beside her widowed mother, who runs a modest but respectable business in the slums.

Funny Girl resembles *Little Nellie Kelly* in that the man in her life is of her own faith. Nicky Arnstein, unlike Fanny, is from the start polished and urbane, one who seems to have completely assimilated to American ways. Playing the romantic Prince Charming of *Funny Girl*, he chases after her, finds her back in her parent's tenement bar, and woos her there, fully cognizant of her humble roots. They wed, but there is no happily-ever-after; this Prince has a gambling problem that threatens Fanny's romantic and economic dreams. Unlike *Little Nellie Kelly*, *Funny Girl* lets our heroine see past her lover's ethnically acceptable façade, showing that an ethnic match and economic duress does not equate with happiness. Even then, Fanny never retreats ala Nellie back to her modest Henry Street roots to find a supposedly more suitable mate.

Of the three, *Funny Girl* most closely, and tellingly, resembles *Sally* in its use of the Cinderella paradigm. Ziegfeld molded Sally to fit his young leading lady so well that it gave audiences the impression that it actually portrayed Marilynn Miller's own rise to success, though it was nothing of the sort. Sally/Marilynn is the poor girl who dances at the ball, which results in her winning stardom in a Ziegfeld show. Since Miller was a Ziegfeld star, this lent credence to the staged myth: audiences adored Miller as Sally, adored her as a Cinderella, and perhaps viewed them as one and the same.

Whereas *Sally* is a fiction that implies the portrayal of a Ziegfeld star's life, *Funny Girl* is fictionalized fact. Fanny Brice was a Ziegfeld star and Miller's peer.[10] In good Cinderella fashion, both shows portray the rags to riches tale of a poor working girl that makes good on the stage. In both shows, the heroine is discovered by the same real-life star-maker, Florenz Ziegfeld, Jr.; it is he who enables them to achieve success specifically on the stage of his New Amsterdam Theatre. Thus, both shows portray Ziegfeld as the millionaire Prince Charming, who rescues our two heroines from impoverished obscurity.

Both shows also measure success more by theatrical stardom than by romantic love or old money. Show-biz is all; you play the role well and you become a star, which equates to achieving the American Dream.

In truth Marilynn Miller's luck with husbands, like Brice, was filled with disappointment and heartache. *Sally* ends with her becoming a star and getting her man; in *Funny Girl* Brice achieves stardom early in the show and spends the rest dealing with the consequences of her questionable marriage. Where Miller's public persona was as a sturdy ingénue who cheerfully urged all to "Look for the Silver Lining," Brice achingly sang "My Man"; and if Sally pranced happily around the stage enabling her good fortune, Brice pleaded passionately not to rain on her parade. Where ever-hopeful Sally passively waits for her chance, Fanny stubbornly insists. Yet, where *Sally* enjoys a fairy-tale ending, *Funny Girl* ends with Brice's romantic dreams shattered, though her professional dreams endure.

It is not just a reflection of one being a musical comedy and the other a book musical (though that is certainly part of it); it is also that our understandings of Cinderellas and of changing American values to enable the emotionally spicier ethnic girl finally to have her chance to shine. With its ungainly looking Jewish heroine, though set in the 1910s and 1920s, *Funny Girl* is as much about the new 1960s acceptance of religious diversity on the American musical stage as it is about the life of one of its greatest stars. In the song, "If a Girl Isn't Pretty" Fanny's mother frets, "is a nose with deviation/such a crime against the nation?" Though clever and cute, it does tell much larger story, of how a woman with a Jewish appearance (i.e. a large nose) had been so forbidden on stage that it seemed almost "a crime." This was also true for the show's star, Barbra Streisand, whose own ethnic appearance at the time seemed so unlikely, especially for romantic roles. Still, Brice, like Streisand in the film version, famously singing while steaming forward on a tugboat's top deck; this Jewish girl was afloat in New York harbor, like countless immigrants before her, and America had better prepare for her triumphant arrival.[11]

That *Funny Girl* still most resembles *Sally* is important because it was *Sally*, of the original three Cinderella shows discussed her, that was shaped to be the most commercial. In order to achieve that in 1920, Ziegfeld created *Sally* by Anglicizing *Irene*, stripping the Cinderella story of its ethnicity. What is so telling about *Funny Girl*, and hence a glimpse into the 1960s changing ethos, was that now ethnicity could be reintroduced into the same basic structure *Sally* so that it could again work its commercial magic. Where in the 1920s ethnic was a handicap, in 1960s it proved a boon.

That *Funny Girl* was also about Fanny Brice, a star of the original Cinderella era, is thus both poignant and telling. She played the Jewish clown, complete with fake Yiddish accent, to win acceptance.[12] By 1964, thanks to *Funny Girl*, we could see Brice as three-dimensional and accepted for both in her Jewishness and her pain. Ultimately, it is Brice herself that is rediscovered, even vindicated, taking her place in the pantheon of American heroines alongside Miller, but with help from Irene, Sally, and even Little Nellie Kelly.

Gender Reciprocity

Unlike the original Cinderella story, most Cinderella musicals featured a reciprocal transformation by the Prince Charming character. The fairy-tale features a European prince, a member of the titled nobility. This means that there is a certain political/legal clout at work to reinforce his personal decisions. Cinderella transforms her appearance in order to attend the ball, but must return to her original modest state. However, when the Prince makes her his Princess, he transforms her permanently and legally into a member of the aristocracy. Others of his class cannot disagree with his choice, let alone pressure him otherwise; there is no sense of his experiencing any loss as a result of this decision, at least in the myth.[13]

But in the Cinderella musicals, the princes are American, enjoying riches but not the same sort of permanent social standing or clout. When an American Prince Charming decides to wed the poor Cinderella they tended to put themselves at risk, in society or economically. In four of the Cinderella shows—*Mary Jane McKane, The Rise of Rosie O'Reilly, Plain Jane and Helen of Troy, New York*—the all-powerful, wealthy father either fires or disinherits his son for wooing a girl outside his class, though by the end of each show the young couple wins out.

The Cinderella musicals thus are aware that there is a transgressive dimension to their stories. We tend to focus only on the two transformations of Cinderella, namely her first for the ball and then her second at play's end. But the character of the Prince often also experiences a comparable double transformation. The first is not at the ball, but rather when he chooses to leave the safety and comfort of his familiar, affluent surroundings in order to pursue his mystery woman, slipper in hand, to her disadvantaged environs and, by doing so, accepting her for what she is. His second transformation is when he then weds her, as, unlike his often private personal search, to wed is public and hence overt. The millionaire prince is now open to scrutiny and criticism, perhaps even exclusion from previously welcoming, fashionable homes.

This transgressive dynamic is certainly present in *Irene*. The fact that our "princess" Irene is Irish means the chances of acceptance are diminished exponentially. Yet, one of the reasons our "prince" Donald Marshall finds Irene so fascinating is that she so differs from the string of bland society girls his mother has foisted upon him. Irene's intelligence and drive is exotic and alluring. To pursue her is transgressive both because it is at odds with his mother's preferences, and because Irene is an outsider due to social class, ethnicity and temperament.

From Transgression to Reinvention

Cinderella musicals like *Irene* also suggest that both the Cinderella and the Prince Charming consciously practice a form of acculturation. Our heroine playacts being rich to attend the ball, and later her performance becomes a reality; our hero playacts hobnobbing amongst the poor and later may suffer the consequences from his peers. However, what makes this a peculiarly American story is that, not only are such marriages possible, but that such transformations are possible on the part of both parties. On the surface it is a mixed marriage. But following the melting pot principle, each finds a commonality through mutual acculturation, thus forming a neutral middle ground that erases (or ignores) difference. That the play ends happily only confirms acculturation's legitimacy.

A show like *Irene* pictures a future world, not only with the poor Irish girl gaining status and wealth, but in which her mate's social class is itself transformed so that it does more than tolerate but rather fully welcomes her into its ranks. It is telling that the father often disinherits the son; this demonstrates the intolerant and prejudice of the older generation, suggesting that such beliefs can be perceived as being "old fashioned" in the face of a modern generation that is trying to dispense with outdated Victorian ways. By accepting Irene and acknowledging her as Irish, Donald Marshall and his ilk transform both the makeup and definition of their own beliefs. This in turn similarly redefines the constitution of their social class and, in a sense of exactly what is "American." Beneath the musical comedy sheep's clothing, *Irene* and its Cinderella ilk all advocate for a more diversely defined Establishment, ultimately a more multicultural America.

Being on the cusp of the Jazz Age, with its dismissal of nineteenth-century Victorian ways in favor of the modern and new, disapproving dads have diminished impact. Tradition be damned. If the sympathetic son is disinherited, he will still woo his Cinderella and go into business for himself. Significantly, this business is usually the brainchild of his industrious Cinderella. But together they will not only make due, they will flourish. After all, the only reason the father had power was because of his money, and that was something the young upstarts could replicate on their own, and do so on their own terms. In America, ultimately it was money that ruled, and with that came greater freedoms and possibilities. True, they might not be acceptable to high society, but they will find their own society. This was exactly what happened with the real-life Irving Berlin-Ellin Mackay marriage. Her father Clarence Mackay initially disowned the couple, the son-in-law was independently wealthy, the newlywed wife was barred from much of high society, and yet they still lived happily-ever-after. America of the 1920s could accommodate this whether it wanted to or not. Welcome the Jazz Age, new uncharted territory for ethnic and nonethnic Middle Passage.

PART TWO: THE PYGMALIONS

Higgins, Quixote, and Curtis: Male Chauvinist Pygmalions

If Cinderella plays centered on women's fantasies, then what of men? The ying to the Cinderella yang would be those plays that still make use of the female character's transformation, but do so from the male's point of view. We have already seen in shows such as *Sally* and *Funny Girl* how it was Ziegfeld who was responsible for recognizing the young woman's talent and who catapulted them on to stardom. Significantly, though, in both shows each woman is in control of her outward appearance, it is she who decides what she will wear "to the ball." So, while Ziegfeld is prominent in both, ultimately both shows center on Sally and Fanny respectively, leaving Ziegfeld as simply a vehicle to "discover" them and then actualize their professional dreams. He is a professional "Prince Charming" who is taken with each woman's talent (rather than beauty) and who then engages them professionally (rather than matrimonially). In good Cinderella fashion, the male ultimately serves the wishes of the female.

The converse of the Cinderella paradigm is what I will call "the Pygmalion paradigm." There are great similarities between the two: both are built upon ancient tales, both center on the relationship between a man and a woman, and both include the outward transformation of the woman seemingly for her benefit. Furthermore, in both the Cinderella and Pygmalion models, the female character is largely passive; it is the change in her outward appearance that ultimately draws the male wooer. In the case of such Pygmalion-based shows, this outward transformation are also directly linked to issues of acculturation, as the changed exterior tends to correspond with an improvement in the woman's social standing. At the start of each show she is both downtrodden and apparently unattractive;

by the end their external transformation signals both increased beauty and a radical raise in status.

Whereas in the Cinderella musicals the Prince Charming characters simply recognize the ingénue's appeal, in the Pygmalion-based musical the male character is himself responsible for transforming the woman's appearance. In the Cinderella shows the prince is a young man, of comparable age to the leading lady; in Pygmalion shows the man is usually a generation older, bringing his knowledge and experience of the world to bear. Yet this suggests that the male is familiar with social norms and seeks to bring the woman to them, whereas in the Cinderella shows it is the woman's very difference that makes her attractive. In the Pygmalion-based show the attraction tends to lie in the young woman's very ignorance, if not innocence. In the end, the older man (Pygmalion), like the Prince Charming, falls in love with the transformed young woman, the difference being that, unlike the case with Prince Charming, the woman's outward appearance is itself a direct creation of the man and hence oddly narcissistic. It is really all about him, not her, and functions to fill his needs, though she herself may benefit from it.

You could argue that to some degree, from the leading lady's point of view, hers is still a Cinderella-like journey. But they are actually pawns in the *uber-mensch's gemeinschaft*, objects to be shaped to fit the establishment to which the male belongs, according to his view of reality and, ultimately in this case, his own view of femininity. In such shows the world is seen primarily through the male protagonist's eyes, with the ingénue going along for the ride, albeit to her benefit, or at least that is what he believes. I call such shows "Pygmalion musicals."

Galatea and Higgins

According to myth, the sculptor Pygmalion shaped a marble Galatea, only to fall in love with her. George Bernard Shaw updated the tale in his play of the same name and added a healthy dose of Anglo-Irish socialism to the mix, having the upper-crust Henry Higgins reshape the Cockney Eliza Doolittle until he could pass her off as a refined lady. This story was in turn transformed by Lerner and Loewe into the 1956 musical *My Fair Lady*, which introduced a romantic happy ending between teacher and pupil not found in the original Shaw.

To use 1970s parlance, Henry Higgins is a male chauvinist pig. For a romantic lead in a musical he is clearly misogynistic, using and abusing Eliza with glee, singing in praise of men at the expense of women.

His interest in her remains essentially clinically distant. He is entirely self-absorbed, concerned only with his own success, never crediting Eliza for her efforts, let alone demonstrating any feelings toward her. In point of fact, how could he do so? As a Pygmalion he demands that Eliza be transformed according to his strictures, to his specifications; he never travels towards her or her world, as a Prince Charming would do. So, in the end, even when he falls in love, it is with his own creation, not with who Eliza really is. He shaped her to fit his idealized image and, once she achieved that, he fell in love with that image, albeit as an *anagorisis*. Early on Eliza does show fire in rejecting of him ("Without You"), but, rather than decimate Higgins, he applauds her even more. Even her declaration of self seems to fit into his conception of a perfect woman! His behavior is pure narcissism, not romantic love for her. Lerner and Loewe salvaged him a bit in the song, "I've Grown Accustomed to Her Face" when they demonstrate his inner conflict, that she (someone other than he himself) has managed to insinuate herself, the other, into his consciousness. So the grouch finds remorse and is then rewarded with her return and affection.

Why would Eliza return to him? True, he has helped her improve her lot, taught her how to transform herself into the guise of a lady and thus enable her to walk alongside London's high society. In the original Shaw made her empowered: we learn that she will purchase her own flower shop and pursue her own life apart. This seems more plausible than what we are given here in the musical version. All that could explain it is that she is in love with Higgins, that perhaps, like we learn through that song, she intuits that he too is in love with her. "Love" will have to suffice to explain her actions and their reconciliation. And ever since she sang "I Could Have Danced All Night" it has been clear that she is infatuated with Higgins and, we the audience, having been schooled in countless romances, know then to root for this Galatea to succeed in her love, no matter how pig-headed the object of her affections.

Though set in Edwardian England, the musical *My Fair Lady* follows the American pattern. Eliza's ability to climb the social ladder through changing her appearance and behavior runs parallel to what Irving Berlin urged in his "Puttin' On the Ritz." Granted her transformation does not include the ethnic component of Berlin, though she is Cockney, but the rest is in keeping with his advice. One suspects that the opening "Why Can't The English Teach Their Children How to Speak?" is a direct descendant of "Puttin' On the Ritz" as Higgins asserts that it is "verbal class-distinctions" alone that makes for societal position; change outward appearance and behavior and a flower girl could be mistaken for a princess.

And the cockney dialect could just as easily be Italian or Yiddish or Puerto Rican if the play happened to be set in America.

And so Eliza goes along with the masquerade. Guided by Higgins, Eliza is meticulously transformed, fools the aristocrats by her ballroom turn, eventually winning the man of her dreams. In many respects it is a Cinderella story, but with some key differences. In a show like *Irene* our heroine only had to don a gown to win acceptance; her behavior was apparently acceptable as is, whereas in *My Fair Lady* Eliza had to learn proper English and oh-so-proper English behavior in order to prove credible. Irene was inherently acceptable; she just needed the outer trappings. Eliza required an entire makeover. As it is her transformed self does attract the aristocratic Freddy Eynsford-Hill who does chase after her, even waiting "On the Street Where You Live" hoping she will appear. But Prince Charming is trumped by Pygmalion, as Eliza spurns Freddy in words meant for Higgins, as she defiantly sings, "Show Me."

Irene is set in democratic America whereas *My Fair Lady* is set in aristocratic Europe. The "social class distinctions" described by Higgins at the opening may well be "antique" but they nevertheless still govern English life and are a key component of that play. According to the American Dream, however, there is social class but the distinctions are malleable and vague. So while *My Fair Lady* works for American audiences because of the parallels and fantasies, it remains firmly rooted in English social norms, even as it parodies them. It resonates with the post–World War II love of all things British, an Anglophilia notably celebrated in the trio of Lerner and Loewe's trio of greatest hit fantasies: *Brigadoon*, *My Fair Lady* and *Camelot*. British culture is idealized for Americans as a remedy for modernism in the first, as a parallel promising both romance and success in the second, and as a model for postwar American Empire-building in the third.

Yet, of the three, *My Fair Lady* has proven the most enduring. It is a first rate-operetta whose underlying Shavian socialism undercuts the aristocratic pretense in a spirit not unlike American iconoclasm. Higgins is an antihero, the most unlikely of romantic leads, middle-aged, self-congratulatory, acerbic, and gruff. Eliza is similarly an antiheroine: whiney, vulgar, spiteful, and ignorant. A match made in heaven. At times they appear to be a possible Beatrice and Benedict, but in truth they are Kate and Petruchio. And like *The Taming of the Shrew*, one suspects that, in the end, Higgins is as tamed by Eliza as she by him.

Still, Eliza remains Higgins' creation. He acquiesces to romance in large part because she becomes exactly what he envisioned. She is the rightful Galatea to his male chauvinist Pygmalion. As such, Higgins, a certified member of the upper class, has taken a Cockney working class girl, and transformed her to his liking, which is to say made her resemble those of his own social class. Even her father ends up reformed by the end, safely wed and ruined by the acquisition of riches. Eliza's Cockney past thus evaporates; she has no where left to go. Caught in middle-passage, she is too Cockney to fit naturally amidst high society, and now too refined to fit in comfortably living amongst her people.

Higgins too is a bit of an odd ball. Though upper crust, he is rather bohemian in his work as a professor, tinkering eccentrically with his experiments and toys. He is too odd to be truly proper and too proper to be truly odd. So what he creates in Eliza is actually a perfect match for his own real circumstances and she cannot fit in anywhere else with any happiness or success. He has tailored her to fit him and his world. As long as they end up a match this can work, but she is far too specialized to fit in anywhere else, including with the amorous Freddie. In Shaw's *Pygmalion* she is independent in the end, as is Higgins, but her future is uncertain; in Lerner and Loewe's *My Fair Lady* she ends up with Higgins, thus resolving both characters' plight, in the only setting for which either can fully function. It is a great disservice in the Shaw because Higgins plays with another person resulting in abandonment. Or perhaps it is a greater service, since it suggests that, ultimately, the bird has to leave the nest and fly on its own, independent of its creator, regardless of the risks. But American Dreams are formed of fantasies, not morality or realities.

For Higgins, romance was an unexpected, perhaps even unwanted side effect of his experiment. For the audience, it is a satisfying resolution, reassuring in its innocence. Not once do we fear for Eliza living in a man's house; Higgins never seems to pose such a threat. Besides, there are the two chaperones of the maid Mrs. Pearce and also Colonel Pickering. It is all quite on the up and up. And as for the issue of an aristocratic male transforming a working class female, by its very nature it never would have worked without Eliza's consent and active participation. She wants to be transformed, she wants to become a lady, and, she dreams of a life, other than her own, in which things would be "lover-ly." Initially that dream does not include Higgins. It is only after the "The Rain in Spain" number that she begins to have feelings for him, and that is quite a ways through the play. When she triumphs at the ball she expects recognition and appreciation; instead it all goes to Higgins, which is when she rebels, largely because of being ignored. And, yes, in the song "You Did It" she largely is being discarded, moving from centerpiece to side adornment, neither respected nor loved. She believed the dream; apparently Higgins did not.

In *My Fair Lady* Higgins is the all-powerful aristocrat who deigns to transform the poor, unschooled girl to fit his fantasy. It appears fairly innocent. It is not as if he was transforming her with the intention of satisfying his own sexual needs. It is crucial to the story that that be the case, that his intention is purely intellectual, even scientific, even if self-serving. Higgin's goal is to prove he is right, not create some sort of love-slave. Furthermore, since he is a "confirmed old bachelor" who is highly critical of women, this lends him greater viability, making his intentions all the more sincere and pure, however warped. It is only in the very last moments of the show that he is transformed, that he realizes and acknowledges romantic feelings for Eliza. This protects him from censure in our eyes and, since Eliza comes back entirely of her own volition, and because even then all says to her is to get his slippers, the domestic ideal is preserved, even if, in the end, they actually do end up romantically linked.

How unlike *My Fair Lady* is from the Cinderella shows, especially *Irene*, where the woman's situation is often as an equal by play's end. Higgins asking for his slipper also reinforces the notion that, at some level, she will always be a servant to him and his male needs. Let's not kid anyone: despite appearances to the contrary, the Cockney girl remains at heart a Cockney girl, and the aristocratic male remains entirely an aristocratic male. No revolution here; the status quo is safely (and reassuringly?) preserved. Perhaps it is because Higgins will always know the truth about Eliza's modest beginnings, whereas a Freddy only loves her polished exterior; perhaps Eliza finds both solace and reassurance that Higgins knows that and accepts her accordingly. It is an odd story then of identity politics, of ultimately being loved because of who you always were, after two-and-a-half hours of striving to change and find acceptance there instead. Pygmalion loves Galatea, not only because she was created according to his image, but also because he alone knows and appreciates she emerged out of stone.

Galatea and Quixote

A similar pattern appears in *Man of La Mancha*. Again we have an aristocratic, middle-aged oddball of a hero, Don Quixote, who, in the course of his work decides to rescue and transform a lower class woman. Aldonza will become Dulcinea. In the musical, she is at first shown to be a tavern wench, one step removed from being a whore. Like Eliza, Aldonza is tough and fiery, a real survivor, accustomed to looking out for herself amidst the poor.

Along comes Don Quixote who, rather than see her for who she has become, chooses instead to see her as he wants her to be. It proves a powerful remedy. By play's end, Don Quixote's chivalrous behavior towards Aldonza does result in her treating herself with greater self-respect, causing her to become in some ways the very Dulcinea he seems to envision. Don Quixote's idealistic delusion causes him to view her as gentle and virtuous, even though we the audience saw her violently fending off unwanted suitors just a moment before. Unlike Higgins, Don Quixote does not physically transform Aldonza, he does not change her clothing or her behavior, but rather he simply changes her by insisting upon the reality of his imagined perceptions. The beauty of the play is that, to those closest to him, his ennobling fantasies take on the substance of fact.

So while less deliberate than Higgins, Don Quixote still functions as a sort of Pygmalion, though a Pygmalion who sculpts dreams rather than stone. And, significantly, Aldonza, like Eliza, slowly complies, refining her behavior to fit his vision of her. She too is thus transformed in such a fashion as to match his male fantasy of her. But it is more than gender-based. Like Eliza, this lower class woman chooses to take on a more refined bearing and behavior, rising to meet Don Quixote's expressed ideal. And, like Eliza, she has her momentary lapses that she manages to overcome. And, like Eliza, Aldonza comes to love her shaper, though, in this case, her love is entirely platonic.

Man of La Mancha also resembles *My Fair Lady* in that it is set in Europe, takes place in the past, and, given its source, is similarly highly literary in tone. Yet as Don Quixote sings his "The Impossible Dream" he may as well be singing of the American one. Though set in a foreign place and time, the show is constructed along familiar American musical lines, with its romantic dreamer protagonist accompanied by the sexy wench and his lovable clown companion, Sancho Panza.

However, while few ever criticize Don Quixote, his fantasies of Aldonza can be seen as highly chauvinistic and disrespectful. He never really "looks" at her, never really accepts her for who she is, in her own terms. Rather he uses his passive aggressiveness to entangle her in the web of his fantasies simply by insisting her to be someone other than who she is and implicitly urging her to act accordingly. Clearly the audience and Aldonza applaud this because of Don Quixote's beneficial intentions and harmless foolishness. But picture the situation was reversed: what is she was a Dulcinea and that Don Quixote's fantasy life insisted that she was a sluttish Aldonza and that he treated her accordingly, expecting her to act in that fashion? We tend to forgive his behavior, not consider them hegemonic when she complies. In the end, Aldonza, by playing the role of Dulcinea, has been tamed and, as a result, found herself defenseless in the face of more powerful forces. Unlike a real Dulcinea, she lacks the authority to intercede on Don Quixote's behalf, and we know she can only return to the life she previously had led, now less-equipped to function as effectively. She no longer belongs there, any more than did Eliza still fit in amongst the Cockney.

There is no place in European society for someone truly to advance. Unlike America, class distinctions not only exist, they are binding. A hallmark of the American Dream, and indeed the society itself, is the possibility for social mobility through self-improvement. "The pursuit of happiness" has led many an American to reinvent themselves if they so choose to do so, a freedom not evident abroad. As we have seen, this is most often tied to acculturation. Perhaps *My Fair Lady* is a comedy because Eliza's assimilation bore fruit: she succeeds in marrying up (or that is at least implied) and will live amidst a higher social class as a result. If so, then *Man of La Mancha* is a tragedy for Aldonza, because her efforts at acculturation come to naught socially. You could argue that she does improve her spiritual lot, that she is a sort of Mary Magdeline to Don Quixote's martyred Jesus, which might be the case. But her external situation, her place in the material world, does not improve as a result of her efforts. In fact, all she would earn is scorn for her misguided pretensions. Yet, in the end, she herself insists on being Dulcinea and being treated as such. Perhaps it is a form of madness, the same madness that haunted Don Quixote, but it does result in her insisting on being treated better, having ironically gained self-respect because of Don Quixote's lie. She believes in him and in the value of how she views herself. She is thus left living in her head, apart from hostile realities. For her there is no America, it is at best only an "impossible dream."

Galatea and Curtis

A third show example of the Pygmalion model is *Dreamgirls*. On the surface the show has marked differences from *My Fair Lady* and from *Man of LaMancha*. *Dreamgirls* is set in America and features African American characters enacting a storyline modeled on 1960s popular culture.[14] And where the other two shows could be categorized as American operettas, here the Motown rock idiom prevails. But beneath the external trappings, *Dreamgirls* is built upon the same structure as its two progenitors; it is simply an updated Pygmalion story built to reach an interracial baby boom audience.

Dreamgirls also features a successful, more experienced male who transforms several downtrodden women to match his idealized vision, eventually falling in love and marrying one of his own creation. Curtis becomes the agent for the black girl group, the Dreamettes. His ambition and tough business practices help the group rise to the top, as he has an affair with lead singer Effy. But eventually he sees greater success if the group can crossover, away from rhythm and blues and more toward pop. He shapes the group according to his vision, kicks out Effy, and makes the more polished and bland Deena the group's lead singer, eventually marrying her instead. The story continues as Curtis tries to enforce his vision onto others, only to have them eventually rebel, one by one. Eventually Effy returns with a hit of her own, performed contrary to the commercialism promoted by Curtis. He fights back, but in the end Effy is reunited with the Dreams as Curtis realizes that Effy's daughter is in fact also his.

Like Higgins and Quixote before him, Curtis strives to shape the perception of the young women, asking them to change themselves according to his specifications in order to attain commercial success. And like Eliza and Aldonza, the Dreamettes do so willingly. Unlike the other two, though, a split occurs in *Dreamgirls*, with Effy going one way and Deena the other. It is not just one woman who is thus transformed but rather the entire group itself. The Dreamettes start off on their own terms, but are at the bottom of the showbiz ladder, but as Curtis reshapes them, they gradually climb that ladder toward success. This is right out of the Irving Berlin School of Assimilation, right down to the show business setting. But *Dreamgirls* starts to diverge and, consequently begins to challenge those immigrant-based assumptions. The crisis point comes at the end of Act I when Curtis and Deena fire Effy because she is not following those guidelines, because she is acting impulsively and according to her feelings rather than conforming to Curtis' take on how one needs to behave in order to gain crossover acceptance. Though the strongest singer, Effy is most closely tied to her black cultural roots and either cannot or will not compromise them in order to adjust to others (i.e. White culture) in order to succeed. Curtis and Deena, on the other hand, are willing to sacrifice their racial identity on the altar of ambition and economic success.

At every turn, Curtis uses his growing authority to control the appearance and behaviors of his clients. He makes Deena a star. He struggles to keep the commercially appealing pop sound and resists new musical trends such as funk, sounds more akin to black culture. But deep in his soul he remains tied to his black cultural roots as attested by his recognition and acceptance of having fathered Effy's child. It is this acceptance that ends the play.

It is also important to note that it was unlikely that Effy's more African sound would have found commercial acceptance had it not been for the pioneering strides of the Dreamettes. Curtis' efforts did create a market for mainstream black music, which in turn then expanded to include a broader range of black sound. In other words, had it not been for the success of the Dreamettes there would be no crossover commercial acceptance for funk or for the kind of music expressed by Effy. In other words, there would have been no Broadway show called *Dreamgirls*.

The musical ends with Effy reuniting on stage with Deena et al as a reformulated Dreamette lineup. Effy may have drifted into more traditional sounds for a while, but in the end she opts for show business. Her inclusion suggests that her appearance and sound are now an acceptable part of what the Dreamettes can now become; progress has been made, in part because of and in part in spite of Curtis's efforts. His acceptance of Effy's child is his acceptance of his ethnic roots, but it also asserts that the world has changed, in part due to his efforts, so as to enable the black experience to find commercial expression on the crossover stage. Even as the audience applauds Effy and the Dreamette's success, ultimately it is Curtis who is acknowledged as the progenitor of them and of the generation to follow. It is his Pygmalion vision that fathered them all even as that brainchild took on a life of its own.

Pygmalions and Societal Norms

So what have our three Pygmalions to do with Jews? It is not so much a question of ethnicity as it is one of one's place within the larger societal norms. While all three—Higgins, Quixote, and Curtis—are far more powerful than their female charges, each is in fact actually an outsider, operating on the fringe of the very class to which they implicitly promise their Galatea's will aspire.

Higgins is a member of London's high society; this is made evident both by his participation in the "Ascot Opening Day" number as well as his attending the ball. Yet he is an oddball, an English eccentric who shuns societal norms and is berated for this by his mother. Higgins is an overage child and acts the part. Ironically, he helps Eliza come of age to such a degree that she outgrows him. Her willingness to "fetch his slipper" is more that she accepts his need for a mother, more than as his servant. Furthermore, Higgins is essentially a revolutionary, skeptical of the very traditions that define his class. His opening song argues that the only real distinction between the upper and lower classes is elocution, suggesting that the upper class is built solely on pretence. He doesn't even argue the case for merit; only appearances count in his view.

The musical fiddles with Shaw's British original because it presents an American dimension. Yes, Eliza does successfully transform her outward appearance to fit Higgins' upper-class model, but she also grows in understanding and awareness, which was not part of the original plan. Her newfound understandings lead to rage, but rather than discard her Higgins becomes infatuated; this was something he had not anticipated and appears to be the root of his love for her.

In the end we understand that Higgins is an aristocrat armed with working class scorn, whereas Eliza is a member of the working class who aspires to gentility. Neither truly fits in with the lot to which they were born, and end up by the play's end meeting somewhere in the middle. In a Diasporic sense, Higgins marrying Eliza cannot harm his standing appreciably because he was already something of an outcast. Yet Eliza, thus transformed, can no longer survive in the world of Cockney London.

Much the same is true of *Man of La Mancha*. Don Quixote is similarly an outsider, a dreaming, loose cannon, riding off into a chivalric Never Never Land. By story's end he is captured (or "rescued" according to his family) and placed under a physician's care, soon to die. He was born to nobility, but his behavior is unorthodox, a source of ongoing embarrassment to his relations and class.

And the worse of it is that both his page and his lady love are of the lower classes. Sancho Panza and Aldonza are not appropriate companions for a man of Quixote's birth and their presence serves to undermine, even ridicule, aristocratic pretense, suggesting as they do that they could fulfill those more upper-class functions. Not unlike Higgins', Quixote's choices iconoclastically challenge the legitimacy of the powers-that-be and the basic premises upon which those class distinctions are determined. Unlike Higgins, the changes in his companions are not based on their outward transformation, but rather their transformation in Quixote's (and the audience's) eyes. So a middle ground is similarly struck, akin to that of Higgins and Eliza. The eccentric Quixote, unable to fit into amongst his own class, triumphs through fantasy and imagination, a hero to his lower class companions, just as he idealizes them. Together they meet in an imagined middle ground, a dream world that can accommodate such mixing and applaud the integrity of their aspirations. The story is Cervantes, but the implications anticipate the democratic American Dream.

In *Dreamgirls*, Curtis makes himself an outsider. He begins his life and career in a ghetto neighborhood, drawing upon its being a cradle of black music. Yet his aspiration is not to remain there, satisfied amongst the traditions and ethnicity of his own people, but rather to crossover, to become part of the exclusionary world of the predominantly white entertainment business. In terms of the American Dream we applaud his ambition and, unlike the European roots of both Higgins and Quixote, we understand that the pattern of American assimilation make such ambitions plausible. But Curtis is black. Is assimilation truly plausible for one who cannot alter their outward appearance? Are the economic rewards familiarly commensurate with assimilation truly within his reach?

In essence, Curtis redefines pop music to include blacks, but he himself becomes culturally lost. He idealizes the white world but does so at the expense of the black, the members of which he increasingly suppresses. Ironically, he makes himself a pariah to the world in which he was born. He takes black soul music and makes it pop, bleaching the color out of it and its performers, and viewing his more traditional brethren with scorn. Curtis comes to thumb his nose at his native class and culture no differently than Higgins did his. He discards the more "African" Effy in favor of the more "white" looking Deena, thus alienating himself further. Curtis' efforts to distance himself and the Dreamettes succeeds in that enables them to become stars. But by the end he is isolated and alone. He is ironically rescued by the reemergence of Effy, and his acknowledgement of their shared child signals his reclamation. Nevertheless, Curtis will continue to exist in a Diasporic reality, living between worlds, not quite acceptable to either, akin to what we have seen with our other Pygmalions and the Galateas they created.

IN SUMMARY: CINDERELLAS OR GALATEAS?

Each of our three Pygmalions improved the lot of their respective Galateas. Yet since each Pygmalion themselves functioned outside societal norms, it is questionable just how far their mentoring could really empower or open doors for their respective mentees.

It seems that the Cinderellas faired far better than the Galateas, largely because our Irenes and Sallys and Fanny's demanded acceptance for who they truly were. They were not as trapped in contradiction between appearance and reality as was largely the case of our strong but essentially dependent Galateas. Still, together, our Cinderellas and Galateas represent complementary though contrasting paths for women choosing romance as a means to achieve the American Dream.

6. Turns of the Century: Dreams of Progress, Dreams of Loss ∽

PART ONE: WHEELS OF DREAMS—*RAGTIME* AS MUSICAL MIDDLE PASSAGE

Oh Sarah, it's more than a promise,
It must be true.
A country that lets a man like me
Own a car, raise a child, build a life
With you.

Coalhouse Walker sings "The Wheels of a Dream"

The 1998 musical *Ragtime* is a study in transitions, a portrayal of early twentieth-century America as a world in flux. Almost every character in the play transforms himself or herself in terms of their social position, almost each of which is motivated by unexpected and unwanted forces beyond their own doing. Based on E. L. Doctorow's 1975 novel of the same name, the musical examines social, cultural, racial, and ethnic changes in turn-of-the-century American culture. While the novel and the musical reflect late twentieth-century sensibilities, both rely heavily on the novelties that transformed American life during the early 1900s, particularly the explosion in every kind of travel—car, steamship, and train. These innovations sped up not only the pace of American life, but also the ability of its diverse diaspora communities to move, intersect, and occasionally collide. Thus the characters in *Ragtime* are shown not simply on a series of "middle passages" but often actually *mid*-passage, and the audience is offered insights into how the journey, whether by car, train, or steamer, is shaping the new identity of the travelers.

The ragtime musical theme is itself emblematic, marking a major shift in the demographic makeup and consequent values of nineteenth-century

American society and culture toward that of the twentieth. The blessings of the previous century enable America to become the land of opportunity, the seemingly prosperous and welcoming destination for any number of outsiders, forced from their foreign homes. In one sense, then, the musical portrays a reshuffling of the societal deck, in which characters either rise or fall by play's end. And though it portrays, through use of archetypes arranged in montage fashion, their stories variously intertwined, a composite snapshot of the nation as a whole, *Ragtime* actually centers on a series of cultural shifts marked by redefinitions of individual, national, and diaspora identities.

Mid- and Middle Passage in *Ragtime*

Every social group is shown in mid-passage in *Ragtime*. By "mid-passage" I am suggesting the existence of a shared liminality, whereas "middle-passage" tends to mean a complete dislodgement. There are characters in *Ragtime* who leave their social position by choice, and yet still remain and consider themselves Americans. Yet they no longer fit in where once they did and are, as such, now liminal, operating outside of accepted norms. This is particularly true of the individuals who comprise what I call "the Family" (the Father, Mother, et al.), but comes to include other characters as well. They are displaced rather than expelled, and redefine themselves as much as they are redefined by others.

In *Ragtime* we are introduced to Jewish immigrants, fleeing pogroms in Russia via steerage on ships, clamoring at America's Ellis Island gate, welcome and yet not. As they are they will only experience poverty and Lower East Side isolation. Only Tateh's eventual assimilation liberates him and his daughter from slum lives, yet as the Baron Ashkenazy he will remain a prisoner, caught between two conflicting worlds. We are also introduced to Coalhouse Walker, riding the wave of a newfound respectability thanks to his success playing ragtime piano. Coalhouse triumphantly rides his middle-passage "ship" of a Model T Ford. He is, unfortunately, thrown out from his ship by a group of racist firemen, a displacement that ultimately results in his radicalization, madness, and death. Father flees his predictable American life to accompany Admiral Peary on his ship, duty bound charting new waters with a Christian, nationalistic fervor. And while he is gone his wife finds Coalhouse and Sarah's bastard infant. Mother did not ask for the new child, yet decides to raise this African American child as her own. In turn her journey will lead her away from Father and toward a new life wed to the equally transformed Tateh, raising a multicultural brood together. Evelyn Nesbitt, the former showgirl, endures public scrutiny due to her mid-passage "traveling" on a red velvet swing, to the delight of her powerful lover, the now deceased architect Stanford White, murdered by her rich husband. Younger Brother, who, infatuated first with Evelyn and later with the ideas of Emma Goldman, also abandons his unhappy respectability. In the end Younger Brother assists Coalhouse in laying siege to the Morgan Library via explosives.

Steamships bring immigrants fleeing Russia; ships remove Father, forced by nationalistic duty to explore and conquer. Cars represent the initial triumph and ultimate undoing of a black man and his dreams of family; cars also thus inspire black militancy. Trains carry Tateh toward becoming Baron Ashkenazy, and, along the commuter train path to New Rochelle, cause him to first intersect with Mother and her son. At the end of the musical, the Baron and Mother, standing on the shore, look immediately out to the beach to view their children playing, but are they also looking out toward the sea, toward the future, with hope and also with uncertainty: If they wed will they also be displaced? If they raise an interracial brood, what will the future hold for any of them? Will they too be dislodged or accepted because they differ?

Early in *Ragtime* Walker and his fiancé Sarah pause to picnic. There they sing an inspired anthem, "Wheels of a Dream." Thanks to Henry Ford's auto, the American Dream, a dream of transplantation and redefinition, seems entirely possible. Walker has, for the moment, successfully redefined how African Americans should view themselves in America— instead of as former slaves, disenfranchised victims, he envisions African Americans as middle-class citizens, enjoying on equal footing the fruits of the American Dream. Technological progress as represented by his auto reflects social progress, pointing toward an empowered future. Of course, this is before Walker is forced from his car and it is trashed in the mud and muck, his dreams of a newfound identity along with it. It is worth noting that this assertion of the American Dream is made right at the play's center, and, immediately afterward, trouble begins to brew, leading to their individual and collective downfall.

The issues of middle-passage, usually assigned to the conveying of African slaves across the Atlantic, are applicable throughout *Ragtime*. It is evident in the play's use of characters and plot, language and themes, though surprisingly less so in its use of music. In order to consider this application, let us first look at the basic construct in which the Middle-passage experience can be understood. African captives lost their identity when sold as slaves; they lost their humanity when transformed into commodities. They were stripped of items that indicated their geographical home, their social status, anything that defined them as individuals, forcing them to experience what sociologist Orlando Patterson has called "a social death." Theirs was an involuntary displacement that led to the annihilation of identity, on the road to eventual sale, and further displacement, once sold in the Americas. The passage across the Atlantic, where slaves were crammed indiscriminately into the holds and deprived of proper nourishment, only accentuated this deracinating process.

Once in America an African became a slave. He or she was an object that could be bartered for goods. The language of the slave traders denied difference in their effort to portray a slave as something that could fetch a good price. Any sense of humanity or dignity was lost in the transaction: a commodity cannot think or feel.

Issues of Identity: Language and Music Shape Humanity

The portrait of America introduced in *Ragtime* reduces all characters into representative social roles and types. There are three categories of characters in the play: actual historical figures, characters known only by their social role, and two characters that are actually named. In the first group are Evelyn Nesbit, Harry Houdini, Emma Goldman, J. P. Morgan, and Henry Ford. Unlike Doctorow's book, Terence McNally's libretto paints each entirely two dimensionally. Consequently, each simply represents a particular dynamic present in period America: Nesbit represents sensationalism, Houdini escapism, Goldman socialism (not anarchy), Morgan wealth and power, and Ford industrialization. When they interact it is simply the collision between competing forces, not a realistic interpersonal exchange. Collectively, they form the various often-conflicting forces that comprise period America. We are also introduced at the start to the family. This group is composed and defined only by traditional familial roles: Father, Mother, Younger Brother, and Little Boy (who is occasionally called "Edgar").

One might think that this impersonal collective forms a forbidding society that any newcomer or outsider would be daunted approaching. But the second category also includes most of the remaining fictional characters. Tateh is a Jewish immigrant from Latvia, accompanied by his young daughter. But "Tateh" is a Yiddish term for father, and thus is no different in delineation from any in the American-based family. At the start of the play he purposely instructs his young daughter never to tell anyone her name, so she too remains a blank slate throughout the play, referred to only as his daughter. We also meet the dynamic Coalhouse Walker. Yet his first name is not a name at all but rather a location, an occupation, and an almost comedic reference to his skin color, as if it was the soot found there that made him black. It is a nickname, not a given name. Thus, he too remains distant and something of a mystery, along with most everyone else around him. At the play's end, we find that his baby is also called "Coalhouse," but that is not until the play's end.

The only two major fictional characters in the play who have actual names are Sarah and Willie Conklin. Since Sarah is not given a last name, it is impossible to refer to her formally; she remains thus vulnerable due to this intimacy. Willie Conklin, the Irish fire chief, is given a full name perhaps because his name becomes synonymous with bigotry and foolishness, and is trumpeted in the press as the cause of Walker's murderous rampage, thus verbally tarred and feathered. So knowing his exact name is crucial to the workings of the play.

If almost all of the characters are robbed of their human dimensionality due to Doctorow's use of non-names, then who are the slaves and who are not? I would argue that all the fictional characters in this play suffer a comparable displacement; they all endure a middle-passage of some sort. In order to emphasize this displacement Doctorow begins by defining each according to the role within the society that they have fulfilled. The very fact that they take actions that go against their roles then asserts their complex humanity, the contradictions that declare them as people, operating below the stereotypical social role suggested by their names. Thus "Father" proves to be far more than just a father, "Mother" more contradictory than a mother, and so forth. But the play asserts at the start that America is strictly defined by everyone knowing his or her social roles and playing them properly. The fact that they do not becomes the story of the play.

Both the use of language and of music define identity in *Ragtime*. Some of this is played out in character names, as already explained, but some of this resonates with the treatment of slaves. Most notable amongst them is the battle between Mother and Father over Sarah's baby. To Father the child is an object that can be disposed; to Mother it is a life she intended to protect.[1] And, as is the case in all musicals, the musical underscoring functions to shape the audience's emotional reaction to the subject at hand. Evelyn's trial becomes a great circus in "Crime of the Century"; Coalhouse's request that his men spread his gospel becomes reverentially moving in "Make Them Hear You." We are being controlled by the medium, much as the characters' names shape our perceptions and assumptions. So Evelyn becomes a cartoon whereas Coalhouse becomes a prophet, all due to what the music directs.

Music is also used to define each of the three major ethnic groups in the play. There are examples of various native American music, from period-sounded ballads such as "Goodbye, My Love" to the industrious "Henry Ford." There is the black music of songs such as "Harlem Nightclub" or the haunting "Sarah Brown Eyes." There is the Jewish music of "A Shtetl Iz Amerieke." Such songs tend to segregate the play's communities into ethnic stereotypes. However, to its credit, the musical also functions to unite those groups into a patchwork whole. This is shown at *Ragtime's* start by the title number, sung by everyone, with internal musical references to each separate community. "Ragtime" is sung again at play's end, again in unison without the internal distinctions, and everyone then joins in to reprise that psalm of American technological and social progress, "Wheels of a Dream." With even the presence of Coalhouse and Sarah's ghosts, the moving ending suggests a rosy future of multicultural racial harmony and freedom. This reassures us but ignores the less certain social ambiguities and imminent dangers introduced by the libretto just prior to the finale. Hence the music overpowers the play.

Issues of Identity: On Coalhouse and Sarah

Let us look more closely at the examples of Coalhouse and his courtship of Sarah. We learn in the play that Coalhouse came from St. Louis where he heard Scott Joplin's music and, as a result, took piano lessons. He worked as a stevedore before coming to Harlem. He also spent time on the road as a musician and proclaims that he no longer wants that life, that his job with Jim Europe's jazz band allows him to stay put, and that he is thus now able to wed Sarah. So Coalhouse too is an immigrant, coming as he did from another city and culture.

Coalhouse's efforts to redefine his culture are in keeping with the slave experience in America.[2] Denied of his ancient African roots, he goes about reinventing them, or perhaps inventing alternatives, once here. He is something of a proselytizer, spreading the gospel of ragtime that he learned from hearing Scott Joplin in St. Louis to Harlem, and from Harlem he manages to spread the "good news" via his piano playing in the Family's New Rochelle homestead to white America. When he travels in his new Model T from Harlem to New Rochelle he is a sort of immigrant, crossing not just geographical boundaries but vast cultural and class boundaries as well. He finds a haven in the Family's New Rochelle home, but the town itself proves an unwelcoming diaspora, as made clear by Conklin and his cohorts.

As an outsider, Coalhouse takes actions that are not the local norm: he dressed well (the point is made that members of his gang stand out because they dress like him in Harlem) and carries himself with a pride that the Irish view as "uppity." Coalhouse also purchases a Model T Ford and transgresses geographical and social boundaries by driving out of Harlem and into affluent WASP New Rochelle. This so shocks the locals that they peek out from behind their curtains. It is also interesting that Walker knocks at the Family's front door, and that he behaves impeccably according to nineteenth-century rules of formal propriety, both in his interactions with the Family and with Sarah. In short, Coalhouse's newfound affluence has enabled him to purchase his freedom and he revels in his ability now to assimilate into the American middle class. This is accentuated first by his desire to wed Sarah and claim her baby as his own, thus forming a respectable bourgeois family unit. He is proud to be an example of one who achieves the American Dream. That he intends to act respectably is marked by his calling on the resistant Sarah on Sundays. Now perhaps that is because, as a musician, it is his day off from work. But this does make a point, as it is the Sabbath and makes his visits holy in intent. Had he visited her instead, say, on Saturday night one would think his intentions decidedly less honorable.[3]

The regularity of Coalhouse's visits enables a relaxing of boundaries between Coalhouse and the Family. This in turn leads to him playing their piano as he waits for the long-delayed Sarah. Walker fills their WASP house with ragtime music, much as his new music filled and thus transformed America itself. It also seeps up the stairs to the hiding Sarah, until she finally relents and dramatically descends the stairs to join him. Immediately the scene changes and we see Walker, Sarah, and their baby sitting on a blanket by the car in some undefined, lovely countryside setting. The family is complete and Coalhouse has found his family, his dignity, and his freedom, empowering Sarah as well as he sings "Wheels of a Dream." Like so many Americans, Walker could afford a Model T and it in turn opened up the roads, enabling him (like others) to escape the city and roam freely, experiencing both power and affirmation because of that freedom. At that moment Walker is living the American Dream fully and sees a rosy future for his family and himself. Thus, his car is his vehicle for change; it represents more than a means of transportation, as it is a symbol of his affluence, his dignity, and his freedom.

The car also hearkens back to the slave ship. Escaped slaves tried to return to Africa, but were unable to do so lacking an adequate ship and the know-how to sail it. They were thus entrapped on the American continent. Thus, the ship not only became a vehicle of enslavement but also the possible vehicle to freedom, to the restoration or return away from the diaspora. It is thus an important practical and functional object. In a sense, Walker's auto plays exactly that role. It is his return "ship" that will take him out of slavery and return him to freedom.[4] It is a step up for the man whose name means that he looks like he worked in a coalhouse, sardonically blackened by soot, and whose usual means of transportation is by foot, in other words, a walker.

In *Ragtime* we are presented with three types of vehicles: steam ships, trains, and automobiles. The auto differs from the other two for a black man in that no one can decide whether to allow you on board or where to sit once there, and that the driver has the freedom to go wherever the roads can take him or her, whenever he or she wishes to go. The driver is in charge and, particularly with the introduction of Ford's Model T, you no longer had to be rich to afford one, making every man a king, to borrow from Huey Long. It gave one a sense of empowerment. Unlike a ship or train one is not as governed by preexisting, fixed routes and it is far easier to cross conventional geographical boundaries, and, in Walker's case, boundaries of ethnicity and class as well.

Sarah too begins the play invisible. Unlike Walker, though, she finds solace and safety in her invisibility. We know that she was a fan of Walker's in Harlem and that she became pregnant from him. She apparently fled without telling him where she was going, and without telling him of his newborn son. In her song "Your Father's Son" she compares the rescued infant to its father, reflecting her intention to kill the memory of both father and son when she abandoned the child to die. Sarah took at job as a washerwoman in the household of the Family. This is akin to her returning to slavery, as she and her condition are largely unknown by Mother or Father, or even the Irish maid who discovers the abandoned child. Sarah wishes to remain invisible, not be found by Walker, and certainly not continuing her relationship with him. It is telling that during Walker's regular visits she remains hidden upstairs, again invisible. Perhaps it is Walker's respectable intentions or perhaps it is simply the appeal of his music that eventually draws out Sarah from hiding, willing to join him as his wife. The staircase thus becomes a motionless vehicle, alive with anticipation of her hoped-for descent.

There is something here about Sarah viewing herself as a commodity. She has had sex with Coalhouse, became pregnant, and, without telling him about her pregnancy, ran away. She acts as if all that would matter to Coalhouse would be her body and that the child spoiled everything. In that spirit she tries to kill her child, that it is an object of pain to her, not something human. In other words, she treats it much as she feels she is being treated by her situation, and who she perceived Coalhouse to be. That her baby is rescued sends the message that it and she do in fact matter. That Coalhouse then searches her out, and then persistently and respectfully comes to court, that his intentions are honorable, all give meaning to her as a person. He fills the Family's house with music, much as he had perhaps earlier filled her with his soul and given her life. Rather than letting her trash her child and herself, Coalhouse asserts a different truth, that she is in fact worthwhile, that she is no longer a slave at heart but rather an enfranchised, respected woman. In time, Sarah complies and comes downstairs to him. Thus Walker brings the socially dead back to life, restoring her to her identity and her humanity, a slave no longer. To one living in fear, one beaten down and commodified, this is both terrifying and revelatory. It is an extraordinary gift and marks the shift in cultural values Walker strives to instill in her and in the era itself. He is an instrument for healing and for cultural change.

Walker has made it because he believes he fits in as a full-fledged participant in the American Dream. He has achieved that Dream, even if he didn't invent it. It is a Dream that was sold to him as much as his car, and which he bought into fully. If Walker can achieve the Dream then he must be like everyone else, measured by his character and talent and perseverance, not by the color of his skin. This is not to say that Walker wishes he were White; it is clear from his later actions that that is not his intention. Walker views his own acceptance in multicultural terms, that he too has a place in the national composition.

But Walker's achievement also proves his eventual downfall. On the way back from the countryside with Sarah, his auto is blocked by a group of pugnacious Irish fire men who resent Walker's dignity and affluence. By trashing the car they are trashing the black man, putting him back in his place. Believing he belonged and asserting that his actions were the norm, Walker was blind to his conspicuousness in the eyes of others.

Walker, and with him Sarah, felt comfortable and safe presenting themselves as a respectable middle-class couple. Walker's musician's flamboyance tended toward public display, but Sarah was shy and fearful, more comfortable when invisible. Convinced that America accepted and enfranchised them, Walker approached the firemen with dignity and without fear. After the firemen trashed his car, Walker went down many roads, appealing to the various powers-that-be for the justice to which he was due. But to them Walker was still invisible as a black man. So ironically, his high visibility resulted in the firemen's attack and his later appeals similarly worked to push him back into a state of invisibility. Sarah similarly suffered. Worried about Coalhouse, she rushes the stage of the Republican presidential candidate (significantly standing on the rear of a train) seeking his help. But no longer invisible, Sarah is now "seen" as a threat and the guards beat her to death. She was safe when invisible, hidden away in the Family's home; Walker's assurances made her visible and, once so, she too became a target for violence. After Sarah's death, Walker became radicalized; if you can't join 'em, beat 'em.

Issues of Identity: On Father and Mother

While Walker's story dominates the action of the play, the other story lines are just as compelling as examples of the struggle against dehumanization. In the case of Father, America's materialistic rewards proved empty, compelling him to explore the North Pole with Admiral Peary. He had no plans to change, however, and when he left he yelled lengthy instructions for Mother to do the same. As he left on Peary's outbound boat it passed the rag ship carrying Tateh and his daughter, traveling inbound for New York's Ellis Island. Tateh spots Father and proclaims him a fool for leaving Eden. Later, Father will return, find his world turned upside down, shifted from a now-dissatisfied wife to a murderous police. And if Father's ships carried him to and fro, note that when he rushed from Atlantic City to serve as an intermediary between the police and the besieged Coalhouse, Father took a train appropriately called "the Cannonball." The man who thought fireworks entertaining discovered the true meaning of explosives in the end. Younger Brother gets it right when he finally accuses a puzzled Father, defining Father's failings, if not his cultural morass: "You are a complacent man with no thought of history. You have traveled everywhere and learned nothing. I despise you."[5] One suspects that Father left on the doomed Lusitania in 1915 in order to escape a world which he no longer understood or had a part.

If Father despaired at the loss of nineteenth-century roles and values, Younger Brother did what he could to expedite their collapse. He viewed them as a prison, at odds with his rebelliousness. Younger Brother traveled surreptitiously to New York to ogle at the shapely Evelyn Nesbit, to applaud the disruptive ideologies of Emma Goldman, and, inevitably to abet Walker by supplying the dynamite and know-how that enabled the taking of the Morgan Library. In short, Younger Brother was drawn to anarchy and chaos and it was he who transformed fireworks into explosives. A member of Walker's otherwise all-black gang, Younger Brother safely escapes the Library in Walker's infamous Model T auto. Later, he travels south and ends up making bombs for the Mexican revolutionary Zapata. So, if Father's most notable vehicle were two ships, Younger Brother's vehicle of choice was traveling in the materialized legacy of Coalhouse Walker, carrying on with violent change.

Geographically, Mother travels the least, but spiritually she travels the farthest. When Father leaves with Peary she sings of her dissatisfaction with her limited role and states her intention to redefine it. It is she who takes in the abandoned black baby; it is she who welcomes Walker into her home; it is she who takes the trolley to Mamaroneck to take over supervision of Father's plant; it is she who defies Father on his return, resisting giving up her business work, and also refusing to surrender Sarah's baby. When she next travels it is by train to Atlantic City where she meets the Baron Ashkenazy, a transformed Tateh, and clearly connects emotionally with him. We only later learn that after Father's death Mother wed Tateh and embarked on her final journey, traveling with him to California. That she welcomed Coalhouse to her home and later welcomed Tateh's gentle advances puts her at decided odds with the New Rochelle WASP world she initially inhabits. Her righteous beliefs have made her a pariah amongst her own and she risks much in connecting with those whose skin and religion markedly differs from her own. Consequently, by rejecting her original community's status quo, Mother is forced instead to live in diaspora.

Issues of Identity: On Tateh

Tateh might well travel the farthest geographically and socially, but he never escapes himself, eternally caught in an internal middle-passage. He flees Latvia with his daughter upon a rag ship steamer. We next see him in the Lower East Side Jewish neighborhood of New York, selling his silhouettes from his next vehicle, a peddler's cart.

It is useful to note that Tateh is an artist who sells images of others. On the Lower East Side he does on-the-spot silhouette cutouts of his customers. As silhouettes he is translating his white clients into black shadows of themselves. Tateh clearly sees no difference, nor do his clients, yet the image is powerful and evocative in terms of identity, race, and boundary crossing. He is an artist whose art form is both aesthetically classical and socially liminal. Later on he becomes a movie director, again a master of casting moving shadows on the wall, again in silent black and white.[6]

Tateh then escapes the New York tenement by taking a trolley to New England, pausing in New Rochelle along the way. The train then takes him to Lawrence, Massachusetts where he gets caught in the infamous Bread and Roses labor strike. Sensing danger, he packs his daughter on a train to safety, but when beaten by a policeman he runs after that same train, catching on to escape once more. When next we see him it is in Atlantic City and he has transformed himself into the successful movie director, Baron Ashkenazy (again a "role" name, as Ashkenazy is the term for European Jews). How did he get to Atlantic City? That is unknown, though most likely via train. He remains there, beside the same ocean that first brought him as an émigré to America, until the end, when we learn he again travels westward to California, now wed to Mother.

Tateh thus attains the American Dream in his outward appearance and level of affluence. But when we see him with Mother in Atlantic City he is uneasy, plagued by doubt. He admits to her that he feels a fraud, that in his mind he is still a poor immigrant Jew. Tateh then hesitantly goes one step further, asking if a woman like her could ever accept a man of his sort. That she does so is revelatory to him, for he remains in diaspora despite his materialistic success, never sure that he is entirely welcome. How unlike Coalhouse, who starts out with a sense of entitlement and belonging, only later discovering otherwise. Yet Tateh, whose skin color, unlike Walker's, enables him to pass, remains tentative. Walker first assumes, and later demands, that America accept him and it never does, killing him instead; Tateh does find a measure of acceptance once he outwardly assimilates, but he is never at peace. This is even reflected in his choice of Baron Ashkenazy as his new name: even given that "Ashkenazy" would mean little to most Americans, the use of "Baron" suggests he is of foreign aristocracy, which might be romantically acceptable in America but still delineates him as an outsider.

Unlike Walker, Tateh the immigrant came to America voluntarily. That is not to say he left Latvia entirely by choice: his precautionary warnings to his daughter imply the dangers they have faced. He is an émigré and subject to the dangerous uncertainties of the diaspora. Granted they are poor and their options limited. But they have chosen America, whereas they could have gone elsewhere. Walker's ancestors had no such opportunity.

Meetings

It is geographical travel, by means of the various vehicles, that enables change in *Ragtime*. It implies that, if people stayed put then there could be no change within a given community or ethos, let alone have the various transgressions, boundary crossings, that give birth to new configurations and significant transformations. This is not to say that travel is always desired. In fact, in almost every instance, use of transportation signals an effort to escape from an unpleasant or unhappy situation. Historian Stephanie Smallwood writes that when a slave left a community that community was forever changed due to the loss.[7] Had Father not left for the North Pole then Mother would have not been able to enact an entire series of changes, ranging from her decision to keep the abandoned baby to her experience managing a business to her being able to act out her general dissatisfaction that eventually led to her being with Tateh.

When the characters leave one setting they are now in a position to interact with a new circle of people, different from themselves. At this point they must decide whether to accept or reject those who differ, the "Other." The play even opens with a promenade of three conflicting ethnic groups—WASPs, immigrants and blacks—delicately trying to avoid bumping into one another, keeping to their own safe boundaries. But it usually happens at moments of transit throughout the play. It is no coincidence that the ships of Father and of Tateh pass in the night and that the two men, strangers, signal to each other. It is no coincidence that it is on a trolley platform outside New Rochelle that Mother and her son first interact with Tateh and his daughter. That same trolley no doubt carried Younger Brother back and forth from New York for his assignations with Evelyn Nesbit, Emma Goldman, and later to join the Walker gang. In this new century, differing races and classes could rub shoulders in public spaces, and, in the process, overcome traditional taboos in the unspoken American caste system.[8] With everyone becoming thus dislodged, with everyone a sort of émigré driven from where they came and moving toward an unsure future, America itself becomes a Diaspora nation.

The nation of immigrants theme is made early in the play. When Father is onboard ship with Admiral Peary, and Peary's African American First Officer Matthew Henson, Peary speaks disdainfully of the human cargo aboard the distant, "ghostly" rag ship:

FATHER: What's that in the distance? Such a ghostly glow.
PEARY: They're called rag ships. Immigrants from every cesspool in western and eastern Europe. Most of them become very patriotic Americans. They're your future customers.
HENSON: My people were also brought here on ships.
PEARY: Good watch, Henson. (exits)[9]

The chauvinistic Peary views the immigrants only as commodities, worthless in human terms since they come from "cesspools." Henson challenges his commander's surprising disdain, noting his own slave ship roots, linking the immigrant's experience to those of the slaves. To Peary such newcomers are only objects, lower than he, fit for patriotism but not for any sharing of power. But under his very nose is his second in command, who, rather than being in diaspora, seems to have a share in the ship's command. So just as the two ships, native and immigrant, converge in transit, so too do Peary and Hanson and Tateh converge on their respective decks, suggesting America historically as an ever changing society.

Of course, once dislodged from the known, each character becomes vulnerable, susceptible to the vicissitudes of the unknown. When one stays put, they are familiar with the terrain. Societal expectations are generally known and clear. One toes the line, plays their designated role, and does not in any way threaten the status quo, even when the truth or happiness might lay elsewhere. In short, the individual cedes their individuality to the dictates of the group. Ironically, this is itself a sort of slavery. No wonder both Mother and Younger Brother, who is after all her brother, are the two that stray. Even their Irish maid Kathleen appears to want this hegemony after Mother takes in the black baby; the next time we see a maid in their household, when Father returns from the North Pole, a different maid is in place. No wonder they can sympathize with the underprivileged, indeed the rebellious. All this offended the intolerant New Rochelle bastion of WASP supremacy and Father's Victorian sense of propriety. However, the loss of social role also means the loss of an acceptable identity. Paradoxically, the loss of identity is a step used by slavers to commodify their African captives to assimilate them into becoming slaves.

It is interesting that whereas Mother seems to become ostracized from her WASP community, Walker, when on his rampage, is embraced by his black Harlem community. Even though he has crossed boundaries away from black culture, dressing and acting like a middle-class white, he is forgiven. In fact, his example is followed by his gang, all of whom dress and behave as does Walker. Unlike those in New Rochelle, Harlem will tolerate individuality.

The one person in the play seemingly lacking in community is Tateh; the play portrays him as uniquely isolated. Unlike even Walker or the Family, the only person Tateh brings or meets is his young daughter. There is no evidence of any other personal connection. Ironically, this isolation enables Tateh to move more freely in America, to leave the Lower East Side and go were he wishes. And there is similarly no evidence of him having formed any connection with his fellow workers in Lawrence. Except for his daughter he remains essentially alone, until he connects with Mother. Smallwood notes some resemblance between the slave and the immigrant when she writes that, "...for Africans as immigrants the most socially relevant feature was their isolation, their desperate need to restore some measure of social life to counterbalance the alienation engendered by their social death."[10] Both Tateh and Coalhouse believe that the solution to this isolation is through the formation of a new family. Where Coalhouse succeeds (albeit briefly) in achieving this by bringing together his baby and its mother, Tateh succeeds in this by patching together rags torn from other American diaspora peoples (i.e., the WASP Mother and Little Boy, and the African-American child of Walker's). Interestingly, Coalhouse Walker III is the linking member of both of these families.

As a side note, it is notable that it is Mother's the Little Boy who initiates conversation with Tateh's the Little Girl on the New Rochelle trolley platform. Had he not done so, propriety would have kept Mother from interacting with Tateh. The connection is made through the children, by the children. Later, in Atlantic City, Mother and Tateh (aka Baron Ashkenazy) connect again, this time as they both watch those same two children at play on the beach, and sing together of "their children," which foreshadows their future marriage. Of all the characters in the Family, the Little Boy is the only one who is sometimes called by his given name, Edgar. It is he who is also the seer in the play, who initiates the future (as just shown) and who also can see beyond. On the platform, after Tateh and the Little Girl leave, he states that they will see them again. And four times in the play the Little Boy confronts Houdini with words that come out of his mouth but which he admits are otherwise meaningless to him, "Warn the Duke." The "Duke" in question is of course the Archduke Franz Ferdinand of Austria. If you chart the events in *Ragtime* they begin with Evelyn's trial in 1906 and end just prior to the Duke's 1914 assassination, which triggered World War I. It is fitting, given our themes, that the Duke was assassinated in an automobile while traveling through a foreign city, Sarajevo. The Little Boy is a seer in part because he will live beyond the play's events. He is also the linking character, actively tying together the various threads that comprise the overall plot. No diaspora character he; he introduces the play to us at the start, and provides projector images of what was to come near play's end. More so, he, along with his step-siblings will form the nation's future.

As for the Little Girl, Tateh keeps her tied to him with a rope, so they will not be separated. Tateh also instructs her never to tell anyone her name. When the Little Boy asks her how she feels about this she replies that she feels "safe." In truth, of all the characters in the play, we the audience come to know the least about her. She never strays from Tateh, even once the rope is removed, remaining ever in his sight. It is a parental umbilical cord, albeit to her father, as Tateh declares her mother dead. We only learn that by the time she is in Atlantic City she has grown and is now beautiful. Yet that really only serves to note the passing of time, to account for the time it took for Tateh to succeed and transform himself into the Baron. After that we are only told that she is playing on the beach; we never actually see her. Ironically, we almost know more about her at the start of the play than we do at the end. She remains only the Little Girl, locked into her role, eternally innocent and opaque. As such she is the inverse of every other fictional character in the play. Her function seems to be to provide a desperate impetus for Tateh to overcome all his adversity, to define Tateh as not only more than an artist but rather one who is accountable beyond himself and hence a wholesome suitor to Mother. And, finally, as one who will represent a fresh future, she is a Miranda to Tateh's Prospero. But if so enslaved she seems content. Unlike Mother who itches for empowerment and change, and unlike Sarah who gains value through domesticity, the Little Girl remains passive and strangely old-fashioned. I think this might make more sense in the context of Doctorow's original novel. The novel had Tateh's wife travel with him from Europe, not dead as explained in the musical. But she sleeps around when Tateh is gone and the enraged Tateh throws her out and disowns her. Such harsh behavior is too dark for a romantic lead (which Tateh certainly is in *Ragtime*, though granted an unorthodox one). But if the wife was an improper mother, then Tateh does become both father and mother to the girl. Furthermore, he would not want her to stray, as her mother did, in ways other than simply becoming lost or stolen. Still, according to diaspora terms, she remains a sort of slave, devoid of identity and kept at bay. It is ironic that Mother rebels in almost Feminist terms against the traditional social role, but ends up parenting the Little Girl who seems to embrace it.

Collisions

The action of the musical culminates in Walker's gang laying siege to the J. P. Morgan Library in New York City. Four of our characters converge at the Library: Coalhouse, Younger Brother, Father, and Booker T. Washington, who preached black appeasement as a means toward acceptance. Thanks to Younger Brother's expertise the gang has lined the Library with explosives and threatened to detonate them unless Walker's demands are met. An agitated J. P. Morgan, oblivious to the human cost, urges immediate action because the Library's collection contains, "Four Shakespeare folios! A Gutenberg Bible on vellum. The treasures of civilization are at stake!" Emma Goldman counters Morgan, incorrectly claiming that Walker acted "for all oppressed people," thereby similarly ignoring Walker's humanity by assigning her own political agenda to the mix.[11]

By taking the Morgan Library, Walker and his men took over the very heart of New York City and the moneyed interests it embraced. It took money to purchase the treasures of religion and of culture (i.e., Gutenberg and Shakespeare), as they had been co-opted by the wealthy elite; Morgan seemed to believe that by owning those items he owned Western culture; certainly those items were more valuable, since irreplaceable, than gold or silver. In the first half of the play Walker captured American culture through his ragtime music; in the second half he replaced music with dynamite in order to capture America's materialistic soul.

His decision to trap himself and his men within the Library reflect a slave sensibility. In other words, they have made themselves prisoners and threaten to blow up themselves along with the Library. It is a passive choice. And no one is under any illusions about why the police are kept at bay: it is the objects contained in the Library, not the men, that have sufficient value to prevent an attack. Once more lives are juxtaposed against commodities and found lacking. As actual slaves Walker and his men would have monetary value, but as freed blacks they have none, especially when placed beside treasures that are assigned far greater worth than a human life.

Walker demands that Willie Conklin be found and that Conklin clean and restore Walker's Model T in full view, outside the Library. Walker also wants Conklin himself. It is a slave transaction. Walker uses his leverage to force Conklin to work for him, to redress his grievance by having to clean up the mud and defecation himself. By doing so, Conklin is debased publicly, far worse than even Walker had been by the firemen. Walker also demands Conklin himself as an act of long-delayed justice. That Walker had murdered numerous firemen in rage against Conklin's actions, for the police to surrender Conklin meant certain doom. Yet they are fully willing to do so. Walker is trading the treasures of the Morgan Library for the restoration of his own smudged dignity in the form of his car and of his former oppressor. By trading objects for Conklin, objects for a human life, Walker does to Conklin what America had done to his people: he makes Conklin into an object, makes Conklin into a slave. And Walker proves that the police and civic officials outside are no better than their ancestors, still willing to deal in the transaction of a person in exchange for a pot of gold. That they do only proves Walker right, however cynical and sad that may be.

At one point during the siege, Booker T. Washington is allowed to enter the Library to plead with Walker. Washington is outraged at Walker's use of violence, after spending a lifetime favoring a strategy of black appeasement of whites. Though Walker ultimately ignores Washington's pleas, it is an opportunity to engage in a discussion about blacks in America. Walker had tried to fit in and was rebuffed; following Sarah's death he became radicalized. Instead of running away he decided to stay and fight, thus demanding attention and respect. The presence of Booker T. Washington offers the juxtaposition of two opposing strategies for black acceptance, and hence an end of slavery's diaspora. It is not so much about violence versus nonviolence, appeasement versus the use of brute force. It is that both men actually have similar goals, which is to make a place for blacks within the fabric of American culture and society.

Yet, in the end, Coalhouse wanted to believe what Father believed: both wanted to have faith in America and the sincerity and authenticity of nineteenth-century values of honesty, integrity, and honor. Trusting his beliefs, Father persuades Coalhouse to surrender by giving his word that he would be taken alive. Trusting Father, Walker complies and is immediately gunned down to Father's horror. Either America had changed or those American values proved an empty myth.

Walker had struggled mightily throughout the play against being commodified. Yes, he purchased a car, but it was never the car itself so much as what it represented that held special meaning for Walker: his freedom and his dignity. In the end, Walker could not be traded for an object; he gave the car to allow his men to escape. But the diaspora sensibility still hung with him, as even he could still agree to be traded, though for a high-principled dream. By "selling" himself for an ideal he proved his soul.

So why do both Coalhouse and Sarah die?

So why do both Coalhouse and Sarah die in the play? On a superficial level, that both die adds urgency and poignancy to their characters, enhancing their position as sympathetic victims of injustice, hence damning the society and systems that caused their demise. This dynamic is further enhanced because we get to know them personally, root in good theatrical fashion for Coalhouse both in his courting of Sarah and in Sarah's consequent blossoming forth. We also root because their son, rather than ending up dead as intended by Sarah, instead seems to find a home and with it a future (again, "Wheels of a Dream"). Opposed to their happiness and well-being are first the obnoxiously malicious firemen under Willie Conklin and then, to make matters worse, a group of murderous policemen who are essentially faceless, an impersonal menace. Just as Father is shocked that the police break their word of honor by shooting down Walker, so too are we confirmed in our fear that the system is ruthless in destroying our hero. In other words, as Walker grows increasingly complex, sympathetic, and real to us, so too do the authorities become increasingly distant and brutish; they function as foils, with one functioning to accentuate the contrasting dynamics of the other. That Sarah dies appealing to an impersonal system on Coalhouse's behalf underscores the sincerity of her love for him; that Coalhouse goes mad following Sarah's death, says much the same. That both are destroyed by a culture that is insensitive to their humanity only reaffirms our dislike for its biases, encouraging us to do better.

The second reason both Coalhouse and Sarah die is that it makes their baby son an orphan, though fortunately under the fervent guardianship of Mother. Later, when Mother weds Tateh they will form a new family together. Mother's WASP son and Tateh's Jewish daughter will be joined by little Coalhouse Walker III, making for a decidedly unorthodox multicultural family. The comment is made near the end that this brood later inspired Tateh to create the Little Rascals film series. Though that was really done by Hal Roach to show how children actually behaved, Doctorow uses this to expand his themes. Like so many Jewish filmmakers (and composers of musicals), Tateh will use his craft to shape a vision of America that includes small-town values and a spirit of inclusiveness. It is a modification of the American Dream, one that not only portrays economic possibilities, but also an accepting society for those otherwise doomed to perpetual diaspora.

There is a particular irony in this dimension. After all, we the audience are watching just such a musical. It is based upon a novel written by a Jew, with lyrics also by a Jew. And the show clearly challenges the old America in an effort to propose a better, more accepting America in the future. This is a metatheatrical aspect, intentionally self-conscious and overt in intent. If it was true in Doctorow's novel, this dynamic is further heightened when placed on an actual stage, before a New York audience, approaching the end of that same once-new century.

The third reason both Coalhouse and Sarah die has more Biblical associations. As stated before, though Sarah is not technically a slave, she certainly still acts like one until Walker helps her see differently. She is thus a woman of an oppressed slave class who abandons her baby, only to have it discovered by the affluent Mother, who will raise it as her own. It is not a coincidence that when first discovered, the Irish maid Kathleen refers to the child as a "Baby Moses." Mother's rescue directly parallels how Pharaoh's daughter discovered and rescued the Jewish slave child from amidst the bulrushes. Moses grows up then as an affluent Egyptian, with all those rights and privileges. It is only when he is well into adulthood that Moses acknowledges that he is a Jew, when he kills an Egyptian slave-master for beating a Jewish slave. As the story goes, Moses appeals to the powers-that-be (i.e., Pharaoh) on behalf of his people, but the Pharaoh hardens his heart, forcing Moses to lead a mass migration of the Jews out of Egypt. But the story does not end there. Due to their impiety, the Jews are forced to wander the desert for forty years, long enough for those with memories of being slaves to die out. Thus, those who enter the Promised Land know only of being free. Amongst those who never reach the Promised Land is Moses, victim of a cruel fate.

Sarah and Coalhouse lived with memories of being oppressed; their son, raised by Tateh and Mother, with his mixed siblings, presumably does not. In one sense you could argue that Coalhouse is a Moses, teaching his people dignity, leading them towards freedom. And though he himself perishes, it does not happen until he first makes sure that his followers escape to freedom in his Model T, armed now with instructions to carry on his beliefs. It is a new world that Coalhouse helped create but will never live to see. But the analogy works better when applied to Coalhouse and Sarah's son, for he is the one who will be raised in affluent freedom as an American, with parents doing all they can to make him feel accepted, not living in diaspora, even to the point of his stepfather making films to confirm that that condition does in fact exist in America. Like Walker and Sarah, we the audience really do not know what will happen to Coalhouse Walker III, but the parallel to Moses implies that someday he too will prove a leader of his people, using his knowledge and character to help lead them towards civil rights in an ecumenical style reminiscent of a Martin Luther King, Jr., another Moses whose dream indicated he himself never made it to the Promised Land he helped to create.

In *Ragtime*, the nineteenth-century America gives way to twentieth-century America, as the two ships pass in the night, foreshadowing how Father will be replaced by Tateh (the Jewish Father), thus homogeneity by diversity. Out with the old and in with the new. And so it will be that Mother with Tateh now will raise the new American family, whose makeup will differ from the nineteenth-century model seen at the play's start. Will this "new" America be a place so defined that an inclusive diversity becomes the norm, or will the Other remain spiritually enslaved, despite the public surface, in a perpetual diaspora? The play ends hopefully, but the outcome is unclear, even to late twentieth-century audiences who know what was to come.

In a sense you could argue that it is a play of rags. At the turn of the twentieth century, homogenous America became increasingly a patchwork of different peoples, a collection of other nation's discarded rags, stitched together to form a new, cohesive American quilt. With *Ragtime*, the twin stories of Tateh and Coalhouse are both defined by the "rag." For Tateh it begins with his arrival on a rag ship and continues in a sort of Horatio Alger fashion, following Tateh's journey from rags to riches. Coalhouse's journey upward, and then downward, is enabled by his success playing ragtime piano. And what is ragtime music? It is "ragged" because the melody is torn apart, in contrast to the steady stride-piano left hand beat, appearing spontaneously and unpredictably, yet infectiously. But rags are torn cloth. What is torn here is America from its nineteenth-century roots, as it gives way to the new century, dominated by the rags of modernity—jarring, brutal, perhaps amoral—yet filled with new possibilities. Tateh has been torn away from his country of origin, along with all the other immigrants whose story he represents. He must mend or refashion his "cloth" in order to fit in to this new nation, altering it (and himself) to assimilate. The rags of another country become the cloth of the new, as he is then allowed to succeed. And when Coalhouse tries to dress in finery, they try to cover him in muck, reduce his car, his "clothes" to rags. He demands his car be restored and no wonder his young gang of apostles also dresses well and behaves immaculately. No rags for them. The Little Boy tells us that the ragtime era was about to pass and that the old world was about to erupt into the flames of war. Having learned our history, we the audience know that that war only ended thanks to American intervention. The former rags of Europe, those forced into diaspora, would return to save it, launching the American century.

Ragtime is thus a musical play in which every character is an immigrant, repeatedly dislodged from his or her familiar moorings. Essentially a story of middle-passage, *Ragtime* is replete with various means of transportation repeatedly used as characters move from location to location, from situation to situation, station to station, seeking safety or freedom. Lives are consistently in flux, never completely by choice, and each, exposed to new territory, remains vulnerable and anxious, trying desperately to find acceptance and peace. But no one really does achieve that state in the play, though it ends suggesting that possibility for future generations in a reconstituted America governed by a modified American Dream that can somehow incorporate the inherent dynamics of the diaspora experience.

PART TWO: DANCING FORWARD, MARCHING BACK — MYTHOLOGIES OF ASSIMILATION IN *RAGTIME* VERSUS *PARADE*

At the very end of E. L. Doctorow's novel *Ragtime*, the character Younger Brother, disillusioned and radicalized, escapes New York and drives Coalhouse Walker's restored Model T Ford southward. He travels to the bohemian artists' colony in Taos, New Mexico, and then continues on from there to detonate explosives, fatally, for the Mexican revolutionary Zapata. But Doctorow notes how Younger Brother first drove through "small towns in Georgia...." where "...citizens spoke of hanging the Jew Leo Frank for what he had done to a fourteen-year-old Christian girl, Mary Phagan. They spit in the dirt."[12] And so the stories of *Ragtime* and *Parade* first converge.

How did late twentieth-century American Jews, approaching a new century, choose to view the Jewish experience at the beginning of their own century? To what degree do their later perspectives color those earlier events? And to what degree did those initial immigrant hopes and aspirations, sold to them as the "American Dream," encouraging them to adopt American behaviors and customs, actually come to fruition? Was this earlier negotiated deal deemed successful, in the eyes of their end-of-the-century descendents? Were late twentieth-century Jews sufficiently secure as Americans to consider the Dream's possible failures as well as indulge in an ongoing desire for it to be true? Did the realities of their twentieth-century experience in fact live up to the aspirations of their fantasies, even as they were approaching a new millennium?

The 1998 musicals *Ragtime* and *Parade* both explore the dynamics and implications of Jewish acculturation in the early days of the twentieth century. Both shows ultimately center on the circumstances and results of relative acceptance. Whereas *Ragtime* portrays and suggests optimistic rewards for assimilating (at least for the immigrants), *Parade* harshly depicts a key instance of the failures, the pitfalls of assimilation, a case where the American Dream turned nightmare.

Ultimately, were late twentieth-century American audiences, both Jewish and Gentile, sufficiently comfortable with the relative success of immigrant acculturation so as to accept, not only the optimistic fantasies, the kept promises, of the American Dream, as depicted in *Ragtime*, but also sufficiently secure in America to welcome the direct, darker examination of its failures, as depicted in *Parade*? Were Americans only able to accept the reassurances of joyfully dancing forward to the strains of a lively ragtime cakewalk? Why did audiences, in turn, resist the reliving of fears required to march grimly back in time to visit a disturbingly non-nostalgic, albeit somewhat sentimentalized, Memorial Day parade of our own?

Taken together, *Ragtime* and *Parade* encapsulate retrospectively conflicting attitudes towards the possibilities and ongoing fears of the twentieth-century Jewish-American experience, as captured on the musical stage.

Genesis

The origins of both *Ragtime* and *Parade* have much in common. The Canadian company Livent, under the direction of Garth Drabinsky, produced and presented both shows. Drabinsky had built an impressive organization, modeled along the lines of a 1930s Hollywood movie studio. He spent lavishly on talent, gave them relatively more time to collaborate and assemble a series of epic shows. In only a few years, Livent had great Broadway success with a string of hits that included *Kiss of the Spider Woman* and a major revival of *Show Boat*. It also built the massive Ford Center for the Performing Arts in New York, which would house *Ragtime* during its New York run, and had built several other playhouses in Canada and the United States.[13]

In the case of *Parade*, Livent worked out a special arrangement with New York City's Lincoln Center Theatre to coproduce the new work; its theatre offered a more intimate setting for what was considered a more serious musical endeavor. Hence, *Parade* was one of three musicals that formed the Lincoln Center's 1998–1999 season. Lincoln Center proudly announced that all three dealt with the difficult issues of identity politics and tolerance, a fitting subject with which to approach the oncoming millennium. The artistic leadership of Lincoln Center believed its audience would appreciate and support work of so serious a bent. Both *Ragtime* and *Parade* received critical praise upon opening, for the quality of their artistry, music, and theatricality. However, where *Ragtime* would proved commercially successful (it would run two years), *Parade* quickly failed (running only three months).[14]

If both musicals were of comparable artistic merit, then why did one succeed and the other fail? The surface reasons are many and complex, much having to do with the business of show business. But the real bottom line had to do with relative audience receptivity. In order to assess that fully it is important to first consider the history of each production.

Ragtime and *Parade* both deal with historical events of the early twentieth century. *Ragtime* was a musical dramatization of a novel whereas *Parade* drew directly from actual events in almost journalistic style. E. L. Doctorow wrote his novel *Ragtime* in 1975. It was only a few years after Watergate and the turbulent 1960s, an optimistic historical moment where national and international problems seemed finally resolved, just in time to celebrate the nation's bicentennial. Doctorow's novel was subsequently made into a successful 1981 film, featuring a Randy Newman musical score that hauntingly echoed times past. A decade later, Drabinsky assembled an impressive team to rework the novel into musical form. This group included composer Steven Flaherty and lyricist Lynn Ahrens, playwright Terrence McNally, and director Frank Galati.

By comparison, *Parade* was the very personal brainchild of playwright Alfred Uhry. His family had owned the National Pencil Factory where Leo Frank and Mary Phagan both worked. Uhry grew up a Jew in Atlanta where no one dared mention Leo Frank's name or his supposed crime. According to Uhry, it was in a Jewish community that took to celebrating Christmas and Easter and imitated "Episcopalian" manners as a direct result of their fear following Frank's racially motivated murder. Uhry mentioned the idea to his friend, producer/director Harold Prince, who in turn suggested they create it as a musical. Uhry wrote the book and Prince was to direct. Composer/lyricist Stephen Sondheim was originally involved, but withdrew largely because he had just come off writing the highly emotional musical, *Passion*. Prince and Uhry instead turned to a then 23-year-old prodigy, Jason Robert Brown, to write both words and music. Uhry conducted extensive historical research before writing, including reading through the personal correspondence between Leo Frank and his wife Lucille. This formed the basis of the show's second plot line, the evolution of their marriage through the course of the troubling events.[15]

Double Fantasies

Before continuing, it would be best to recount each musical play's plot. *Ragtime* opens in 1902 with the musical promenade of three separate ethnic groups, all destined to converge or collide: the pristine White Anglo-Saxon

Dreams of Progress, Dreams of Loss 155

Protestant (WASP) establishment, the lively African-Americans, and the timid immigrant newcomers. Of them, respectively, Father and Mother live comfortably in New Rochelle, New York; Coalhouse Walker is a Harlem piano player who has found success playing the new ragtime music; Tateh and his young daughter live in New York's congested Lower East Side. *Ragtime* also interweaves a bevy of historical figures into its plot: J. P. Morgan, Henry Ford, Booker T. Washington, Emma Goldman, Houdini, and the scandalous former showgirl, Evelyn Nesbitt, caught in a highly publicized trial because her crazed husband, the wealthy Harry Thaw, murdered her lover, architect Stanford White. Meanwhile, Coalhouse Walker has fathered an illegitimate child with Mother's black maid, Sarah. He decides to court her, reclaim their child, and, as a family, build toward the future. But Irish firemen trash Walker's car and Sarah is later killed, causing Walker to become radicalized. With Younger Brother's help, Walker's men seize the Morgan Library, demanding that his car be restored. It is, but Walker is then killed. Meanwhile, Tateh has translated his art into filmmaking and reinvented himself as "the Baron Ashkenzy." He weds Mother and together they will raise her Christian son, his Jewish daughter, and Coalhouse and Sarah's African American child as one family, pointing to a multicultural American future.[16]

The musical *Parade* opens with a lone figure, a young Confederate soldier who sings lovingly of Georgia. In mid-song, he transforms into an old crippled veteran attending Atlanta's 1913 Confederate Memorial Day parade. Teenage Mary Phagan, on her way to the parade, stops by the factory to collect her pay from its manager, Leo Frank. She is later discovered raped and murdered in the factory's basement. Leo is accused of the crime. The Brooklyn-raised, Jewish Leo had recently wed Lucille, an assimilated Atlanta Jew. Leo is peevish, Lucille spoiled, and their marriage is coolly distant. Atlanta's newspapers hype the case for their own gain. In the trial, District Attorney Hugh Dorsey, under political pressure, uses anti-Semitism to discredit Leo, thus stirring up a virulent local popular opinion against him. Dorsey also relies upon the false testimony of an African American plant worker, Jim Conley. Leo is convicted of murder. In prison he learns the law to protest the verdict and raises public protest in the North. Lucille becomes Leo's advocate, causing her personal growth and strengthening their marital ties. She provokes Governor Slaton to investigate the case and, learning the truth, he bravely commutes Leo's death sentence to life. Newspaperman Tom Watson stirs up bigotry against Slaton and Leo. Leo and Lucille realize their love, but shortly thereafter Leo is kidnapped by Klansmen from the prison farm and lynched. He leaves

Lucille his wedding ring. She dons it as the annual Memorial Day parade goes by, now with Hugh Dorsey as Georgia's new governor.

The plot description illustrates that *Ragtime* and *Parade* share much in common. Both recreate flag-waving historical events from the early part of the century, weaving together fact and fiction. Both deal with issues of family caught in the web of larger social crises born of struggles for change. Both portray conflicting social classes as well as the intersecting concerns of WASPs, Jews, and African-Americans, and feature plots constructed out of the issue of nativism, racism, and bigotry. Both *Ragtime* and *Parade* climax with the martyr-like death of a central character, the culmination of growing societal discontent. Both shows contain an awareness of history itself, a sense of the past and of the future, that colors the action of each respective story. Both stories use a romantic relationship as pivotal to what ultimately occurs in each play. Lastly, both plots explore the possibilities and limitations of the American Dream.

In Quotation

Despite their similarities, the style of presentation of the two shows differed greatly. The musical *Ragtime* was presented as if in quotation marks. The play opens with the young son speaking directly to the audience in presentational theatrical style. While it is not unusual to stage book musicals so that the songs are sung directly for the audience's benefit, it is unusual to acknowledge the audience within the framework of the action itself.[17] In *Ragtime*, director Frank Galati seems to have used this device to both acknowledge the audience and to assert that what they are about to see is in fact the reenactment of a book, rather than of the historical events themselves. We the audience are hence encouraged to view the actions on stage as a fiction rather than as a fact. We are kept at a certain arm's length away from the play's action, encouraged to observe and consider the events portrayed, but discouraged from becoming too emotionally involved.[18]

The "quotation mark" theatrical style steadily reminds us we are watching the reenactment of a book. This style is then carried forth throughout all of the production elements, creating a comparable, posed effect. The scenery reminds us of sepia-tinted period photographs, the settings and costumes remind us of historical scenes as found in textbooks. Add to this actual historical figures closely associated with that era, none of whom were quite as prominent in later years. It was a period of ragtime music, as changing American sensibilities and tastes started to change.

The nineteenth century's smug Victorian homogeneity suddenly gave way to twentieth-century diversity and social strife. Viewed from the more knowing perspective of 1975, or 1998, these long-ago changes had long since been resolved and *Ragtime's* settings and events consequently seem charming and innocent. The musical deliberately works to reinforce this dynamic. It doesn't ignore the period's real-life strife—it portrays immigrants behind Ellis Island bars, it portrays the masses literally pressed down beneath the descending weight of bloated industrialists; it recreates the passionate, agitating declamations of an outraged Emma Goldman—and yet it is all bathed in nostalgia as quaint reminders of times past. To see Emma Goldman or Houdini alive on the *Ragtime* stage, no matter how sincere, is to see an image, not a still threatening force for change. Nor is J. P. Morgan any less a threat to our present existence as shown here. Both are long dead, along with the ragtime era itself. And we the living are reassured by a theatricalized staging that works to romanticize their onetime forcefulness by portraying them as picture-postcard idiosyncrasies.

Ragtime's use of music is similarly written in a quotation style. It too functions to remind us that we are watching a fiction and comparably quotes mythically from period songs and long-ago styles. The play opens with a stately promenade, sung in stilting manner to a lovely but sedate ragtime melody. There is a formality here not all that different from Moss Hart's famous staging of "The Ascot Opening Day" number in *My Fair Lady*. We see the beautifully dressed elite almost frozen in propriety as they sing. It is a stillness reminiscent of that required to take period photographs: any movement on the part of the subject would blur the picture. The scene actually doesn't differ much from *My Fair Lady* in that the initial number dissolves into the introduction of raucous aliens into their staidly genteel midst. In the Lerner and Loewe show it was only Liza Doolittle, not yet sufficiently tamed as to prevent her from jumping around screaming profanely as the horse race begins. In *Ragtime* this stiff propriety is similarly invaded, both the arrival of ragged, cautiously hesitant immigrants and a group of jazz-dancing, lower class African-Americans. Taken collectively, the photograph is complete. The three groups circle each other, cautious not to interact.[19] When a stray wanders too far into the space of another group, he or she quickly rushes back to the safety of his or her own kind. But there is nothing that one group actually does that actively threatens the "strays"; there is no apparent actual danger portrayed on stage per se. Even the danger is therefore suggested, as if, again, in quotation marks.

In point of fact, the sense of distance one feels from the musical is inherent in the original novel and is consequently carried through onto the musical version. Except for the celebrity figures, the only character in the entire show whose name we truly know is that of the doomed maid Sarah. We never learn Walker's true first name, we only know him for his minstrel-like nickname, "Coalhouse," suggesting the blackened face. The WASP family members are only known by their domestic roles: Mother, Father, Younger Brother. And the same is true for the Jewish immigrant… The word "Tateh" is Yiddish for Father. So in essence, at the play's end when Mother weds the Baron Ashkenazy, she is simply marrying a Jewish version of what she had before. As for the name "Ashkenazy," it is the term for a Jew who comes from Europe, as compared to someone with Spanish-Jewish roots, who would be Sephardim. So even in reinventing himself, Tateh reverts to delineation. As for the historical celebrity figures, we really know little about them, especially in the musical version, beyond their symbolic function; they are only walking, talking two-dimensional cutouts. Add this up and one realizes that all the characters in *Ragtime* function as archetypes, each representing a particular aspect of turn-of-the-century American culture, in some sort of Expressionistic-like display. It is history viewed through a stereoscope. That handheld device juxtaposed two identical flat photos, placed side by side, to give the illusion of three-dimensionality, when in fact there was none. In *Ragtime*, two-dimensional moments are given depth only when accompanied by music.

In *Ragtime* the music dominates the action. There is relatively little dialogue to the piece. And the songs themselves most often echo musical and corresponding dance forms prevalent in the ragtime period (i.e., 1900–1918). We have ragtime numbers, cakewalks, marches, gospel, and vaudeville. The music is fresh, yet formal in tone. Again, it is as if it were all in quotation marks, as if to say, "see, this sounds just like a ragtime would sound!" a dynamic in contrast with the rollicking, unpredictably spontaneous freedom of authentic ragtime music. All here is controlled, an Epcot-style sampling that outwardly resembles the original, but is sanitized and safe. That is not to say that the show is without its musical moments. "Your Daddy's Son," sung by the doomed Sarah to her newborn infant, is exquisite and moving, "The Crime of the Century" is raucous satire, and "Wheels of a Dream" is a powerful anthem to the future. Add to that the catchy title number and the heartfelt "Make Them Hear You" and the show's musical merits are considerable. No, I do not mean to diminish the quality of the musical accomplishments, only to note that they deliberately remind us of a particular time and place, long ago and seemingly distant from ourselves. And with the possible exception of "Make Them Hear You" the music seems to comment rather than involve, urging the listener to think rather than feel, to consider events rather than galvanize audiences to action. Each element of the show therefore keeps us at a safe distance, much as it promises us that the events portrayed are also at a safe historical distance and hence harmless, reassuring us of our own security. We may be inspired by *Ragtime*, but it does not ask anything more than that. There is no need for us to address the play's social ills. Because the music draws so heavily from the ragtime period, it comforts the audience by placing the action, not in the troubling present, but rather in the long-resolved past. The problems it portrays, no matter how unjust, have already taken place long ago, within the timeframe and fabric of the era shown on stage, the world of our grandparents, forever remote, frozen in time.

If *Ragtime* was written in quotation marks, *Parade* is intended to use every theatrical device to grab us by the lapels and shake us awake. *Parade* is divided into three sections, four if you add the ending coda, and five if you add the opening prologue number. It is crafted to make use of both the operetta and the vaudeville roots of the American musical, but unlike *Ragtime* (which draws on the same forms), *Parade* uses music to involve and manipulate the audience emotionally. There are no "quotation marks" here. If *Ragtime* works to remind the audience that it is a novel, *Parade* is a piece of investigative journalism, bent on setting the story straight. It loudly demands its audience become involved, demands they sit up and take notice. *Parade* strives to erase any misconceptions and lies, forcing us to look the facts directly in the eye (as much as an American musical is able to do). No fantasy or denial here; the events are actual and the theatrical elements designed to get you to address them directly and unflinchingly. The events leading up to, and including, Leo Frank's lynching are disturbing. The authors appear to play up the counterpoint story of the evolution of Leo and Lucille in an effort to add some element of romantic beauty and hope to a piece which otherwise would only disturb. But despite those more gentle intentions, *Parade* ultimately demands we move back in time and reexperience those harrowing events as they unfold before our eyes, as we sit helplessly unable to change their historically inevitable course.

Where *Ragtime* is blithely anonymous *Parade* is entirely personal. Where *Ragtime* seeks to construct a comforting myth, *Parade*'s intention is to shatter a fraudulent myth by confronting it with fact. The characters are mostly all real. Where they are not they are composites of actual figures involved in the Frank/Phagan case. As stated before, author Uhry built the Leo/Lucille relationship directly out of reading their letters. And a careful reading of Steven Oney's history of the case, *And the Dead Shall Rise*, confirms that most of what happens on stage is reasonably close to the actual events themselves.[20] Each character is introduced to us—the audience—in specific and fairly complex terms. They are specific and they are reasonably three-dimensional, a fact underscored by our awareness that each corresponds to an actual historical figure, but here human in their fallibility. It is played out in key moments. For example, Lucille sings the haunting and quietly accusatory "You Don't Know This Man" to newsman Craig, which suggests both to him and to us, the audience, that there is much more to know beneath the public/performative surface, well beyond what we think we know, things that she herself knows to be true. It challenges both Craig and us to reflect more deeply, to look more closely, to challenge whatever assumptions we may have as being superficial and, as such, insufficient and ultimately false. The play throws down the gauntlet, demanding that we become active in our observations and thought, not simply passive and accepting. That Craig then challenges her with the observation, "You're sayin' he's decent, you're sayin' he's honest, but you're not sayin' he's innocent" refutes the relevance of her words and the things we want to believe of him. In another show, the authors would simply let the song stand as a definite, righteous statement; in *Parade* the comforting sentiment and its assertion of a moral high ground are quickly and brutally shot down; the bubble of sentiment is popped by the sharp truth of the newsman's legalistic retort. We are not allowed to believe what we want to believe; it will all have to go to trial.

Craig's words are more than a retort; they are a rebuke. In addition to their legal implications, in a more personal sense they question whether Lucille herself really knows Leo. In a sense she does not; the play suggests a distance between her and him, as well as the sense that perhaps they have not even consummated their marriage. I say this because it is clearly the opposite of when the two last meet, where Leo and Lucille's relationship is shown to have reached a level of genuine closeness, respect, and understanding. You could argue that when Lucille sings that song she describes an image of Leo more than describing someone she really knows. Hence Craig's words really hit home and she scurries away. She never does answer his question.

Furthermore, to what degree does the audience really know Leo? His actions seem to suggest his innocence, but how can even we be sure? It was only in recent years that Frank was finally exonerated by the state of Georgia, and historians now believe that Jim Conley was the actual murderer.[21]

All this differs from the surface characters of *Ragtime*, who never suffer any crises of identity, self-knowledge or what they construe as truth. But *Parade* is considering deeper questions than does *Ragtime*, and the portrayal of characters is central to its message. *Parade* is essentially concerned with issues of identity, of truth in the face of stereotypes, whether disparaging or admirable. It argues that it takes work to uncover both truths and lies, that rights cannot be taken for granted, that anyone and everyone is susceptible to ruin when lazy, inaccurate images are superimposed upon people, be it by others or done by oneself. It is the lesson of Iago, Shakespeare's master of deceptive and damning innuendo, who is adept at reframing reality to destroy others for his own gain. But Iago can only succeed if others accept his imposed perceptions without question or thought. Leo is not guilty because he is a Jew; nor is he innocent for the same reason. Nor is he guilty or innocent for any reason other than the facts themselves. In *Parade* Leo is accused because his behaviors are considered alien and odd. He is indicted because the prosecuting attorney paints him with an anti-Semitic brush. His sentence is commuted because the Governor reveals the truth, negating both the lies and the damning distortions. Leo is then murdered because the Georgian public still choose to cling to Civil War era issues and beliefs, denying both the present day and its unwelcome truths. In *Parade*, myths kill.

Designs on Parade

Harold Prince staged *Parade* in more conventional musical style than had been the case with *Ragtime*. Songs are often done presentationally, but otherwise the action remains entirely on stage, suggesting we are watching actual events as they unfold, a staged reality, rather than remind us, as does *Ragtime*, that we are watching a fiction. If this dynamic is achieved through the storytelling and through the play's use of character, it is also conveyed through its design elements.

In the case of costuming, *Parade*, like *Ragtime*, relies upon historically correct costumes. Not only do the costumes situate the play in a particular time and place, and not only do they reassert the sense of us watching actual history, they also serve to define identity and change. For example, at the start, Leo's formal clothing reinforces his awkward discomfort and sour personality. However, near the play's end, he is wearing informal prison clothing and behaves far more comfortably and confidently, even nonchalant about a knife wound he received. The point is also made that he requests, and is granted, being covered with a coat so as to preserve his dignity once hung. In a parallel progression, when we first see Jim Conley he is dressed shabbily as a janitor. When brought in as a witness, his appearance is drastically transformed, wearing neatly tailored clothing which is noticeably at odds with his earlier demeanor and appearance. The last we see of him is also in prison garb, sweaty and defiant, as part of a chain gang. In the case of Leo, the costuming marks his personal internal transformation. In the case of Conley, the costuming contrasts his true self from his staged courtroom appearance. Throughout *Parade*, we never see the sort of pristinely clean costuming that permeates *Ragtime*. Again, *Ragtime* is intent on building dreams where *Parade* is determined to tear them down.

If in *Ragtime* we are treated to scenic elements reminiscent of nineteenth-century architecture and design, *Parade* lives closer to the earth. Victorian homes in New Rochelle may have long ago been razed, but the red Georgian earth and its corresponding southern forests still endure. In the original production of *Parade* the set was dominated by a broad, old tree whose single branch extended above the stage, overhanging all the action. This set piece suggested that its younger self had survived the Civil War of some fifty years earlier and was still a presence through 1915, perhaps even to today since it is apparent so ominously before us on stage. It's life runs parallel to the now-elderly, crippled Confederate veteran who sings of "The Old Red Hills of Home" at the play's start, suggesting that the roots of those Confederate beliefs still run deep in the South of the 1910s, as deep and as wide as that tree's root system must surely run. The old soldier has lost a leg; the tree is mostly represented by a large, single limb. And though the settings may shift from scene to scene throughout the play, the tree remains, overshadowing all, both literally and figuratively. It is only at the end that we, the audience, fully realize its dark purpose: it is from that sturdy old Southern limb that Leo Frank is finally hung. Symbolic? Yes, but neither distant nor in any way quaint.

The music in *Parade* is similar to that found in *Ragtime* in that it sometimes echoes the music of the period. Both shows also use vaudevillian-style numbers when portraying the crowd, but rely upon operetta-style ballads to portray higher truths and more genuine feelings. But where *Ragtime's* music echoes nostalgia, *Parade's* underscores ongoing danger and is filled with suspense; it works to unsettle where *Ragtime's* music seeks to reassure.

(Re)construction

Parade is constructed as three movements, and the music follows that structure accordingly. In the first third of the show we are introduced to each character and the situation as it unfolds. It is all exposition and the music and lyrics together function to reinforce the values and beliefs of each figure. Hence "How Can I Call This Home" reinforces Leo as an outsider to the southern culture and values; "The Picture Show" shows Mary as young, lively, and flirtatious as well as linking her to the impulsively young Frankie (the same Frankie who will later push the table out from under Leo, causing his death); "Big News" introduces us to the bored, alcoholic newsman Craig who sees in the murder his big break, and, due to its vaudeville musical style, also the notion that that reporting is showbiz. But the music, much like the characters, only show us each character's surface beliefs, however accurate and true. Ultimately, it is cartoon music, used to define cardboard characters.

The second third of *Parade* centers on Frank being tried for murder. Here the music serves to reinforce the plot. If the first third of *Parade* simply depicts events, the trial is a play within a play. The master of ceremonies is District Attorney Hugh Dorsey who aims to reshape the events and all its participants into melodramatic caricatures. Under his deft direction dead Mary's mother becomes the grieving widow, the young factory girls wronged innocents, the testifying janitor Newt the ignorant black man, fellow janitor Jim Conley the repentant sinner, and, above all, Leo is painted as the grotesque stage Jew: a lecherous, avariciously plotting sybarite. Dorsey's ability to alter our perceptions rival that of Iago, and it is all played out to equally melodramatic music and words. We are suddenly no longer in the modern age but rather in the tawdry, popular theatre of stereotypes, of angels and devils, heroes and villains, and, as in the case of the piano music accompanying a silent-movie melodrama, the music here reinforces Dorsey's efforts as it functions to manipulate the audience's emotional response. It tells us what to believe, how to feel, whether to cheer or boo. It is age-old shabby theatrics—with the emphasis on "tricks"—providing comfort rather than truth. With Hugh Dorsey "writing" the script, all are encouraged to view Leo in virulent anti-Semitic terms, as a drooling devil who gleefully murdered an innocent young girl. And we the audience are jury to the jury; we see how Dorsey distorts opportunistically, how Leo's attorney Rosser does nothing. It frustrates us that we can do nothing to stop it. And the reason we know better is because we saw a more objective version of the events in the first third of the play and believe Dorsey's take to be all lies. We are modern and sophisticated; we can spot the cruel distortions and can recognize them as hateful bunk. "Why can't the onstage jury see the same!" we ask. If we were the jury, we would surely act differently.

The last third of *Parade* is devoted to finding the truth, to debunking the destructive myths Dorsey imposed upon Frank in order to win the case. It is here that Lucille persuades Governor Slaton to investigate, where each testimony is proven false, where the Governor commutes Leo's sentence. However, even though we see the truth unfold, it does not win out. The hate persists, fanned by Tom Watson's politicized, anti-Semitic tracts, eventually resulting in Leo's murder. In this last third of the play, just as the story gains complexity and the characters mature, the music responds in kind, becoming deeper and more emotionally compelling. Most telling are three numbers: "Blues: Feel the Rain Fall," "All the Wasted Time" and "Sh'ma." The first is where Slaton interrogates Jim Conley to reveal his perjury. It is done as a traditional chain gang blues number, a black work song filled with monotony, frustration, and rage. There is nothing "performed" here per se, as had been the case during the trial scene; rather, Brown's music pushes forward an authenticity of experience that matches the insolent authenticity of Conley's behavior toward the Governor. It is defiant and honest, however distasteful. The second song is that sung by Leo and Lucille immediately after they make love, just prior to Leo's abduction. It is in the operetta tradition, a song of sincere love, a shared ballad of mutual appreciation and respect where their voices weave together much as do their bodies and their lives. Much like Conley's song, it reveals an honesty and depth beyond anything we have seen before. The final song to note here, sung when Leo, rope around his neck is about to die, sings "Sh'ma", the Jewish prayer of faith. Brown leaves the ancient Hebrew words intact, but composes a new melody for them. The tune is difficult, unpredictable, haunting, and Jewish in its sacred tone; it fully reflects a Jewish man of faith at life's end. Again, there is nothing "stagy" or false about it; it shows the man just as he is, in his final moments. There is an austerity to all three songs that is at odds with the two-dimensional theatrics of the trial scene. It is as if the composer was trying to scour the infectious muck of the melodramatic trial and its tawdry associations and accusations from our consciousness and replace it with images and sounds now authentic, real, and true, however disheartening their context. As such, *Parade*, as a musical, soars high above by the end, displaying an integrity that transcends the ingratiating schmaltz that usually ends such entertainments.

Unlike the music of *Ragtime*, which is often distant and pristine, the music in *Parade* is more immediate and urgent. *Parade's* music sometimes echoes ragtime styles, but more often it is more contemporarily flavored, more distinctively show music of the 1990s. The music does not take you to an earlier time; rather, it takes the "earlier time" and drags it into our present day. Given the difficult subject matter, this is itself most disturbing. It denies us the possibility of keeping the events at a safe historical distance. Even when most austere, *Parade's* music, much like the play itself, is designed to draw you in, get you involved and worked up, making the people and events real and immediate, figures toward whom the audience is expected to develop strong feelings, whether positive or negative. We are not allowed to sit back in our seats and observe dispassionately, as is mostly the case with *Ragtime*; *Parade's* music insists we become involved and take a stand. We are thus encouraged to feel outrage at Leo's treatment and remorse at his cruel end and driven to want to do something about it. This is of course ironic given that the play "accuses" Hugh Dorsey of using similar tactics to manipulate the jury and push popular opinion against Leo. But while *Parade* plays similar tricks, it reverses who are the heroes and who the villains to promote definitively Leo as innocent victim and Dorsey and his cohorts as evil opportunists.

Another comment about *Parade*: This musical play opens with a parade and it ends with a parade. However, the trial that composes its center is itself a kind of parade. Like the jury, like those keeping tabs via the press, we, the audience, are regaled with a steady flow of people and stories, one following breathlessly on the heels of the other, designed to inspire and provoke. It is courtroom drama at its most entertaining. This onstage trial presents one witness after the other, much like a float following a marching band, traveling down the street before our waiting eyes. There is also a trial in *Ragtime*, and though sensationally billed as "The Crime of the Century" it only centers on the sordid deeds of a few celebrities and lacks the substance and punch of the Frank ordeal.

Fact versus Fiction

In *Parade*, Leo is depicted as an outsider from the very start. Even though the real Leo, Frank, was born a southerner (in Texas), he was raised in Brooklyn and attended Cornell before moving to Atlanta and marrying Lucille. He was a highly acculturated, upper-middle-class American Jew, president of the Atlanta's *B'Nai Brith*, whose wife belonged to a prominent southern Jewish family. Jews had long found acceptance in the south: the Confederacy counted many Jews amongst its leaders and heroes. The anti-Semitism invoked by the trial shocked and surprised many of Atlanta's Jewish leaders as they had long viewed themselves as little different from their neighbors. Different than that shown in *Parade*, the real Leo's life in jail was not particularly uncomfortable. He was constantly surrounded by family, friends, and well-wishers. He ate well and regularly played bridge. The shock of the accusations against Leo came in part because the police chose to believe the highly questionable account of a disreputable black man over the words of a Jewish pillar of the community. Leo may be assimilated in Northern terms, but he is not in southern Atlanta's terms. It is his difference that makes him vulnerable to suspicion. To Georgian sensibilities, African-Americans belonged, they had their place and deferentially "knew their place." But as a Yankee and a Jew, Leo had two strikes against him; Frank was an outsider. That he was also affluent only alienated working class Georgians all the more.

After Leo was found guilty the Jewish community sought to help, but was worried that high-profile support would backfire and spark national resentment against Jews. *The New York Times* went against policy and campaigned on Frank's behalf. Many Northern cities had rallies and thousands signed petitions protesting Frank's guilt. National celebrities also spoke up for Frank. However, all this only stiffened southern resentment that viewed them as Yankee outsiders again trampling on state's rights. This fed resentment against Slaton's commutation of Frank's sentence with thousands literally marching on Slaton's home intent on murder. Not only did it result in powerful southern leaders orchestrating Frank's abduction and subsequent lynching, it also refueled interest and support for the long-dormant Ku Klux Klan.

The Jewish response was the formation of the Anti-Defamation League. But the Klan gained prominence and power in the years following Frank's death. Tom Watson's opposition to Frank catapulted him back to national prominence as he was elected to the Senate representing Georgia. As stated earlier, by 1924 the Klan was so powerful that it came close to taking over the Democratic Party at its national convention, mostly in opposition to the candidacy of the Irish Catholic Al Smith. The coup failed. But when the Coolidge-led Republicans came to office they enacted national legislation that effectively closed the doors to significant immigration, especially of those from Eastern and Southern Europe (i.e., Jews and Italians).[22]

The battle over Leo Frank was then essentially the battle between the forces of homogeneity versus the forces of pluralism. It signaled the start of a new Civil War fought to determine the direction and composition of the American democracy. As Jews increasingly acculturated to American life, critics like Horace Kallen struggled to redefine Jewish identity to fit this new diaspora condition. And yet what was the value of becoming an American, perhaps at the expense of one's ethnic identity, if that could not guarantee some measure of acceptance and security? Was the American Dream a lie?

Though the musical *Parade* is built on historical fact, playwright Uhry changed significant elements in shaping his book. First, *Parade* makes no mention of attorney William Smith and the pivotal role he played in the trial and beyond. It was Smith, initially working for the prosecution, who coached Jim Conley, but who later had second thoughts about the case. It was Smith who later demonstrated the impossibility of Frank having done the crime, who came to question the legitimacy of Conley's testimony, and who later concluded that Conley was the probable murderer. Uhry's version ignores Smith completely.

So why alter the facts? This enabled Uhry to expand Lucille's role and to illustrate her personal odyssey. At the play's start Lucille is self-absorbed and meek. She initially does not plan to attend Leo's trial claiming she is afraid to be seen, frightened that people will point. She later overcomes hers fears and becomes a highly visible and effective advocate, confident and formidable. Hal Prince compared Lucille to Eleanor Roosevelt in this regard; both women overcame great shyness to become active and outspoken surrogates for crippled, absent husbands. Uhry thus portrays Lucille as a heroic Jewish woman, struggling for truth amidst rising anti-Semitism.[23]

In the play, Lucille resourcefully relied upon the legal system as the means to overcome local intolerance and injustice. Her efforts force the governor to investigate and then commute Leo's sentence. This seemed an affirmation of faith in truth and that the system would ultimately protect the rights of the few in the face of the many. Lucille's very effectiveness demonstrates that Americans can overcome hate and that justice will prevail. However, the governmental system can only go so far. Leo's subsequent death occurs beyond the established system's reach, and it is that which proves most frightening.

Dramatically speaking, just as Lucille becomes a new Eleanor, so too does Leo become a new Franklin. Leo and Lucille's matching advocacy cause the doomed couple to gain in stature, to mature individually and as a couple. They grow confident in the success of their rightful cause even as they achieve warmth and intimacy. They come so close to triumph that their sudden unforeseen downfall only accentuates the pain of their loss. This dramatic reversal is wrenching to the audience.[24]

In a second major instance of altering fact, playwright Uhry portrays the lynching itself differently than what really occurred. It was not a group of unlettered Klansmen who kidnapped Frank, as shown in the play, nor was there any disagreement amongst them about whether or not to hang him. Nor did the lynching result from the impulsive, vengeful act of a teenage boy. In fact, Frank's abduction was carefully orchestrated by civic leaders from nearby Marietta, Georgia. They believed that they were righting a wrong, believed that they were carrying out a legal verdict that had been subverted by outside pressures from a tampering North, which undermined Georgian autonomy. Most participants reportedly believed they were performing a grim but necessary duty, however distasteful.[25]

It is better dramatically to blame Frank's murder on a divisive few. It reinforces the sense that chaos ensues from an irresponsible press stirring up hate, and that Leo's personal goodness might have come close to swaying them to his side, even with a noose wrapped about his neck. We hope his insistence on his innocence would have some say even as he teetered toward death. The truth that Frank's murder was as much due to politics and regionalism, that it was planned by state leaders for reasons beyond Frank himself, is too abstract. It detracts from the play's focus on Leo himself and its story of corruption and hate generated primarily by personal ambition.

By Century's End

Over seventy years passed between the closing of America's doors and the debut of both *Ragtime* and *Parade*. The book musical in particular had long advocated a vision of America that was inclusive, that portrayed ways by which any ethnic group, Jews in particular, might negotiate cultural waters and find some measure of acceptance through taking America at its word and becoming Americanized. The great bulk of those shows reached their peak in the 1950s and began to wane in the decade that followed. By the 1990s, it was unusual to find book musicals of the older ilk, particularly after a wave of English megahits that read more like bloated, self-aggrandizing operetta than any American-bred show.

Under Garth Drabinsky, the Canadian production company Livent began to produce works of an older sort. They made a fortune producing *Phantom of the Opera*, but followed that with a string of musicals centered on more serious, thoughtful social issues. A show like *Kiss of the Spider Woman*, with its focus on social and political injustice, served as a precursor to *Ragtime* and especially *Parade*.

Both *Ragtime* and *Parade* evoke the traditional American book musical, and both embrace its themes of acculturation and inclusiveness. However, *Ragtime* is a throwback musical, though presented in stylized form. In *Ragtime* the character Father represents justice and public life where the character Mother represents mercy and domesticity. It is when Father is away exploring with Admiral Peary that Mother finds the abandoned infant and vows to look after it. Mother is hence open to outsiders. When Father returns he challenges Mother's decision, but she stands firm.

Mother's actions are key to this musical-as-assimilation paradigm. It is a clear instance of how the WASP establishment might function in relationship to immigrant newcomers, an instructive demonstration of how the American society could be reconstituted, re-envisioned along more culturally pluralistic lines. Doctorow, like his Jewish forbearers, portrays America as welcoming the immigrants with open arms, offering freedom and opportunity, a new Canaan for those fleeing persecution.

Later in the play Mother weds the Baron Ashkenazy (i.e., Tateh). The earlier baby rescue (like Pharaoh's sister rescuing the baby Moses) suggests that Mother would have welcomed Tateh as is, without his assimilation, without his abandoning of his ethnic identity, without his having to reinvent himself. But the fact is that their romance only begins once he is thus transformed. Therefore, Mother is open to accepting others, but they needs must first adjust themselves as well. This represents a negotiated deal, since Mother is being asked to leave the safety and security of her first homogenous situation, to change her standing in the community (no doubt risking gossip or expulsion); it only makes sense that the Jew should make a comparable possible sacrifice so as to meet her halfway.

And yet *Ragtime* is not of the earlier book musical, nor of the era of *Oklahoma!* or *Guys and Dolls*. Its ethnic characters are placed sympathetically in the forefront and their possibilities are the possibilities of the 1970s or 1990s. *Ragtime* happily culminates in an intermarriage. This is a rare theme for a musical, particularly as it pertains to a mixed couple living in America. As far back as *South Pacific* the musical stage saw a mixed marriage (as well as another mixed couple), but it was set far from the American homeland and the couple would never have to deal with local prejudices. By the late 1990s though interfaith marriage was common in America and generally accepted, though its potential impact on preserving Jewish religious practice are recognized as seriously problematic. Yet there was no mention of this being in any way controversial or disturbing, a sign of how New York audience values, both Jewish and Gentile, had changed over time. It was a given that acculturated Jews often wed Gentile women, and that that did not necessarily mean a loss of ethnic or religious identity. Doctorow's multicultural vision of the future, written in 1975, proved prescient. And in so symbolically written a piece as *Ragtime*, there are few real moments of character inner conflict, let alone any expression of personal feeling, so as to suggest that this might be a problematic within the play. One might argue that this represents a kind of American stoicism, but it also a benefit of writing stories built around archetypes rather than real people. It enables the acting out of ideals without concern for the troubling difficulties presented by actual life. *Ragtime* is a myth that promotes further utopian fantasies, riff variations of the American Dream.

Raining on *Parade*

In February 1999, Harold Prince and Alfred Uhry appeared on the Charlie Rose television program. The program began as publicity, but ended as a plea for money. Garth Drabinsky had been charged with fraud and summarily dropped from Livent. Despite the scandal, Prince argued that *Parade* was forced to close because Drabinsky was no long able to sustain it financially through the normally slow winter months. Prince argued the show's merits and predicted that, if it could continue, it would win multiple Tony Awards which in turn would result in a strong box office. If so, he went on to say, it would surely run through at least the following Broadway season. It was all a matter of generating some $500,000 to carry the show through to the spring. Apparently, none came forward to help and *Parade* closed at month's end.[26]

Years later Prince inadvertently admitted that *Parade* closed because it did not draw sufficient audience. Though he had produced *Fiddler On the Roof*, the highly assimilated, southern born, German-Jewish Prince never related to the material. But, to him, *Parade* was different, as he shared with interviewer Abigail Pogrebin:

> 'I felt *Parade* was as close as I could get to doing my *Fiddler*,' says Prince. "And when it was rejected in terms of popular entertainment, I was very hurt. Because I loved the show and still do. Its reception could have put it right where it belonged, but instead, it was completely unappreciated where it mattered....
>
> "I ask how it connected him to his Jewishness. 'What did it mean to me? Everything,' he says. 'I related to Leo Frank. But see, that's a southern family.'[27]

So in 1999 Prince blamed *Parade's* closing solely on a lack of cash, suggesting that it enjoyed sufficient critical and popular support otherwise to survive. Yet the later interview reveals its real problem lay in its inability to draw playgoers.

The same fact has held true in the subsequent decade. Revivals of *Ragtime* are far more common than revivals of *Parade*, despite the obvious artistic merits of both shows. So why did *Ragtime* succeed where *Parade* failed? The first obvious argument is simply who wants to watch a musical about an anti-Semitic lynching? And who wants to spend two-and-a-half hours listening to people sing about dread, fear, and hate? Fair enough, but there is much more to it than just that. After all, as Prince himself noted, the book musical often dealt with a difficult subject matter. From *West Side Story* to *Cabaret* to *Kiss of the Spider Man*, there is a long and distinguished array of musical shows that dealt with troubling topics resulting in dark endings. But *Parade* was different.

First, the other shows' portrayals of hate often took place amongst other populations, in other countries. *West Side Story* centered on Puerto Ricans and whites, even though the original conceptualization was to have been between Jews and Irish Catholics. *Fiddler* did deal with Jews, but the ending was sad, not tragic, and suggested an ultimate happy ending when they would eventually reach America. *Cabaret* did deal with anti-Semitism, but that was Nazi Germany, not America. *Parade*, on the other hand, was a story of American anti-Semitism. And though Stephen Sondheim had successfully constructed in *Assassins* a musical out of the unlikely subject of American hate, its essential tone was satiric, not emotional.

Second, as stated earlier, unlike *Ragtime*, all the theatrical elements of *Parade* worked to draw in the audience emotionally and intellectually. Its melodramatic devices acted to work up the audience, to prevent them from keeping a safe, self-protective distance. It demanded you care. That this then all resulted in Leo Frank's doom, despite heroic efforts, made the show a bitter pill to swallow.

Third, though Uhry, seemingly with Prince's encouragement, embellished the evolving romantic relationship between Leo and Lucille so as to add romance to the otherwise stark story, in some ways that very device backfired. It is a lovely story and it does work to dilute the despair, bringing a personal richness and meaning to the piece that does tend to transcend Leo's grim fate. But this also added to the feeling of senseless loss at the play's end. Still, the play does end on more of a spiritual and thoughtful note, rather than one exploitative of the audience.

I think there are two more significant reasons why *Parade* failed commercially. I also believe it to be an extraordinary musical in its own right, and, as Prince observed, one most worthy of finding an audience. The first reason has to do with its being a musical. Had Alfred Uhry simply written a drama of those same events, much as he had done with his *Driving Miss Daisy* and *Last Night at Ballyhoo*, the play would have stood effectively on its own two feet. It might not have been done on Broadway, but it certainly would have had a life on the stages of American regional theatres.

Serious stories about the dysfunctional American often draw crowds and win awards. But it was Prince who suggested they try it as a musical. Artistically, we are certainly richer for his courage and vision: *Parade* is a brilliant and wonderful show. But in part it failed because it was done as a musical. Had it been only a drama one suspects it would have found its audience and been accepted as is.

His suggestion was quite daring. Had it worked commercially, *Parade* would have opened the doors to the next chapter in musical theatre history, demonstrating further the book musical's possibilities. In essence, Prince was suggesting that the musical form itself was capable of the examination and exploration of the most delicate, the most serious, the most difficult subject matter, and do so in a serious way. Prince had regularly challenged the American public, directing or producing musicals that consistently reinvented the form in terms of subject, stylization, and aesthetics. His career reads like a litany of Broadway's most challenging and successful new works, including the aforementioned *West Side Story*, *Cabaret* and *Kiss of the Spider Woman*. It also included *Company*, *Pacific Overtures*, *Candide*, *Follies*, *Evita*, and *Sweeney Todd*. Prince took risks and they usually panned out, to Broadway's artistic and commercial benefit. He was drawn to serious subject matter with a consistent faith in the musical's capacity to accommodate in order to make the otherwise difficult subject matter palatable. In one sense, the history of musical theatre boasts a series of landmark productions, works that proved successful despite the fact that, when first produced, they challenged the audience's assumptions by daring to present then-provocative subject matter. Prince saying that he "loved" *Parade* and that its rejection left him "very hurt" is no small statement. It should have been the next logical step in the ongoing evolution of the musical form. The musical "sweetening" worked to counter various forms of hate as seen in Broadway shows from *Show Boat* through to, yes, *Ragtime*. With *Parade* it hit a wall. *Parade's* subject matter proved too disturbing, too objectionable, for audiences to allow the musical form, no matter how reassuring and aesthetically pleasing its elements, to presume to counterbalance its story or to overcome the potential audience's perceived level of distress.

The Limits of Acculturation?

I believe that the second reason for *Parade's* failure, as well as *Ragtime's* success, had entirely to do with issues of acculturation and the American Dream. Ironically, the strength of the book musical form was its ability to transform itself; at one level it was a protean form, ever changing and ever changeable within the parameters of its basic structural elements, its defining vocabulary of theatrical devices. In other words, the musical itself proved a hearty chameleon, whose very survival was based in its ability to transform itself to match changing times. In other words, the musical itself was accustomed to acculturating to American life. It is ironic that it failed to do so when it addressed a play depicting the failure of acculturation itself.

Ragtime, regardless of its degree of historical distance or quaintness, was built entirely upon the principles of acculturation. At its start we witness the 1902 American status quo that, by play's end, would be recalibrated. The affluence and comfort enjoyed by the archetype Father and Mother represent American possibilities, that which both the immigrant and African American characters aspire to achieve for themselves. By the play's end the immigrant characters do achieve that American Dream, though, by doing so they redefine its composition. There is only so much room at the top, it suggests, as Tateh could never wed Mother had Father not first tumbled. Nor could Coalhouse Walker have succeeded in occupying the Morgan Library, thereby gaining some measure of respect, without Younger Brother's help, which resulted in Younger Brother's fall from grace.

The tragedy of *Ragtime* is what happens to Coalhouse Walker. On the surface his personal tragedy is the loss of his beloved Sarah and his subsequent death after holding New York City in siege. But his deeper tragedy is that he is denied the opportunity to acculturate. At the play's start we see Walker at the piano, presumably in a Harlem club, enjoying his newfound success thanks to the ragtime. We soon learn he has fathered an illegitimate child, a behavior that corresponds with lower class mores. But with his professional success Walker decides to become middle-class. As was described in Doctorow's novel, the onstage Walker dresses nattily, has purchased an automobile, and has decided to court Sarah in the manner of a middle-class beau, ever patient and ever polite. His goal is domesticity, to redefine his brood in family terms, according to the rules of genteel respectability. Walker dreams the America Dream as surely as does Tateh. But the obstacles of prejudice interfere with Walker's attainment of it. Walker's newfound affluence supports his ability to dress and behave like a white man, but his skin color betrays him. The firemen's abuse is designed to demean him, to put him "back in his place," which is to say below them in the social ladder. That Sarah was a black woman approaching the stand resulted in her death; one suspects that a white woman would have been treated better. Coalhouse becomes radicalized because he is denied what he thought was promised. His militancy is in sharp contrast to the passive acceptance preached by Booker T. Washington in the play. Walker fights not so much for the restoration of his automobile, but rather for what he believes is the restoration of the dignity and respect due to him by the tacit promises of that same American Dream. He is calling America on it, challenging the nation to keep its words, to live up to its promises, and he dies in the process.

The Jew Tateh, on the other hand, is able to reinvent himself so as to pass as white. Tateh realizes the promise of the American Dream in ways Coalhouse could not. And, in part, Coalhouse's failure serves to underscore Tateh's success. Because Tateh could triumph, and do so by being allowed to work through the system, he becomes positioned as a member of the reconstituted American society, to shape a better future. His ability to acculturate accommodates his wedding to Mother, his newfound wealth and influence, his ability to raise his daughter and his two stepchildren in a comfort and ease that he himself never experienced. But as a filmmaker, he could invent and disseminate a vision of America that was inclusive and diverse. As Count Ashkenazy, Tateh would redefine the American Dream so as to include the possibility that future Coalhouse Walker's might succeed and thrive, rather than fail and die.

This is a most comforting image and message for the 1998 Jewish-American audience. It is a reassuring and empowering myth, justifying a range of otherwise controversial choices ranging from acculturation to intermarriage to secularization. *Ragtime* similarly comforts other ethnic groups as well, for similar reasons. It suggests that there was a larger payoff for the sacrifices our ancestors made upon coming to the New World. Old religious practices have given way to self-actualizing, reassuring Culture. Sitting as we were at the tail-end of the twentieth century, we could look back nostalgically at that century's start with a sense of satisfaction and reward. Progress has been made, we really are better off then we were back then, though we are ourselves secularized, we live along the same guidelines as a Tateh, direct descendants fulfilling his vision of a better American world. Based as it was on Doctorow's 1975 vision of America, *Ragtime* enables us to relive the idealism of the preceding 1960s: through it we can still support the civil rights of the downtrodden black man. American Jews have made it; it is now up to us to fight for "his" rights as well. It is comforting, it is impersonal, it is mythic; it is also smug and presumptuous when compared to messier realities of historical experience.

Parade might actually be a better religious exhortation. Not the sort of comforting religion preached by *Ragtime*, but rather something more along the lines of the ancient Jewish prophets, raging at injustice and demanding change, no matter how uncomfortable or unpopular that call-to-action might be. Whereas *Ragtime* promotes a reassuring myth that we as Jews have made it and can be content with our achievement, *Parade* brings everything into question. It seems to say, "if we are so secure, then we should now be able to examine a real-life instance of murderous rejection."

As stated, Harold Prince called *Parade* his greatest disappointment, the show he identified with and in which he most believed. It was the logical next artistic step for him and should have been for his audience as well. Here they all were, at the cusp of a new century, in an historical position to look back at a century of accomplishments as Jews in America, as well as the musical form's ongoing ability to adapt to changes in musical styles and shifting cultural and political issues. *Parade* should have been the next step, the culmination of a century of successful American lives and an opportunity to thumb their collective nose at past prejudice, to declare that Jewish-Americans had made it and that the prejudicial past was dead. But the optimism of Prince, and the underlying optimism required of an audience to relax and enjoy *Parade*, was sadly missing. Ironically, rejecting *Parade* denied the possibility of collective closure, symbolic or otherwise.[28]

So in the end Prince was right to view Uhry's ideas as a viable source for his next musical. Had *Parade* succeeded it would have represented as important a step forward for the musical form, and the audience that supported it, as *Show Boat* had been some seventy years earlier. But advocating for blacks is not the same as Jews advocating for themselves. It was always easier for Jews to find acceptance through use of a black imagery and culture with which they could identify, or at least project their own painful history and contemporary angst. Blackface brought an acceptance on stage that Jewish beards, accents, and shrugs could not. *Ragtime* perpetuates this myth of solidarity. It can do so because it deals exclusively in idealized archetypes. Coalhouse Walker becomes the heroic martyr, dying while fighting for the dignity to which he is entitled. And though Tateh does not fight shoulder to shoulder with Walker, in his own more indirect way he too fights the same fight through his artistry. But myths are too often fantasies, far simpler and neater than the facts themselves, too often subject to wish-fulfillment rather than practicalities.

The interracial portrait painted by *Parade* is far different. To Jewish eyes, *Parade* shows the betrayal of all the forces that should have protected Leo Frank, and potentially other future Jewish generations as well. Leo is deemed guilty large due to the false testimony of a black man. He is also betrayed by the legal system, betrayed by the powers-that-be, betrayed by the press, and betrayed by the public at large. All the societal elements that usually serve to protect any minority's rights conspired to murder an innocent man, seemingly because of his Jewish faith. But though Jim Conley is treacherous, the other black janitor, Newt Lee, is trustworthy. *Parade* also includes a song sung by four black characters expressing their own situation in their own cultural terms, irrespective of any other societal group, ethnic or not. It is a far more complex and authentic picture, devoid of sentiment, understandable and accurate, than found in *Ragtime*. No mythologizing here, no group personalities. Stereotypes are shattered and individuals stand for themselves in face of the faceless mob.

Musical Limits?

Had *Parade* proved successful, it would have shown that the musical form could handle the portrayal of the most sensitive of subject matter, particularly for the New York audience. It would mean that the form itself had the integrity and power, the flexibility and scope, the structure and aesthetics, to explore any and all phenomenon, no matter how provocative, delicate or profound. It also would have meant that the American Jewish community would have sufficiently evolved in its sense of self-acceptance and national acceptance to relax its grip and be able to begin a public dialogue via the show. But this did not come to pass. The New York audience, Jew and Gentile, did not feel sufficiently secure to accept and support a musical that explored the possibility that the American Dream might have turned nightmare. Leo and Lucille thought that, by acculturating, they were accepted and protected; the events in Atlanta proved them wrong. What hidden demons of hate might still exist in 1990s America? Rather than opening the proverbial "can of worms" to expose possible latent hostilities or even dangers within, best simply to ignore. So on the verge of a new millennium, New York audiences were not sufficiently secure to support a show that might have purged them of their secret anxieties and fears.

In 1998 Livent produced two companion shows: *Ragtime* and *Parade*. Which vision of American assimilation and acceptance would contemporary audiences accept? Would it be the impersonal optimism of *Ragtime*, ever insistent that the American Dream worked—except for heroic African-Americans? Or would it be the dark and confrontational *Parade*, suggesting that acculturation ultimately does not work, that, under certain circumstances, it is ever ready to reemerge, disastrously, within the seemingly welcoming American landscape? In looking back almost a hundred years, with thoughts ahead to the coming century, did Jewish-Americans believe that acculturation worked enough to support a work that suggested otherwise? No, they did not. They instead still sought the comfort and reassurance of a rearticulated American Dream as found in *Ragtime*. Better to be soothed than frightened; better to indulge in flattering dreams rather than explore one's nightmares.

In Summary

Onstage, the portrayal of history functions as spectacle. There is a special magic in seeing actors dressed in period clothing, in historical settings, recreating past events. But one of the reasons historical dramas work is because those events are perceived by the audience as being long- resolved. Controversial subject matter has often been portrayed in times past to enable a hearing on stage, which is to say the material may be highly timely but that the historical setting provides sufficient distance to enable its production.[29] In the case of *Ragtime*, even the title suggests a distant era, one long gone and happily resolved. But in *Parade* the events are apparently not resolved, despite its historically specific characters and setting. As its title suggests, a memorial "parade" recurs annually and functions to relive and commemorate past events. *Ragtime* is locked in its lyrical, toe-tapping Scott Joplin past; *Parade* stubbornly comes marching back and its unresolved issues continue to haunt us.

7. Fiddler's Children

Harold Prince has said that when approached with the idea to develop Shalom Aleichem's stories into a musical, he felt ill prepared to do so. As a German American Jew he could not identify with the material. Better to ask Jerome Robbins instead, as his family had come from Russia and could better identify and hence work with the material more effectively.

Prince had done much to move forward the notion of what material could make for a musical. By the early 1960s his most significant production probably had been *West Side Story*, significant in that it portrayed New York City gang life. In another couple of years he would break through more doors by placing Nazi Germany on stage in Cabaret. Prince was a risk taker. But he had to relate directly to the material.

So it was that Jerome Robbins came to develop, choreograph, and direct *Fiddler on the Roof*. Robbins had always been an innovator, a classically trained ballet dancer, and world-class classical choreographer. Like his friend Leonard Bernstein, Robbins traveled easily between the worlds of classical music and musical theatre. Together they had collaborated to create *On the Town* and later *West Side Story*, each an attempt to blend together high art and popular culture, and thereby elevate the American musical to a new aesthetic level.

In many respects *Fiddler on the Roof* was the culmination of fifty years of American musicals as traced in this book's first chapter. It brought ethnicity entirely to the forefront, creating not an American world, but rather a Jewish world on stage. Several Rodgers and Hammerstein productions had been set abroad, but always included at least one Western character with whom the audience could relate as either American (such as *South Pacific*) or as an American surrogate (as it could be argued is Anna in *The King and I*). No such cultural bridge characters exist in *Fiddler on the Roof*. Instead the oppressed Jewish milkman Tevye addresses us directly, assuming we can relate to him and his family.

And if earlier shows of the Golden Age of American Musicals tended to relegate its ethnic figures to secondary comic roles, *Fiddler* presents them prominently and seriously. Set in a turn-of-the-century Russian Jewish *shtetl*, *Fiddler on the Roof* deals with large issues, even if it does so with a philosophical shrug of the shoulders. Tradition gives way to modernity forcing Tevye to reconsider a lifetime of beliefs, challenging his presumptions and prejudices along the path. Tevye was already struggling to make ends meet. In the show he also negotiates the politics of small-town life exacerbated by growing anti-Semitic hostilities. In the end the entire town of Anatevka is displaced and old friends scattered. Jerry Bock's music and Sheldon Harnick's lyrics faithfully recreate this lost world, with mournful melodies and haunting imagery; joy is melded with sorrow, hope tempered by despair, the pall broken by wild Russian dance, softened by songs which echoed Jewish liturgical music.

Fiddler opened less than twenty years following the Holocaust, which effectively destroyed countless Anatevkas and slaughtered their inhabitants. The children of Russian Jewish immigrants who came to America would view Anatevka as the world left behind, a nostalgic reminder of an impoverished, set-upon past, thus underscoring the blessings bestowed by America, the intended destination for Tevye and his family.

Fiddler's characters are colorful and lively, the dance flowingly reminiscent of Hasidic movement in swirling post-Impressionist blurs. Set designer Boris Aronson created sets inspired by the Jewish Russian spiritual dream world of artist Marc Chagall, and the costumes followed. But it was a fantasy shtetl. When my own shtetl-raised grandmother attended the show she was outraged, saying, "It was never like that! It was never pretty, never so nice!"

But the bulk of *Fiddler's* Jewish audience was of a later generation, largely raised in America and now largely assimilated and feeling sufficiently secure in America to indulge in a refined reminder of their not so pleasant roots. For *Fiddler* succeeds in portraying that past world as one troubled by hate, one with a dim future at best, with its world-weary protagonist trying to make some sense of it all and encouraging us to do the same.

Hatching Robbins

Jerome Robbins had changed his name while still a teenager from Rabinowitz, which meant "son of a rabbi," to Robbins. Why? Because he did not want to be seen as an immigrant. Wanting to be a classical ballet dancer he assumed, perhaps rightfully, that being a Russian Jew would impede his ability to gain acceptance. Hence "Robbins." And indeed he did build a distinguished career first as a dancer, then as a classical choreographer, before designing dance for Broadway.

In the mid-1950s, Robbins teamed with composer Leonard Bernstein to codevelop, choreograph, and direct *West Side Story*. They originally planned an update *Romeo and Juliet* set in contemporary New York City, with a Jewish boy and an Irish Catholic girl finding love amidst sectarian strife; it was to be called *"East Side Story."* But as they wrote, the city's demographics shifted; hence, the native-born Jets now fought Puerto Rican Sharks.

Regardless of what might have been with *West Side Story*, it is significant that Robbins felt sufficiently accepted and professionally secure by the early 1960s to work on *Fiddler on the Roof*, especially given the terms described by Hal Prince. His story thus marks the major cultural shift in America: in 1930, being Jewish was a handicap, an impediment to acceptance; by the early 1960s Robbins could publicly acknowledge his Jewish identity and roots.

Rabinowitz or Robbins?

Jerome Robbins changed his name to help him gain success in America. In 1944 the twenty-five-year-old classical dancer achieved that success with the choreography for his debut ballet, *Fancy Free*, with music composed by a then-unknown Leonard Bernstein. Robbins was an overnight sensation and the offers suddenly came pouring in from the worlds of classical dance, Broadway and Hollywood. One of the first things Robbins wanted to do was to change his name back to Rabinowitz, before fame cemented him as Robbins. Apparently, having achieved fame and fortune via his Americanized nomenclature, he felt he no longer needed the disguise and wanted to be known by his Jewish self. In other words, now that he made it, he felt it no longer necessary to appear assimilated.

Ironically, it was his parents who stopped him. Rather than changing his name back to Rabinowitz, they decided instead to change their last name to Robbins. After a lifetime of having their Jewish surname, they proudly declared themselves according to the success of their Americanized son. So Robbins remained Robbins.[1]

One wonders if most stage performers would have had the same option available to them. Robbins worked in the rarified air of classical ballet, of high culture, which enjoyed both status and cosmopolitanism. Robbins may have worked with the transplanted English choreographer Anthony Tudor, but he also worked with the Russians Michel Fokine (a disciple of Diaghilev) and George Balanchine. Along similar lines, *Fancy Free* was the first compositional success for Robbins' collaborator, Leonard Bernstein. Bernstein was a protégé of both Serge Koussevitsky and later Dmitri Mitropoulos, both prominent conductors. The international glamour could blind Americans to the names Rabinowitz or Bernstein, much as it did to an Arthur Rubinstein or Vladimir Horowitz. Most stage actors, in contrast, needed to maintain local or national popular appeal in order to sustain their livelihood and could rarely escape into a comparable international arts scene.

One of the reasons *Fancy Free* achieved such renown was because Robbins choreographed with an eye toward creating an American idiom. Agnes de Mille had had success in 1942 with her choreography for Aaron Copland's *Rodeo*. Robbins similarly used classically trained dancers to dance in an American milieu. But Robbins went one step further in that his settings were contemporary and the movements echoed everyday behaviors and interactions of the sort found on any New York City wartime street corner. So as de Mille made American folk dance classical, Robbins transformed American vernacular into high culture. Robbins had three American sailors take the place of Russian exotics like Petruschka or the Firebird, and had them move as American sailors might move. Robbins thus elevated the prosaic into the realm of art, making everyday American life his muse. Jewish classical composers were doing the same: Aaron Copland found musical inspiration in the nation's folk traditions, and Leonard Bernstein would even compose an opera out of suburban American domestic squabbles in his *Trouble in Tahiti*. All won their spurs via training in the classical, European traditions, but sought to define an American classical music distinct from the European, which reflected both their pride in being Americans and their acceptance of an American, rather than ethnic, identity.

What is most interesting here is that, just as Rabinowitz became Robbins, so too did the man's capacity to create enduring art choose to express itself in American stylistic terms. The art itself was thus Americanized. Similarly, Leonard Bernstein's music became an amalgam of Jewish liturgical music, classical music, jazz and pop. This is found in his classical compositions as well as in his Broadway scores. Much like the Jewish Hollywood film moguls invented and popularized a wholesome image of small-town America, so too did Jewish classical musicians invent and celebrate American vernacular as high art.

Robbins Sings

Robbins' sense of security was short-lived. His fame also brought him attention from the House Un-American Activities Committee and in May of 1953 he testified as a friendly witness. HUAC threatened to expose him, not as a Jew but as a homosexual, thus destroying his professional career. Nevertheless, it was Robbins' anxiety over being a Jew that resonated with him. In the 1980s Robbins was called for jury duty, reigniting his tortured memory of those hearings. He confided to his diary, "The HUAC returns and I can't escape the terrors of that catastrophe—the guilt, betrayal, cowardice, but most of all-the about-to-be-discovered-Jew by the Aryans."[2] His success did not protect him from such scrutiny or from underlying insecurities about his safety as a Jew living in America. Because he named many names, he was despised by many.[3] But his artistry was such that even the most ardent overlooked his discretion in order to work with him: both Zero Mostel and Jack Gilford[4] agreed to do so even though each had suffered enormously by being blacklisted.

Half-a-decade later Robbins was a guest of Jack and Jackie Kennedy at the White House. Much like Irving Berlin before him, Robbins suddenly found acceptance and hence assurance by inclusion amongst at the nation's highest levels. Perhaps it was this that freed him to delve again into his Jewish roots to create ethnic art; perhaps this freed him to do *Fiddler*.[5]

Preliminary Steps

Robbins worked on many Broadway shows during the 1950s, as director, choreographer, or as play doctor. The list includes work on *The King and I*, *The Pajama Game*, *Peter Pan,* and *Gypsy,* along with *West Side Story.* Whatever the project, Robbins took great pains to research the material thoroughly, to familiarize himself with the intricacies of each culture. He combined his scholarship with his creativity and skill to create a series of enduring shows. Each foray into a new culture also paralleled his personal search for identity and acceptance.

Even *Peter Pan* can be seen to express Robbins' concerns. As shaped by Robbins, Barrie's story centers on how a group of children are chastised by their father for not behaving. They are put to bed and then visited by the elusive Peter who whisks them away to another world, one where children can run free and be enfranchised, especially after they defeat the comically menacing Captain Hook and his (adult) men.

Conformity governed 1950s America's dominant culture and hence the times spawned a series of nonconformist heroes: whether a motor cycle–riding Marlon Brando or explosive James Dean, or an Elvis Presley or Chuck Berry, or a Jack Kerouac, or J. D. Salinger. But the notion of conformity takes on extra pressure and meaning for those whose identity itself leaves them out of the mix, for reasons of ethnicity or religion, race, gender or sexual preference.

In *Peter Pan,* the children flee from conformity, from having to grow up and hence surrender themselves in order to fit into societal norms. Better to fly away to a place where one can remain a child forever, to preserve their individuality and innocence eternally in a land where such nonconformity is celebrated, even if that place is a never, never land. As we will see, Robbins' *Peter Pan* is the antecedent to shows like *Hair* and its disciples in expounding this sentiment.

Building a New Tradition

When Robbins was a child of six he and his sister accompanied his mother back to visit Rozhanka, the shtetl from which their father came, to meet their grandfather and spend the summer. He found the little Jewish village joyful and freeing.[6] After the war he returned to find the town destroyed, the townsfolk liquidated and the buildings obliterated.[7] He lost his personal never, never land, but managed to rebuild it lovingly by creating *Fiddler on the Roof.*

Though Prince viewed the material as too culturally specific for himself to understand, Jerome Robbins and the rest of the creative team found a way to open up the story so as to transcend those potential limitations. This is achieved in the opening number, "Tradition" that situates the story to follow. Consequently, *Fiddler* enjoyed worldwide success as productions sprouted up in nations lacking any overt Jewish presence. The show had hit a responsive nerve. All nations and peoples struggle with the conflicts between the allure of the new and the security of the old, the conflict between the modern and the traditional. All are eager to embrace the latest ideas and technology and yet fear being cut off from the same parents' beliefs that had defined, protected, and preserved them as a people.[8]

Fiddler on the Roof proved an enormous commercial success. It was the first show to run for over 3,000 performances, a record that stood for over ten years. In addition to the world tours, it was made into a major motion picture in 1971, with Topol taking the place of that force of nature,

Zero Mostel. The show has enjoyed many revivals in the decades to follow. The 2004 New York revival drew criticism because it lacked a Jewish cast, though Alfred Molina eventually gave way to the gay, Jewish gravel-voiced Harvey Fierstein as Tevye.[9]

Far From the Home I Love...

Even given *Fiddler on the Roof*'s remarkably broad and lengthy commercial success, it deserves to be considered in still more profound terms. I think *Fiddler* was one of the most important American musicals ever produced. It represents a real turning point in American culture, and paved the way for many others to follow, not only because of its precedence but also because it served as a model that others later followed.

Fiddler on the Roof is groundbreaking because it presents a world apart from America for an American audience, a world that is entirely ethnic, in this case Jewish. Whereas various shows portrayed Jewish (or pseudo-Jewish) characters before, they were always depicted in American settings, trying to make it in American life. *Fiddler* does not do so in part because it predates the twentieth-century Jewish American experience and is thus largely a world unto itself. True, just offstage the gentile peasants, police and soldiers dwell, with their anti-Semitic animosity, and occasionally drift into the onstage Jewish setting to toast a marriage or conduct a pogrom. But aside from their intrusions, we the audience witness Anatevka as an encapsulated Jewish community, featuring its own set of quirky town folk, laboring under the archaic ways of an ancient people. While Tevye, ever affable, reminds us that hostilities are being precariously kept at bay, most of his time and attention is spent trying to preserve his family and faith, to marry off each daughter, to dream of better days. And "better days" are not only charming in their materialistic modesty (one staircase going nowhere, just for show), but profound in their spirituality as he laments lacking the time to spend at prayer.

A Trip to... Belarus?

A popular American musical of the late nineteenth century was *A Trip to Chinatown*. It featured a band of young New Yorkers who on a lark make their way through the city to spend time in the exotic Chinese neighborhood. The show was a huge hit. It featured songs that could imitate Chinese sounds, though still safely American; its scenery showed the foreign-looking settings. It was considered a travelogue, a spectacle whereby the audience could be transported to a less respectable part of New York vicariously, without having to leave the safe familiarity of their theatre seats. The lead characters were us on stage, bold explorers of the unknown, encountering the "other" and reassuringly reacting just as we might do so, even singing a familiar song to reassure that this trip to difference was but temporary, much like riding on a roller coaster.

In contrast, no vestige of America is present on *Fiddler's* stage. Tevye's direct address invites us, the audience, into his world. Rather than asking the minority ethnic characters to understand America, here positions are reversed. *Fiddler* asks for audience empathy. That is a lot more than tolerance or sympathy, or even understanding. Acceptance is a given; now it is up to the audience to participate in the trials and tribulations of the characters and their tenuous world. This is the ultimate in enfranchisement; *Fiddler* has no reason to ask for basic rights; rather, it demands recognition and respect for difference. Perhaps it does so with a gentle charm, with a heartfelt or clever song, but the demand is tangible and real. No Americans are on stage because we the audience are the visitors; *Fiddler's* presentational use of direct address places the audience within the action of the play. It is the great reversal.

Jewish Authenticity

One dance in *Fiddler* that proved most memorable was Robbins' dance of the Hassidim, who move slowly in a line with the wine bottles on their heads, described as "a dancing menorah." Set designer Boris Aronson, also Jewish, wept at the beauty of it. Robbins always did a lot of research and for this show he had a friend sneak him into a Chassidic Jewish wedding where he saw the traditional dances first hand.[10]

Robbins' menorah story is striking because it both resembles and is the inverse of what the Jewish George Gershwin did in writing *Porgy and Bess*. Gershwin spent the summer of 1933 on Folly Beach, a small island just off the coast of Charleston, South Carolina. There he observed the local Gullah community, even attending local church services to witness the call and response gospel music style. It was the same sort of cultural immersion research Robbins loved to do.

The difference here is that Gershwin was dipping into black culture whereas Robbins was swimming in his own Jewish. The result for Gershwin was his classic black folk opera, *Porgy and Bess*, a work both magnificent, but also criticized by its critics for being a white man's vision of impoverished black life. They argued that it was hence neither authentic nor ultimately respectful, regardless of his intentions or the ultimate quality of the work.

George Gershwin created a masterpiece, but it stands alone. There are few imitations of *Porgy and Bess*, few shows that follow its template, by anyone, white or black. Where some skewered Gershwin for what they saw as an ethnic transgression, a root of today's black musical then ironically emerged from this Jewish progenitor.

Jerome Robbins, in contrast, felt able to draw directly from his own personal experiences (albeit conflicted) as a Jewish American artist. If Gershwin's music was ultimately a flattering imitation of others, Robbins' work rang as more true to life, more authentic. Even if such a bottle dance as conceived by Robbins is not actually authentic, it resonated as such and worked to enhance the sense that we are watching a shtetl called Anatevka, watching actual Jewish folk living real, if musicalized, lives. Built from Aleichem's fiction, expanded and honed by an American Jew harboring nostalgic childhood memories but beyond that little actual exposure to turn-of-the-century shtetl life, *Fiddler on the Roof* exudes fundamental human truths that transcend anthropological mimicry and a veneer of authenticity. It is an entertainment that resonates with memory and yet can transcend his cultural specifics and speak to many.

HUAC, or, How Forced Assimilation Backfired

The House Un-American Activities Committee sought officially to purge America of Communists. Perhaps that could be seen in some circles as positive. However, its methods deprived American citizens of rights promised in the nation's Constitution and Bill of Rights. The Committee also seemed to follow in the footsteps of those who hunted "Reds" immediately following World War I, with comparable suspicions of people with foreign-sounding names and differing opinions. In other words, their demand for conformity, a forced assimilation, had tacit ties to Nativism. In 1924 this trend corresponded to the peak of the Ku Klux Klan and the closing of America's open immigration policies; in the early 1950s many of those who were deemed "different" were forced underground, blacklisted from their former professions.

We have seen how Jerome Robbins named names in order to appease the bullying wrath of HUAC; we have also seen how Robbins who, having survived their purge, eventually created *Fiddler on the Roof.* Robbins' work on *Fiddler,* coming only a decade after he testified, represents an historical reversal for him. Forced to hide his identity (both as gay and as a Jew) in order to preserve his career, Robbins' path enabled him to create with *Fiddler* a show that asserted ethnicity, not assimilation, as part of the American identity. *Fiddler's* precedent would eventually open up comparable musical doors to other "fringe" groups similarly oppressed by the sort of asserted conformity practiced by HUAC and others similarly resistant to change. Thus, one could argue that HUAC repressive tactics inadvertently laid the groundwork for a future multicultural musical theatre.

Jerome Robbins named names. Ironically, the other source of musicals built upon the writings of Shalom Aleichem came from a group of those who, unlike Robbins, refused to testify and consequently had their careers destroyed by HUAC. With few professional options, this group turned to their ethnic roots. Where Robbins zigged, they zagged. But both routes led eventually to Shalom Aleichem.

The Blacklisted and the Black

The antecedent for *Fiddler on the Roof* was the 1953 production of *The Tales of Shalom Aleichem.* It was not a musical but rather a play, drawn from the stories of author Shalom Aleichem. Aleichem has been called "the Yiddish Mark Twain" for his stories of Eastern European Jewish folk culture at the turn of the last century. Like Twain, Aleichem's stories are folksy and funny, capturing a particular people, place, and time with insight, irony, and warmth.

In 1953, a group of Jewish theatre people, all blacklisted by McCarthyism, gathered together in New York to do a play using the basement theatre at the Barbizon-Plaza Hotel. The group included Howard Da Silva, Morris Carnovsky, Phoebe Brand (all once members of the Group Theatre), as well as Herschel Bernardi and Jack Gilford. Perhaps because of Communist sympathies, they welcomed a young black couple to work with them: Ruby Dee as an actor and her husband Ossie Davis as a stage manager.

Davis later wrote that this was his first opportunity in show business. He stayed with the group and worked on their productions of *The Dybbuk* and readings of the funny Yiddish tales of Chelm, a town composed of fools. Davis' behind the scenes work gradually gave way to his performing with the group, often in Jewish community centers and synagogues. He developed a love for the material and an appreciation for its ability to portray a quirky, entertaining ethnic community.

When Robbins was casting *Fiddler on the Roof* his colleagues (Jerry Bock, Sheldon Harnick, and Joseph Stein) envisioned casting Da Silva as Tevye because of his work on *The Tales of Shalom Aleichem*. Robbins favored Mostel instead. But the 1953 example was in the mind of *Fiddler's* creators.

Similarly, Ossie Davis drew directly upon *The Tales of Shalom Aleichem* and its ilk in his own writing. While Davis performed stage readings of Jewish material in predominantly Jewish settings with the blacklisted group, Davis tells of how Da Silva encouraged him, saying, "You don't have to read from Jewish material. Do things from your own culture—something you love." Davis later wrote that he drew sustenance and inspiration from the Jewish material's example in trying to formulate his approach to writing for his own people. He also described how the group's simple way of staging led him to realize that simplicity, plus "our passion for great literature," was all they needed "to create a kind of people's theater." And when this company of blacklisted actors actively began seeking scripts from other cultures, Davis began to write a play of his own people. Choosing to write about the South, Davis' first drafts boiled with rage. However, his experience working with the Jewish material caused Davis to modify his dramaturgical approach:

> Meanwhile, every night on stage, a solution was trying to reach me. As I visited again with the delicious fools of Chelm, I found that same ineffable contradiction: that we were both—I and my fellow fools, in a way that was as Jewish as it was black—laughing to keep from crying. My play began to change. My characters from Waycross were beginning to sound like the people of Chelm; and then they became in the end, something else entirely. That something else would finally be called Purlie Victorious.[11]

This dynamic proved groundbreaking. Davis' play *Purlie Victorious* debuted in 1961 and was later made into the 1970 musical, *Purlie*.

On the surface one would not see much resemblance between *Fiddler* and *Purlie*. *Purlie* is set in the Deep South and centers upon the arrival of the title character, the new preacher, who uses his charm and guile to free his co-peers from the clutches of an aging, avaricious Southern white man. In the end, not only does Purlie win, everyone is happy, even the white man, and Purlie even gets the girl.

But where *Purlie* is inspired by *Fiddler* is in its depiction of an encapsulated African-American rural community life on stage. Like *Fiddler* there is a main house, and where *Fiddler* had scenes in the synagogue, *Purlie* had scenes in the local black church. Both used liturgically-inspired melodies.

And the intrusive, white outsider threatens to destroy the lives of the simple black folk. Also, like *Fiddler*, *Purlie* enjoys a humorous folk aura. It is of an earlier time, seems the sort of tale older people would pass on to their children and grandchildren. And though the white man is opportunistic and racist, he is not a slave owner; rather, this is a parable marking the shift when black people first learned to stand up for themselves. Ghosts of slavery may hang over the world of the play, but Davis shows us black characters grappling to preserve their past culture without bringing along slavery's chains in the bargain. And, much like *Fiddler*, *Purlie* appeals directly to the audience, welcoming them into its own world. Tevye's example lives on in *Purlie*.

Rockin' Robbins

In the fall of 1964, the fledgling National Endowment for the Arts awarded Jerome Robbins a sizeable grant that enabled him to found his short-lived American Theatre Lab. In the spirit of the just completed *Fiddler on the Roof*, Robbins worked with a small select group of actors to explore folk imagery and envision new ways of making theatre.[12] Robbins employed the lessons of *Fiddler on the Roof*. He also had the company explore Japanese Noh Drama in his search for communal expression, as well as various newly emerging forms of experimental theatre.

One of the members of Robbins' company was Gerome Ragni. While working with Robbins, Ragni was also working on a script that would become the musical *Hair*. Ragni asked Robbins to direct, but Robbins, burned out by *Fiddler*, declined. Robbins instead referred Ragni to his old associate Gerald Freedman, who was then developing projects for Joseph Papp's Public Theatre.[13]

It is unclear whether Ragni approached Robbins because of similarities in aesthetic approach or because he was professionally opportunistic. *Hair* was a political statement of a musical, and Robbins shunned mixing politics and art. Yet Robbins' inclusion of Ragni in his company does suggest some similarities of interest and approach between the two men, and hence perhaps between elements of their work as well.

Though set within the larger context of Vietnam-era America, *Hair* concentrates audience attention within the self-contained world of "the tribe," a community of antiwar hippies. We learn their values and become acquainted with their ways. Much like *Fiddler*, we see this collective in their own deliberately isolated world and grow familiar with their sensibilities, rituals, beliefs. Like Anatevka, the Tribe is an extended family, one that has developed its own traditions that are being challenged by the outside world. And much like Tevye's daughters are taken away from their family, so too does Claude leave this protective cocoon when drafted to serve in Vietnam. In both shows the community struggles to preserve its ethos against outside forces that threaten its inherent goodness and innocence with change.

This is not to say that *Hair* is *Fiddler*. It is not. But it is to suggest that they share key ingredients that enable both to function effectively on stage as commercial works, though their subject matter would presume otherwise. It is also to suggest that, in a sense, *Fiddler* paved the way for *Hair's* acceptance and success by providing a model by which the audience enters into the community, culture and values of that seemingly foreign world of the "other."

Fiddling Beyond *Hair*

In like fashion, Jonathan Larson's 1993 hit *Rent* is also indebted to *Fiddler on the Roof.* It too presents a community that is at odds with the status quo. Granted, it is a reworking of Puccini's opera, *La Boheme*. Nevertheless, in Broadway terms it relied directly upon the foundation established by *Fiddler*, for the same reasons as had its direct progenitor, *Hair*.

Jonathan Larson was a Jewish composer/lyricist who grew up outside of New York City. His first exposure to musicals came by listening to his parent's recordings of *The Music Man* and, yes, *Fiddler on the Roof.* He later became interested in rock music (his favorite rock musical being *Hair*), and then became a fan of Stephen Sondheim's work. In fact, Sondheim became something of a mentor to Larson, not unlike how Oscar Hammerstein had long ago been a mentor to the young Sondheim.

Following the examples of *Fiddler* and *Hair*, Larson constructs a self-contained community, a sort of extended family, whose survival is being threatened by hostile outside forces. More specifically, the community can only continue if they can find money to pay their rent; unable to maintain their housing, the community will not endure. Where *Fiddler* depicted poor shtetl Jews and *Hair* a tribe of hippies, *Rent* portrays a group of Greenwich Village bohemian artists. They are a twenty-something modern mishmash of religions and races, ethnicities and sexual preferences, unlike the outside world, having found ways to form a healthy community ethos, despite capitalistic pressures. Aside from threats by impatient landlords, the more terrifying culprit to them is the ongoing threat of AIDS, a disease that kills Angel and almost takes Mimi as well. Yet aside from those dangers, we the audience are made familiar and comfortable with this clan's values and beliefs, their rituals and relationship, their ways of providing love and support.

As outsiders we the audience may at first view this bohemian community unsympathetically. But Roger quickly introduces us to each. As we grow familiar with each we discover our commonalities far outweigh our differences. The song "Seasons of Love" functions to assert our fundamental shared humanity, which transcends outward differences. The audience is thus encouraged to identify with the bohemian set, share their joys and mourn their losses. It is we who are the outsiders, generously welcomed into their world and lives. Furthermore, much like *Fiddler*, the characters in *Rent* also primarily deal with the conflict between tradition and change. They are held together by shared assumptions and values, about the century's old role of art and bohemian love, and present not only themselves being threatened by expulsion, but also the survival of their values.

In *Fiddler* and *Hair* and *Rent*, if the action had centered instead in the world outside of each community, we would be encouraged to view each group as being of the fringe, as undesirable outsiders who practiced strange beliefs anathema to our ways. The miracle of these shows is their ability to get us to see the world through their eyes, to accept their point of view as the cultural norm and to root for their perpetuation in the face of enormously unfavorable odds. Furthermore, they do so without asking for pity; each show is a celebration of beliefs and practice and of people themselves.

Part of the ethos of *Fiddler*, *Hair* and *Rent* is that those who people each play insist on preserving their own identities. They redefine the notion of assimilation in the process. Whereas the bulk of the plays studied in this book center on how outsiders tried to adjust to American norms, here in the 1960s and beyond "outsiders" increasingly insist on their right to exist in their own terms, ostensibly not seeing assimilation as a necessity for preservation or success.

Ironically, it is the progenitor of these three that is the most open-minded on the subject. The entire argument of *Fiddler on the Roof* is that, while tradition matters, it is challenged to adapt to a changing world. The question then becomes just how far can tradition bend before it will break? Each successive daughter pushes the envelope a bit further. Tevye tries to accommodate and still retain his beliefs. The first daughter's choice of a husband forces Tevye to challenge the Jewish custom of using a matchmaker; Tevye uses trickery to make this work. The second's choice challenges traditional Jewish religious beliefs in the name of social justice, Tevye respects her decision but suffers when she then decides to leave Anatevka for Siberia to be with him. The third goes farthest, challenging the religion itself by deciding to wed outside her faith. This Tevye cannot accept. Social customs could be subverted for love; traditional approaches to the religion could be challenged, but not the religion itself. As Tevye breaks with her so too do the authorities break with the Jews of Anatevka, forcing them to leave their village in search of a new land.

One could argue that each of the daughter's decisions systematically uprooted another tie between this people and their village. By the end, those roots completely broken, there was nothing left to anchor them and their end-of-play exile was symbolically a search to find and establish new roots, either reestablished or redefined traditions, in a "modern" world. The old formulation of custom/family/religion/village is broken apart, element by element, in the show; what can or will now replace it? They exit into the vast Diaspora in search of new roots and in need of deciding what to keep and what not, with the warning that giving up too much will result in still greater loss. Like most in the Diaspora they will have to reinvent themselves, trying to maintain what they can, adapt to whatever degree is necessary, all in an effort to survive as a people.

There is no evidence in either *Hair* or in *Rent* that such flexibility exists amongst their respective communities. Part of this has to do with notions of time itself. *Hair* is time specific: it is only of a particular generation, a particular era, a particular nation. The future is simply not part of its equation. The tribe's liberal values might continue, but it is highly unlikely that they will continue their onstage way of life indefinitely. The same could largely be said of *Rent*, where we see characters drift away even during the show itself. These are both stories about a group of individuals primarily living in the "now," whereas *Fiddler* is more the story about the preservation of a community, of a people.

Fiddling to a Latin Beat

Playwright/performer Lin-Manuel Miranda has said that his *In the Heights* was directly inspired by *Fiddler on the Roof*, as well as by *Rent*. As such, it too is a descendent of Shalom Aleichem. It operates in the *Rent* mode in its contemporary edginess and its youth culture use of music (salsa, hip-hop, rap, merengue) and wonderfully rhythmic dance. The larger influence though is clearly *Fiddler*.

Following the *Fiddler* antecedent, *In the Heights* is set in its own ethnic enclave, this time the Washington Heights section of New York City, settled primarily by émigrés from the Dominican Republic. Like *Fiddler*, *In the Heights* welcomes us, the American audience, into the Dominican world of the play; where in *Fiddler* it was Tevye the milkman, here it is Usnavi the grocer (originally played by author Miranda himself). Usnavi introduces us to the neighborhood, much like Tevye does at the start of *Fiddler*. We learn about the inhabitants' relationships, their businesses, their daily life, and the traditions that form their collective culture. As in *Fiddler* we see the characters just getting by economically, filled with aspirations and dreams of success, even to the point of fantasizing about what they would do if they had money (an updated, Latin parallel to "If I Were a Rich Man"), similarly charming in its modest simplicity and warmth. Also present throughout the show is the American world just beyond this ethnic, urban village. When the electricity goes out during a neighborhood celebration, and all is plunged into darkness, outsiders come and wreak havoc, not unlike *Fiddler's* wedding festivities interrupted by a violent pogrom. Theirs seems to be a precarious existence, held together by this extended family of a community and their individual and collective hope. Yet the locals retain faith in the American Dream, that hard work and merit will win out in the end.

And part of that Dream to them is a desire to fit in, the parents' tacit belief that their children must assimilate if they are to realize their potential and be able to advance meaningfully in their new homeland. And, like *Fiddler*, it is a daughter that dictates the future. Nina returns after a year at Stanford, wanting to drop out. She is the light of the neighborhood, the hope for the future. But she finds the pressures there too difficult: she is struggling at school with her coursework and is making ends meet, but is especially worried by the sense that she does not fit in culturally.

The last is of course the pressure to assimilate. Whereas in countless earlier shows we have seen assimilation as the goal, here it is directly challenged. Nina abandons her parents' American Dream, convinced that she can find true happiness amongst her own people, remaining within the Washington Heights neighborhood. But even Nina experiences cultural change as she falls in love with Benny, a young black man who works in her family's taxi business. Much like in *Fiddler*, Nina's choice of Benny challenges her family's long-held beliefs, their ethnic traditions and personal preferences. But we the audience see Benny is honest, industrious and sincere and root for his acceptance and the young couple's future happiness. It is a different definition of assimilation, therefore, in that the young man is asked to assimilate to Dominican norms.

This reflects a new definition of America. *In the Heights* takes place in 2007 in an increasingly multicultural New York City, an increasingly multicultural America. What is not clear is to what degree there is a ceiling to what Nina and Benny can achieve by rejecting assimilation, even if the times have changed. Are their possibilities any different than those of previous groups who clung to the ways of the Old Country, living solely in narrowly defined ethnic neighborhoods, feeling no need to learn American ways? Is their declaration of identity ultimately liberating or is it a trap?

Perhaps the biggest irony here is that of the author himself. Manuel is of Puerto Rican descent, born and raised in New York City. He attended Hunter College and then Wesleyan University, where he first developed *In the Heights* for a student group to perform. In other words, Manuel is himself akin to Nina in the show, though, unlike her, he stays in school and assimilates sufficiently to thrive. Is he then Americanized? It appears from the show itself that he is in a liminal position: he is assimilated enough to succeed at an Ivy League college, yet the work he produces is one reliant upon Latin music, culture and dance, celebrating his own ethnicity. Furthermore, *In the Heights* might never have made it to Broadway had Miranda not been sufficiently assimilated: two of his Wellesley classmates encouraged Miranda to expand the piece in order to be viable for Broadway, to which they already had connections.

Regardless, *In the Heights* matters because it celebrated the Dominican culture on the Broadway stage. Its very presence proclaimed the arrival of Latin culture into the American mainstream, and its great commercial success acknowledged a great degree of acceptance by an audience well beyond only fellow Dominicans (or other fellow Latins). The question remains as to whether the show would have worked as well, or perhaps better, had Nina decided to return to college and persist in her efforts to assimilate. Has assimilation grown passé or no longer necessary, or is this show promoting a romanticized cultural fantasy? *In the Heights* ends with Usnavi planning to rebuild the neighborhood thanks to his share from a winning lottery ticket; thus the American Dream is here preserved in the rather arbitrary form of a *deus ex machina*.

Fiddler Speaks With Purple Prose

The Color Purple started out as a novel by Alice Walker that won the 1983 Pulitzer Prize in literature. In 1984 director Steven Spielberg adapted it into a film version, starring talk show host Oprah Winfrey, who delivered a sparkling performance as Sofia. The film garnered eleven Oscar nominations, won none, yet remains highly regarded. In 2005, the story again appeared, this time as a Broadway musical; amongst its producers was Oprah Winfrey.

In the summer of 2009, the road company of *The Color Purple* came to Boston. My wife and I saw it downtown on a Thursday night. Walking from the parking garage to the cavernous Wang Theatre I was struck by the crowd gravitating toward the theatre; it was clearly not the usual Boston theatre-going audience. Rather than the familiar informally dressed, middle-aged white middle-class clusters of playgoers, here the vast majority of the audience appeared well dressed and black. For this group it seemed a special event that merited participation by a supportive community. The energy within the theatre was terrific. Every once in a while you heard audience members call out to the actors in response to a key moment or after an impressive song or dance. It was clear that the audience identified with the performers and the story in more than just theatrical terms.

One thing that struck me from early on in the show was that we were watching an entirely self-contained world; everyone on stage was African American and that, in and of itself, was a very powerful phenomenon and statement. The only intrusion occurred off stage when the tough-as-nails sister-in-law, Sofia, was beaten up apparently by a white man. When we finally see her it is in the jail. This once powerful, large, indomitable woman now sat comatose, with bloodied face and torn clothes, suddenly vulnerable and, worse, defeated. We thus see the impact of outsiders, especially whites. And it was not limited to men: Sofia was beaten for refusing a white woman's request that she become her maid.

The Color Purple shows a black world replete with its own ecosystems. There are good and bad people in this community, users and abusers as well as helpers and givers; it shows the black community as complex and, because of this variation, resisting prejudicial definitions of blacks as only victims or only victimizers, only heroes or only villains. Some characters are successful, some are not; some are likeable, some not. It is a world unto itself. All onstage villains were black men, both because of their race and gender; though not all black men in the show are villains. Most of protagonist Celie's ills were caused by abusive black men; and, in the end, it is the black women who prove the more powerful and who eventually triumph.[14]

Thus, *The Color Purple* is a show which deals with significant change. On one hand it depicts the black experience in America, but it does much more than that. It also features scenes of African tribal life, reminding the audience that black cultural roots run far deeper than the slave experience. Thus the show advocates for a distinctive black identity rooted in strength, independence and pride.

The play begins with women downtrodden by abusive men who use fists and sex as means to assert control; this appears to be the culture's accepted norm, the "tradition." But by the play's end Celie turns the table on that tradition, enacting a sort of revolution in the process. She succeeds because she becomes proactive and accepts herself, as follows: she turns to her African roots (thus bypassing the American black slave experience); she embraces her homosexuality; she redefines her womanhood in positive terms; she uses her seamstress skills to begin a business making pants for women which results in her achieving economic security. In short, Celie achieves the American Dream. Initially beaten down by local norms, she breaks with collective traditions in favor of celebrating her individuality, and finds success as a result. It is an inversion of the assimilation formula. In the end, if anyone is tamed, it is Celie's once-brutal, now meek former husband Albert, his manhood vanquished first by his passion for Shug and later by his desire to reconcile with his wife. It is now his turn to assimilate to them and, by doing so, acknowledge the establishment of new traditions, new norms.

Another thing that struck me while watching *The Color Purple* was its casting. This was not a 1920s musical comedy, with svelte long-limbed dancers of uniform shape and height, parading glamour and sex. Like *Fiddler*, *The Color Purple* presents a more realistic world on stage; it is not about what one could become, but rather a celebration of what one already is. The protagonist, Celie, is short and not even as attractive as her sister, Nettie. Her own husband Albert regularly describes Celie as "ugly." This is not the usual female lead for a Broadway musical. The saloon singer, Shug, is more conventionally attractive in appearance; it is she who later both ignites Celie's sexuality and who declares Celie as pretty. However, in *The Color Purple* it is the secondary couple, Harpo and Sofia, who are the most sexually charged. Where Harpo is average in build, Sofia is big and heavy and round. After Sofia leaves Harpo early in the show (after having his baby), Harpo takes up with the scrawny Squeak, his waitress. But when Sofia returns she quickly claims Harpo back from Squeak, proving herself the more desirable woman. Are these examples of the standard American "ideal" leading lady, namely thin and demure, obedient and deferential? No. These favor women with large bodies and strong, outspoken personalities.

A comparable portrayal of women is found in *Fiddler on the Roof.* True, Tevye's daughters are all slim, but the more mature Golde and Yente are not. Furthermore, like in *The Color Purple*, the women in *Fiddler* prove more formidable than the men: while Tevye makes the decisions, he worries about what Golde will think and uses deceit (his supposed nightmare) to win her over to his side. And tellingly, in the nightmare the two powerful forces against whom Tevye struggles are the Butcher's late wife Fruma Sarah and Golde's deceased, shrill grandmother, Tzietel. In this ethnic Jewish community the women were large, powerful and forceful. Furthermore, keep in mind that it is Tevye's daughters' decisions that dictate the plot of the show.

The obvious pride the black audience took in *The Color Purple* reminded me of the comparable pride Jewish audiences took in *Fiddler on the Roof.* As my wife and I left the theatre I found myself thinking about *The Color Purple* in relation to *Fiddler*, about how much the two shows appeared to have in common. Both shows are historical and rural; both are set in villages that are strangely similar: synagogue/church, the house and its surroundings, the drinking hall. Both show everyday people doing everyday chores; no evidence of any leisure class here. In both you barely if ever saw someone on stage who was not of the central ethnicity (Jewish in *Fiddler*, black in *The Color Purple*); both featured the battle between stern, sometimes oppressive traditions and modernity, causing liberating change, especially for women. In both shows there are the echoes of ancient traditions born in other lands (Jewish ritual in *Fiddler*, reenactments of African tribal life in *The Color Purple*). And both shows have traditions that are challenged by new definitions of "love," ultimately disrupting the core family and forcing them to leave their homes.

If *Fiddler* is cast from a Jewish mold, *The Color Purple* resonates with down-home Christianity. Where *Fiddler* has its Rabbi and *yeshiva buchers* and liturgical-sounding music, *The Color Purple* has its ministers and church ladies, and gospel-based music. In both there is strong presence of the synagogue or church; both preach the importance of family and community. Still, both shows also show the men primarily at work, not idling or gambling. And if there is faith there is also much question about the nature of love in both. And both onstage cultures are endangered by the constant presence of hostile neighbors who are just off stage, just out of sight.

There are also transgressions in both shows. Tevye's liberalism allows his daughters to break time-honored traditions; and while he never breaks his own faith he certainly (respectfully) questions God's intentions. In *The*

Color Purple the transgressions are rife: if there is family there is also adultery; if there is church there is also the gin joint; if there is heterosexuality there is also homosexuality. And one wonders at what point one person's "transgression" is another's act of liberation. In *Fiddler on the Roof* such acts of liberation ultimately foreshadow the community's ruin; in *The Color Purple*, though, acts of liberation add up to revolutionary change that result in a collective healing.

Finally, as in *Fiddler*, in *The Color Purple* we the audience are made privy to the daily life of this town; we see a broad range of characters, entirely ethnic communities formed by the full spectrum of their respective peoples, warts and all, offering a healthy three-dimensionality that happily argues against stereotyping and the dehumanizing prejudice that accompanies it.

Not a Coincidence

After seeing *The Color Purple* and noting its similarities to *Fiddler on the Roof*, I sought to see if there were any actual links between the two shows. I found that the idea of making *The Color Purple* into a musical came from Scott Sanders, a white theatrical producer. The story goes that Sanders read Alice Walker's book and was deeply moved by it. He travelled to Berkeley, California to speak with Walker herself about transforming it into a musical. Walker resisted: the film had been made of it already and she wanted to move on. Sanders persisted believing in the viability of the idea. What did Sanders see in it that convinced him it could work on the musical stage? *The Color Purple* reminded him of *Fiddler on the Roof*.[15]

Therefore....

Fiddler on the Roof is a watershed show because it introduced American audiences to shows featuring peoples secure in their own ethnicity; it is also important because it thus provided an effective model for others to then follow. Prior to *Fiddler on the Roof* ethnic characters in musicals were usually depicted as second-class citizens willing to sacrifice their ethnicity in order to achieve the American Dream. In *Fiddler* and in the shows it inspired, the American Dream is still a viable presence, still a much wished-for aspiration. But *Fiddler* pointed the way to reverse the process of ethnic erosion as a necessary price for success. As such, it proved an affirmation of the legitimacy of ethnic identity (or that of any fringe culture) and set the standard for later shows that dealt with comparable dynamics, even if their cultural particulars differed from the *Fiddler* antecedent.

Ultimately, perhaps what *Fiddler on the Roof* demonstrated and established for the musical portrayal of many peoples to come, was not the suffering of the downtrodden, but rather the fundamental struggle of a community to survive in its own terms and to do so with dignity.

8. Lovable Monsters: An Epilogue ❧

The musical *Beauty and the Beast* opened in 1994 and musically reenacted the classic tale, its happy ending having the beast magically transformed to a handsome prince, the ideal suitor for our beautiful heroine. In 2008, the musical *Shrek* debuted and its happy ending had the beautiful princess magically transformed into a female beast, the perfect match to our ogre hero. This striking inversion signals values had suddenly changed.

Off-Broadway often featured the monstrous as sympathetic protagonists, but Broadway not. For instance, Off-Broadway's *Little Shop of Horrors* (1982), which became a cult hit, enjoyed a successful revival on Broadway in 2003. But *Bat Boy: the Musical* (1997), another Off-Broadway cult hit, has yet to reach Broadway audiences. And when a monster character did appear on Broadway its condition was considered grotesque: 1998's *Carrie* famously flopped on Broadway; 1997's *Jekyll and Hyde* succeeded, but at its end the monstrous Hyde and Jekyll were thankfully dispatched.

Things changed with the new millennium. A slew of shows appeared on Broadway with sympathetic monsters as their leads, inverting conventional expectations. Some have been cute, such as the Muppet-like creatures of *Avenue Q* (2003); some drawn from cartoons, like *Shrek* (2008) and *Spiderman* (2011). *Wicked* (2003) is a variation from the classic film, *The Wizard of Oz*, and *Young Frankenstein* (2007) featured the monster dancing tap. But our list is not limited to the inanimate or the animated; there are also shows that portrayed monstrous people: witness *The Producers* (2001) and *Hairspray* (2002). The hallmark of all of these shows is that the audience's initial view of each show's protagonist is as frightening or distorted, yet, by the show's end we come to view them as normal and cheer for their triumph. The trend reached a point where even the seemingly most conventional can be portrayed as abnormal: in *Legally Blonde* (2007) our heroine, every bit the standard valley girl, battles to gain acceptance and respect. Anyone could now be a victim, everyone deserved acceptance and love.[1]

In terms of assimilation, this plethora of quirky heroes and heroines suggests America has become most open to accepting people as who they are, rather than asking them to conform to a standard cultural norm. It is an era of identity politics and all can be seen as marginalized. Assimilation has become reversed: "the other" has become the new dominant cultural force.

Mel Brooks and *The Producers*

Working as a young gag writer for early television's star comedian Sid Caesar, Mel Brooks once made the star so exasperated that Caesar dangled Brooks by his ankles out of the twenty-third story office window. Caesar's writing team was a brilliant collection of mostly Jewish wits, including Larry Gelbart, Woody Allen, Carl Reiner, and Neil Simon. Subsequently, all contributed heavily to American comedy on stage and screen. Yet it was Brooks who proved most revolutionary because of his consistent assertion of self as a comically sympathetic, unapologetically loud-mouthed Jew.

Starting in the 1960s Brooks proclaimed his Jewishness mostly through recordings and film. His bluntness was jarring. Ethnic America found welcome in mainstream America, but in a sweetly nostalgic packaging. Singer Tony Bennett sang of poverty and the promise of America in his 1950s hit "Street of Dreams." Jewish-American singer Eddie Fisher had a 1952 hit with the German, "Oh My Pa-Pa," which the Italian-American Connie Francis included in her 1960 disc of Yiddish songs. Ethnicity was in the air, but done sentimentally, soft-sold so as to reassure American or Americanized audience ears. Brooks instead loudly trumpeted being an Americanized Jew. His humor featured not so much ethnicity as extroverted anxiety. What is remarkable is that, unlike others, Brooks found broad popular appeal for his work, despite (or because of?) his brash displays.

The films Brooks wrote and directed are mostly loving send-ups of 1930s Hollywood films. Brooks appeared in many of them, sometimes allowing his cartoon Jewishness to explode out. In *Blazing Saddles* he played a corrupt idiot governor, and also appeared as a Yiddish-speaking Indian chief; in *The History of the World, Part One* he played Moses as well as an orthodox rabbi in an over-the-top production number "celebrating" Jewish torture during the Spanish Inquisition. Tasteless? Which?: Brooks' comic reenactment or religious-based torture? There is nothing subtle about Mel Brooks or his humor: he offers no apologies and it cannot be explained away or ignored. Brooks' rude portrayals popped the bubble of anti-Semitic hate and fear, reducing ancient and more recent historical nightmares into the stuff of silly buffoonery.

Why *The Producers* Matters

In this book I have tried to illustrate how twentieth-century American musicals generally concerned themselves with issues of assimilation, following a model largely established by Jewish composers and writers. *The Producers* is important, not only because of its broad commercial appeal, but because it heralds the twenty-first-century shift away from conformity (assimilation) and toward the celebration of difference. Yet *The Producers* is transitional because Brooks consciously mimicked traditional Broadway forms, grounding it in the traditions of Irving Berlin and Cole Porter to create a retro-musical comedy whose sensibilities anticipate the world to come.

Based upon his hit film, Mel Brooks composed music and expanded the script to create his musical, *The Producers*. He relies upon familiar musical comedy devices, but his story defies convention. The two protagonists, Max Bialystock[2] and Leo Bloom, are both clearly Jewish, which is pivotal to the story. In the song "The King of Old Broadway," a Yiddish theatre style lament complete with *klezmer*-style violin accompaniment, Max speaks even of the great Yiddish star actor Boris Tomashefsky with awe. The men's Jewish identity only underscores the humor when they settle upon a play about Hitler as the worst script possible.

Yet their musical becomes a hit. This despite having the worst actors, director, and designs they could find. At first the audience is aghast; they then view it as kitsch and applaud it into a success. There are more than a few ironies here. First, we the contemporary audience for this musical have similarly applauded *The Producers* into hit status, similarly laughing at the onstage Hitler and the show's proclamation of camp. Second, the show is filled with all sorts of potential "monsters," all as would be seen through the eyes of 1950s America. Third, at first the show portrays almost every character as deviant yet by the end all appear relatively normalized. Thus, by *The Producers*' finale, the tolerance of we the audience has been stretched into a broad inclusivity. This is more than a "buddy" story—it is the depiction of the American melting pot as a group of outrageous eccentrics band together to achieve an unlikely collective success. And though Max and Leo wind up in jail, they happily start over, this time with a comparable group, this time comprised of usually objectionable convicts.

The Producers encourages the audience to see everything through the eyes of timid accountant, Leo Bloom.[3] When Leo first meets Max he is shocked, scandalized, frightened, and finally fascinated by Bialystock's larger-than-life persona, aggressiveness, and amoral *chutzpah*. Leo is envious of Max because he is "everything" Leo "is not." In one sense that means Leo too wants to be a producer, but Leo also dreams of becoming successful and free. Leo is no victim here: it was he who discovered how to cook their books and then went along with Max's scheme.

The "monster" Max then takes Leo on the ride of his life. We see Max seducing ancient—and willing—old ladies for their money; Max then leads Leo (and us) to meet a series of what 1950s America would consider freaks (other sorts of "monsters"), from a closet Nazi to a group of not-so-closeted cross-dressing gay theatre artists. The money they collect also finance hiring a tall, sexy secretary after whom both men lust and whom Leo successfully woos. So Max's questionable gambler tactics do enable Leo to realize his wildest American dreams. "Monster" Max ends up as Leo's dearest friend; their *Springtime for Hitler,* portraying the most horrific of monsters as its protagonist and the most horrific of wars as its setting, unexpectedly proves a smash hit. Max's behavior may be vulgar, but it is nothing compared to the vulgarity of Hitler's crimes, so if a mass-murderer can find approval in America, why not a loudly obnoxious, mildly felonious Jew? In the end Leo has fled and Max is put on trial. But Leo heroically returns to plead on Max' behalf via a sung declaration of love and appreciation. Leo demonstrates his integrity by returning at his own risk; Max becomes beloved because we view him through the once-hapless Leo's eyes.

The pattern in *The Producers* is to depict figures as monsters, but, by the end, they all find acceptance and even affection in an America that is more than tolerant, which shows the flexibility to adapt to any and all newcomers. They start out as grotesques, then become familiar, and end as identifiable heroes, able to overcome adversity, triumphant in a singularity at odds with conventional norms. As such it appears that assimilation is no longer necessary, at least as it was defined along twentieth-century lines.

Notes

1 INTRODUCTION: BROADWAY AS A CULTURAL ELLIS ISLAND

1. Not only was the audience heavily Jewish: "The New York musicians union, Local 801, was over 70% Jewish from the 1930s on. Jews were also very active in the writing and promotion of popular music for Broadway's 'Tin Pan Alley.'" See *Encyclopedia Judaica* (Farmington Hill, MI: Macmillan Reference USA, 2007), Volume 15, 219.
2. See Nahmah Sandrow, *Vagabond Stars: A World History of Yiddish Theatre* (Syracuse: Syracuse University Press, 1996). By around 1900 there were three theatres in New York City devoted to Yiddish theatre, collectively drawing about 25,000 patrons per week; by 1917 this number had increased to seven. Also note that Yiddish theatre favored interweaving songs with story, no doubt later shaping Jewish compositions and audiences on Broadway.
3. See Irving Howe, *World of Our Fathers: The Journey of the East European Jews to America and the Life They Found There* (New York: Weidenfeld and Nicolson History, 2000).
4. See Armond Fields and L. Marc Fields, *From the Bowery to Broadway: Lew Fields and the Roots of American Popular Theatre* (New York: Oxford University Press, 1993); also Robert C. Toll, *On With the Show: The First Century of Show Business in America* (New York: Oxford University Press, 1976).
5. See Harley Erdman, *Staging the Jew: The Performance of an American Ethnicity, 1860–1920* (New Brunswick: Rutgers University Press, 1997). Erdman traces the gradual process by which the portrayal of Jewish characters on the late nineteenth-th/early twentieth-century stage shifted from derogatory stereotypes to increasingly sympathetic figures.
6. See Henry Bial, *Acting Jewish: Negotiating Ethnicity on the American Stage and Screen* (Ann Arbor: University of Michigan Press, 2005).
7. "...the purpose of playing, whose end, both at the first and now, was and is, to hold as 'twere the mirror up to nature: to show virtue her feature, scorn her own image, and the very age and body of the time his form and pressure." *Hamlet*, III. ii, 17–24.
8. Long-time Yiddish Theatre star Molly Picon starred in *Milk and Honey*, providing one of the few direct links between the Yiddish Theatre and Broadway.

9. See Philip Furia, "Something to Sing About: America's Great Lyricists," *The American Scholar* (Summer 1997): 379–394. Furia credits the New York City Public Schools for teaching classical poetic forms as part of its curriculum, training a generation of great Jewish lyricists. He points out how Oscar Hammerstein II, Ira Gershwin, Yip Harburg, and Lorenz Hart were all born in 1895 or 1896, as were Leo Robin, Buddy DeSylva, Howard Dietz, and Andy Razaf. Furia writes, "Those pioneers of American song who were born in 1895 or 1896 came from remarkably similar backgrounds. The children of immigrants, practically all were Jews who grew up in New York and learned their English on the streets. 'The Street, not the home, was your life' Harburg recalled. 'Your parents spoke no English. Down on the street you were being Americanized, but in a special ghetto way. Parents were very proud of children who spoke English and could interpret for them. This put the parents in an inferior position.' Nothing impresses upon a child the power of language more than his ability to speak it better than his parents." (381). And to offer a recent perspective on the pressures to assimilate, Wellesley College Theatre professor Nora Hussey, directing *The Last Night of Ballyhoo*, commented on her own experience : "Why do you want to be assimilated? Why not hold on to your culture? These are the questions I wasn't able to ask when I arrived here [in America] from Ireland as a five-year-old. I just wanted to lose my accent so I wouldn't be teased." Quoted in Nancy West, "Assimilating Humor," *The Boston Globe*, January 8, 2011, Globe West Section, 4.
10. Quoted in John Lahr, "The Lemon-Drop Kid," *The New Yorker*, September 30, 1996, 68. Also note a great many Jewish composers had fathers who were cantors, hence raised with close familiarity with Jewish liturgical music, which no doubt shaped their secular musical invention. This included Irving Berlin, Harold Arlen, and Kurt Weill.

2 HELLO, YOUNG LOVERS: ASSIMILATION AND DRAMATIC CONFIGURATIONS IN THE AMERICAN MUSICAL

An earlier version of this chapter was previously published and is here reprinted by permission of *The Journal of American Drama and Theatre*.

1. See, for example, Robert C. Toll, *On With the Show: The First Century of Show Business in America* (New York: Oxford University Press, 1976).
2. See amongst many Gerald Bordman, *American Musical Theatre: A Chronicle*, 2nd Edition (New York: Oxford University Press, 1992); also, P. G. Wodehouse and Guy Bolton, *Bring On the Girls!* (New York: Limelight Books, 1984); also Julian Mates, *America's Musical Stage* (Westport, CT; Greenwood Press, 1985).
3. Max Wilk, *OK! The Story of "OKLAHOMA!"* (New York: Grove, 1993).

4. Hammerstein also depicted potential mixed marriages in *South Pacific* and in *The King and I*, underscoring his advocacy for diversity and ethnic integration. Thanks to Albert Williams for this point.
5. Andrea Most, "'You've Got to be Carefully Taught': The Politics of Race in Rodgers and Hammerstein's *South Pacific*." *Theatre Journal* 52.3 (2000): 307–337. See also Andrea Most, *Making Americans: Jews and the Broadway Musical* (Cambridge, MA: Harvard University Press, 2004).
6. Some refer to the children of immigrants as the "first generation," some call them the second. I favor the latter.
7. Regarding the rising presence of Jews in relation to their portrayal on stage, see Erdman; also see Sandrow: also see Howe. Also, *Encyclopedia Judaica* notes in its entry on New York City cultural life notes: "The half-century following the end of World War I witnessed the entry of Jews in large numbers into every corner of New York artistic and cultural life.... The role of New York Jews as consumers of the arts also grew immensely during these years. It is safe to say that from the 1920s onward Jews formed a disproportionately high percentage of New York's theatregoers.... One rough estimate placed Jews at 70% of the city's concert and theater audience during the 1950s...."
8. See, for example, Oscar Handlin, *The Uprooted* (Boston: Little, Brown and Company, 1975); also, John Hingham, *Strangers in the Land: Patterns of American Nativism, 1860–1925* (New York: Atheneum, 1981); also, Arthur Mann, *The One and the Many: Reflections on the American Identity* (Chicago: University of Chicago Press, 1979). Also, Henry Feingold, "American Liberalism and Jewish Response," *Contemporary Jewry* 9.1 (1988).
9. See, for example, Helen Lefkowitz Horowitz, *Culture and the City: Cultural Philanthropy in Chicago from the 1880s to 1917* (Lexington, KY: The University Press of Kentucky, 1975); also, Lawrence W. Levine, *Highbrow/Lowbrow: The Emergence of Cultural Hierarchy in America* (Cambridge, MA: Harvard University Press, 1988); also, Alan Trachtenberg, *The Incorporation of America: Culture and Society in the Gilded Age* (New York: Hill and Wang, 1982); also Frederic C. Jahar, *The Urban Establishment* (Urbana, IL: University of Illinois Press, 1982).
10. See, for instance, Ethan Mordden, *Ziegfeld: The Man Who Invented Show Business* (New York: St. Martin's Press, 2008).
11. A case in point is the evolving professional theatrical career of Lew Fields and his children Dorothy, Herbert and Joseph, which ranged from baggy-pants Dutch comic routines of the 1880s through jazz musical comedies, and up through the cynical and sophisticated book musicals of the 1960s; See Armond Fields and L. Marc Fields. In another parallel vein, see Lewis A. Erenberg, *Steppin'Out: New York Nightlife and the Transformation of American Culture, 1890–1930* (Westport, CT: Greenwood Press, 1981).
12. See Robert C. Allen, *Horrible Prettiness: Burlesque and American Culture* (Chapel Hill: University of North Carolina Press, 1991); also, Werner Sollors,

Beyond Ethnicity: Consent and Descent in American Culture (New York: Oxford University Press, 1986).
13. The infusion of classical music and, more than that, high culture into the Broadway idiom was certainly not limited to the work of Rodgers and Hammerstein. Snippets of his "An American in Paris" can be found in the score to George Gershwin's *Of Thee I Sing* (1931); Leonard Bernstein zigzagged between classical and popular forms even within each of his four Broadway shows, much as he zigzagged between the classical and pop worlds in his own professional life. Jerome Robbins did the same. The impact of this classical presence did much to legitimize Broadway even to skeptical Jewish eyes. Martin Charnin built a prominent career as a Broadway lyricist and director. He tells the story of how he began. As an art student in New York City Charnin saw a newspaper notice in the paper announcing tryouts for a new musical; it would eventually become *West Side Story*. Charnin, a Jew, needed permission from his religious father to audition. At first his father balked, but upon learning that Leonard Bernstein and Jerome Robbins, both prominent in classical music circles, were involved, he gave his blessing. Their high-culture status gave the project a legitimacy to his conservative eyes of a sort that even a Broadway show did not otherwise enjoy. Charnin was cast as one of the dancing gang members, thus sparking his long career. Martin Charnin's panel remarks at the "Broadway Musical: 1920–2020" conference held at Hofstra University in 2003. The respectability of high culture was a familiar pattern amongst many Jewish American families. It took on the role of being akin to a secular religion. The roots of this probably lay in the German Jewish experience where the invention of Reform Judaism enabled Western European Jews to assimilate, leaving their orthodoxy behind, and finding new spirituality and truths in works of great literature and art. Many Russian Jews coming to America shared in this appreciation and respect. An account of some of the links between the two can be found in David Lehman, *A Fine Romance: Jewish Songwriters, American Songs* (New York: Shocken Press, 2009), 184–187.
14. See, for example, bell hooks, *Black Looks: Race and Representation* (Boston: South End Press, 1992); also, Peggy Phelan, *Unmarked: The Politics of Performance* (New York: Routledge, 1993); also, Judith Butler, *Gender Trouble: Feminism and the Subversion of Identity* (New York: Routledge, 1990); also, a study that applies this more directly to Jewish ethnicity, see Barbara W. Grossman, *Funny Woman: The Life and Times of Fanny Brice* (Bloomington: Indiana University Press, 1991).
15. See Paul Zollo, "Sultans of Song." *Reform Judaism* (Winter 2002), 14–25. Zollos notes a range of Christmas songs written by Jewish composers also include "... 'Rudolph the Red-Nosed Reindeer' by Johnny Marks, 'Let It Snow, Let It Snow, Let It Snow' by Sammy Cahn and Jule Styne, 'Silver Bells' by Livingston and Evans, and the 'Christmas Song' ('Chestnuts roasting on

an open fire...') by Mel Torme." Speaking of Irving Berlin's song "Alabammy Bound," Zollo writes of "...[s]ongwriter Randy Newman, who once said, 'I seriously doubt Irving Berlin was *ever* Alabammy bound,' surmised that the Russian-born songwriter wanted 'to get into America *harder*....'"

16. John Lahr, "Walking Alone: Richard Rodgers's Disappearing Act." *The New Yorker* (July 1, 2002) 90–94. This dark picture of Rodgers is reinforced in Meryle Secrest, *Somewhere For Me: A Biography of Richard Rodgers* (New York: Alfred Knopf, 2001). It is understandably absent from the composer's autobiography, in even the reissued version that featured endnotes by Lahr. See Richard Rodgers, *Musical Stages: An Autobiography* [Centennial Edition] (New York: Da Capo Press, 2002).
17. See Hugh Fordin, *Getting to Know Him: A Biography of Oscar Hammerstein II* (New York: Random House, 1977).
18. Note that though publicly assimilated, Rodgers nevertheless supported Jewish causes. See Andrea Most.
19. Andrew Solt, *The Best of Broadway Musicals: Original Cast Performances from the Ed Sullivan Show* [videotape] (Walt Disney Home Video, n. d.).

3 THE MELTING POT PARADIGM OF IRVING BERLIN

1. See Charles Hamm, *Irving Berlin: Songs from the Melting Pot: The Formative Years, 1907–1914* (New York: Oxford University Press, 1997).
2. Alexander Woollcott, *The Story of Irving Berlin* (New York: De Capo Press reprint of 1924 original), 212–215.
3. Irving Berlin advocated assimilation in much of his life and art. However, while he wed the Irish Catholic socialite, Ellin Mackay, he insisted they live essentially nonreligious lives, only really fighting when she much later returned to Catholicism. Berlin himself weekly attended Shabbos dinner at his mother's until her death, always supported Jewish causes, and late in life maintained a lively correspondence with fellow composer Harold Arlen in which he spoke of himself as being a Jew. See Mary Ellin Barrett, *Irving Berlin: A Daughter's Memoir* (New York: Simon and Shuster, 1994) and also Robert Kimball and Linda Emmet, eds., *The Complete Lyrics of Irving Berlin* (New York: Alfred A. Knopf, 2001).
4. See Andrea Most, *Making Americans: Jews and the Broadway Musical* (Cambridge, MA: Harvard University Press, 2004); also, Jody Rosen, *White Christmas: The Story of An American Song* (New York: Scribner, 2002). For a good account of Berlin's complex and often contradictory feelings toward his own Jewish identity, see Laurence Bergreen, *As Thousands Cheer: The Life of Irving Berlin* (New York: Viking Penguin, 1990); see also Irving Howe *World of Our Fathers* (New York: Simon and Schuster, 1976).

5. Anecdote told me by Alezah Weinberg, May 18, 2004. This was confirmed in my 2004 phone interviews with Seymour Greene, trombonist for Berlin's *This Is the Army* pit band who performed at that event and witnessed it first hand.
6. Philip Roth, *Operation Shylock: A Confession* (New York: Simon & Shuster, 1993), 157.
7. Philip Furia, *Irving Berlin: A Life in Song* (New York: Shermer Books, 1998).
8. Woollcott, *The Story of Irving Berlin*, 95; see also Tyler Anbinder, *Five Points: The 19th Century New York City Neighborhood That Invented Tap Dance, Stole Elections, and Became the World's Most Notorious Slum* (New York: Free Press, 2001); also, W. T. Lhamon, *Raising Cain: Blackface Performance from Jim Crow to Hip Hop* (Cambridge, MA: Harvard University Press, 1998). See also Armond Fields and L. Marc Fields, *From the Bowery to Broadway: Lew Fields and the Roots of American Popular Theatre* (New York: Oxford University Press, 1993); see also Robert C. Toll, *On With the Show: The First Century of Show Business in America* (New York: Oxford University Press, 1976).
9. Between 1907 and 1918 Berlin wrote a slew of ethnic songs. Titles include 'That Cooney Spooney Rag," "Oh! How That German Could Love," "Yiddisha Eyes," "Yiddle On Your Fiddle (Play Some Ragtime)," Sweet Italian Love," "Good-Bye Becky Cohen," "Sadie Salome Go Home," "When You Kiss an Italian Girl," "Abie Sings an Irish Song," "Cohen Owe Me Ninety-Seven Dollars," "It Takes an Irishman to Make Love," "Bad Chinaman from Shanghai." After 1919, he wrote only three more: the two mentioned here and also 1921's "Pickanniny Mose." See Kimball and Emmet, eds., *The Complete Lyrics of Irving Berlin*, and understand Berlin was simply following a popular trend that dated back to the late nineteenth century, if not beforehand.
10. Laurence Bergreen, *As Thousands Cheer: The Life of Irving Berlin* (New York: Viking Penguin, 1990), 220–221.
11. Barbara W. Grossman, *Funny Woman: The Life and Times of Fanny Brice* (Bloomington: Indiana University Press, 1992).
12. Kimball and Emmet, eds., *The Complete Lyrics of Irving Berlin*, 214.
13. Ibid.
14. Woollcott did write a book about the American actress Mrs. Fiske. But this is essentially a book on acting, in sharp difference to his tribute biography for Berlin.
15. Woollcott, *The Story of Irving Berlin*, 223; also note that "Nigger Mike" was the nickname of the owner of the Pelham Café. He was actually a Jew but his swarthy complexion caused him this now-unfortunate moniker, which he appeared to enjoy.
16. For the marriage of Ellin and Irving, and its social class ramifications, see Barrett, *Irving Berlin*.
17. Kimball and Emmet, eds., *The Complete Lyrics of Irving Berlin*, 261.
18. Neil Gabler, *An Empire of Their Own: How the Jews Invented Hollywood* (New York: Knopf Doubleday Publishing Group, 1989).

19. Ironically, Astaire did have some Jewish ancestry on his father's side. Fred Astaire, *Steps in Time: An Autobiography* (New York: Cooper Square Press, 2000). Astaire and Berlin became fast friends, spending many of their retirement years together playing cards.
20. Kimball and Emmet, eds., *The Complete Lyrics of Irving Berlin*, 262.
21. Furia, *Irving Berlin: A Life in Song*, 208.
22. Bergreen claims Berlin revamped the lyrics because tastes had changed and that "coon songs" were no longer fashionable. A more generous explanation might take into account two other possible factors: first, 1920s Harlem had lost its chic glamour by the 1930s, so such musical "slumming" no longer made sense; second, remember this was now post–World War II and the Fascists hated blacks almost as much as Jews. Irving Berlin spent several years during the war touring Europe and the Pacific with his *This Is the Army*, which featured an unheard of integrated cast (again, at Berlin's insistence).
23. Kimball and Emmet, eds., *The Complete Lyrics of Irving Berlin*, 263.
24. Seymour Greene interviews; See also Alan Anderson, *The Songwriter Goes to War: The Story of Irving Berlin's World War II All-Army Production of This Is the Army* (Pompton Plains, NJ: Limelight Editions, 2004).
25. Eric Lott, *Love and Theft: Blackface Minstrelsy and the American Working Class* (New York: Oxford University Press, 1993).
26. Jeffrey Magee, "Irving Berlin's 'Blue Skies': Ethnic Affiliations and Musical Transformations," *Musical Quarterly* 84 (2000): 537–580.
27. In 2007, Mel Brooks reworked his *Young Frankenstein* film into a mildly successful 2007 Broadway musical. Ironically, the one number that stopped the show was not a Brooks ditty, but rather Irving Berlin's "Puttin' On the Ritz." I cite the movie because it is the original creative vision.

4 HOW TO SUCCEED

1. While characters might not be ethnic, often Jewish authors masked Jewish characters in their works as being WASP. See Henry Bial, *Acting Jewish: Negotiating Ethnicity on the American Stage & Screen* (Ann Arbor: University of Michigan Press, 2005).
2. According to the novel *Show Boat*, it is not that Magnolia or Gaylord were Catholic. What happened was that Magnolia was unhappy with Kim's upbringing, as they were sometimes living in bad neighborhoods and she was becoming street smart rather than properly educated. Since they didn't have the money to send her to a top notch private school (which would be Protestant) Magnolia arranged instead to send her to a Catholic girls' school, even though that was considered a significant notch down because they accepted anyone! See Edna Ferber, *Show Boat* (The Country Life Press, Garden City, NY, 1926), 323–329.

3. There really were Mississippi gamblers in the nineteenth-century West, making a living on riverboats and in towns along the river. It was regarded as a legitimate profession at the time, not unlike practicing law or medicine. It later took on a bad reputation as dishonest men began infiltrating their ranks. See www.legendsofamerica.com.
4. The interest in gambling as a musical's theme extends back earlier. One of the first big hit musicals of the twentieth century was George M. Cohan's *Little Johnny Jones* (1904) in which he played an American jockey who unexpectedly wins the English Derby, thus attaining fame and fortune while also affirming Irish American nationalistic pride.
5. In real life Nicky Arnstein was a scoundrel and a card sharp, a man who went by multiple names as he charmed the wealthy out of their money. Brice was drawn to him because he had what she lacked: "One Saturday afternoon, I was introduced to a man who stood then and forever after for everything that had been left out of my life: Manners, good breeding, education and an extraordinary gift for dreaming." In Barbara W. Grossman, *Funny Woman: The Life and Times of Fanny Brice* (Indianapolis: Indiana University Press, 1991), 60ff.
6. *Funny Girl's* producer Ray Stark was Fanny Brice's son-in-law. Because the real Nicky Arnstein was then still alive, the creators tactfully shaped a gentler portrait of Arnstein than perhaps he deserved.
7. See, for example, Horatio Alger, *Luck and Pluck: Or, John Oakley's Inheritance* (Nabu Press, New York, 2010).
8. Michael Alexander, *Jazz Age Jews* (Princetown University Press, Princetown, NJ, 2001).
9. When Lansky was dying, he sought burial in Israel. But then-prime minister Golda Meir, originally from Milwaukee, had him deported back to America instead. Myths that idealize gangsters may appeal to some American Jews, but not it seems to Israelis who protect the Holy Land.
10. Richard Bissell, *7 ½ Cents* (Boston: Little, Brown and Company, 1953). The musical differs sharply from Bissell's original novel, even though Bissell coauthored the libretto with the legendary George Abbott, who also directed the show. The differences here are revealing since they presumably were made to improve the odds of the story's success on Broadway. In other words, the changes demonstrate what most likely Abbott thought would work with the 1954 New York audience. So whereas in the novel Sid is the narrator and the reader knows the most about him, in the musical version we know little; in the book Sid lets it known early that he previously was labor, in the musical it is not till much later; in the book Hasler and Hines are serious businessmen, in the musical they are essentially clowns. The musical also makes Babe the head of the grievance committee, has Sid fire her, invents the characters Prez and Gladys. It also introduces the notion that the picnic happens but "once a year" and that the workers are essentially happy

with that life. Finally, in the book Sid finds out about Hasler's deceit from a guy in the cost department, not from Gladys, and has nothing to do with averting the strike. The book does play up the contrast between Chicago as being ethnically diverse and cosmopolitan in contrast to the small-town, small-minded homogeneity of the Iowa locals.

11. Along similar lines to *How to Succeed in Business Without Really Trying* (1961) is the musical *I Can Get for You Wholesale* (1962). It was created by the same Harold Rome who wrote the score for *Pins and Needles* some twenty-five years earlier. This Harold Rome's show set in the 1930s New York City Garment District where protagonist Harry Bogan (Elliot Gould) ruthlessly makes his way to the top, abandons his mother and girlfriend, loses all, and then is accepted back. Rome's score sounds heavily Jewish, which makes sense given the setting. Significantly, it is the inverse of *How to Succeed in Business Without Really Trying* in that it ends in failure and is sentimental in tone. Unlike the Loesser's score, Harold Rome's score is heavily and overtly Jewish in tone. It has not enjoyed any Broadway revivals, but did mark the memorable Broadway debut of a nineteen year old Barbra Streisand, playing the irrepressibly Jewish Miss Marmelstein.
12. Lyrics to "I Believe in You" can be found at www.stlyrics.com/lyrics/howtosucceedinbusinesswithoutreallytrying/ibelieveinyou.htm
13. A *New York Times* book review also linked Frank Loesser's *How to Succeed* with Kennedy, see David Lehman, "The Man Who Rhymed 'Barbasol'," *The New York Times*, December 7, 2003, found online at http://theater.nytimes.com/mem/theater/treview.html?res=9F03E4DF113AF934A35751C1A9659C8B63

5 CINDERELLAS

1. http://en.wikipedia.org/wiki/Cinderella_(musical); see also *Rodgers and Hammerstein's Cinderella* [original television broadcast of March 31, 1957] (DVD) (Image Entertainment, 2004), directed by Ralph Nelson; also *Rodgers and Hammerstein's Cinderella* [1997 television version] (DVD) (Walt Disney Video, 2003), directed by Robert Iscove.
2. *Rodgers and Hammerstein's Cinderella* [1964 television broadcast] (DVD) (Sony Pictures, 2002), directed by Charles S. Dubin.
3. For descriptions of the various *Cinderella* shows and their period context see Gerald Bordman, *American Musical Theatre: A Chronicle,* 2nd Edition (New York: Oxford University Press, 1992), 345–379.
4. Laurence Bergreen, *As Thousands Cheer: The Life of Irving Berlin* (New York: De Capo Press, 1990), 223; see also Deena Rosenberg, *Fascinating Rhythm: the Collaboration of George and Ira Gershwin* (Ann Arbor: University of Michigan Press, 1997).

5. Boardman, *American Musical Theatre*, 356–357; see also Ethan Mordden, *Ziegfeld: The Man Who Invented Show Business* (New York: St. Martin's Press, 2008) where the footnote at the bottom of page 194 notes, "Sally and her alley comprised a very popular image of a working-class sweetheart, Sally being one of those plain names that tended to incite George M. Cohan to compose an ode, and the alley referring to the lane behind brownstones or row houses where working-class children played."
6. Bordman, *American Musical Theatre*, 376.
7. Anne Nichols was herself Baptist. When *Abie's Irish Rose* debuted it was panned by critics. Nichols turned to the notorious Jewish gambler Arnold Rothstein who agreed to underwrite the show, thus enabling it to find its audience, leading to it becoming a major theatrical hit. It is unknowns if Rothstein gave money because he supported the show's message or because he saw it as a good business investment.
8. The term "burlesque" here means an over-the-top parody of a popular hit, at which the two comedians proved adept in the turn of the century New York vaudeville stage; it has nothing to do with striptease shows. See Armond Fields and L. Marc Fields, *From the Bowery to Broadway: Lew Fields and the Roots of American Popular Theatre* (New York: Oxford University Press, 1993). There is a great deal of research about Jews and blackface, presenting a complex and often contradictory picture. Perhaps the one that shows the complexity best is Michael Rogin, *Blackface, White Noise: Jewish Immigrants in the Hollywood Melting Pot* (Berkeley: University of California Press, 1996).
9. John Bush Jones, *Our Musicals, Ourselves: a Social History of the American Musical Theatre* (Hanover: Brandeis University Press, 2003), 58.
10. Though peers, Brice and Miller never appeared in the same edition of the *Follies*.
11. Barbra Streisand took on the role of groundbreaker for both Jews and women and should be recognized for her considerable contributions to this cause. Though *Funny Girl* made Streisand a star and also introduced our first Jewish Cinderella, Streisand first made a name for herself on Broadway playing a Jewish secretary who sings a lament, "Miss Marmelstein" in Harold Rome's 1962 hit, *I Can Get It For You Wholesale*. Her portrayal of Marmelstein jarred audiences in part because of Streisand's remarkable talent, and in part because it brought Jewish ethnicity directly to the forefront in terms audiences could relate to directly. As for the famous tug boat scene in *Funny Girl*, Streisand mimicked the same image when she directed and starred in the 1983 film *Yentl*. Tellingly, this time the one riding the tug into New York harbor was no longer a glamorous Broadway star, but rather a modest, cross-dressing Jewish *Yeshiva-bucher*. It was as if by the 1980s there was no longer any need to "hide" beneath even the assimilated mask, that the Jewish woman believed it now commercially possible to reveal herself for who she always was underneath the accoutrements, her sexually ambiguous ethnicity in full "parade" display.

12. See Barbara W. Grossman, *Funny Woman: The Life and Times of Fanny Brice* (Bloomington: Indiana University Press, 1991).
13. In real life this may not in fact even be the case, as witnessed by the English King Edward VIII's abdication of the throne in order to wed the American widow, Mrs. Wallace Simpson, explaining that she was "the woman I love."
14. Whereas *My Fair Lady* and *Man of LaMancha* were based on literary classics, *Dreamgirls* is loosely based upon Barry Gordy, who founded Motown Records, and his personal and professional relationship with Diana Ross and The Supremes.

6 TURNS OF THE CENTURY: DREAMS OF PROGRESS, DREAMS OF LOSS

1. Terrence McNally, *Ragtime* (libretto), copy in possession of author, 103.
2. Stephanie E. Smallwood, *Saltwater Slavery: A Middle Passage from Africa to American Diaspora* (Cambridge, MA and London, England: Harvard University Press, 2007), 187.
3. See Philip D. Morgan, "The Cultural Implications of the Atlantic Slave Trade: African Regional Origins, American Destinations and New World Developments," *Slavery & Abolition*, 18:1, 136. Walker's pattern of adopting WASP behaviors and transforming them to his own ends matches a long-standing pattern dating back to the slaves. Morgan writes, "Just as ethnic identities both within Africa and the Americas should be viewed as fluid and permeable, so cultural development in the New World involved borrowing and adaptation, modification and invention. Slaves functioned as *bricoleurs*, to borrow Claude Levi-Strauss's term, picking and choosing from a variety of cultural strains to create something new."
4. Smallwood, *Saltwater Slavery*, 183.
5. McNally, *Ragtime*, 74.
6. Orlando Patterson, *Slavery and Social Death: A Comparative Study* (Cambridge: Harvard University Press, 1982), 45. Tateh's liminal situation closely resembles that experienced by slaves in America.
7. Smallwood, *Saltwater Slavery*, 57.
8. See, for example, Tyler Anbinder, *Five Points: the 19th Century New York Neighborhood that Invented Tap Dance, Stole Elections, and Became the World's Most Notorious Slum* (New York: Free Press, 2001); also, Lewis A. Erenberg, *Steppin' Out: New York Nightlife and the Transformation of American Culture, 1890–1930* (Westport, CT: Greenwood Press, 1981). Both Anbinder and Erenberg provide accounts of how public settings function to enable the mixing of classes and races, in otherwise segregated New York.
9. McNally, *Ragtime*, 11.
10. Smallwood, *Saltwater Slavery*, 59.

11. McNally, *Ragtime*, 106.
12. E. L. Doctorow, *Ragtime* (New York: Random House, 1975), 256.
13. Garth Drabinsky, *Closer to the Sun* (Toronto: McClelland & Stewart Inc., 1995).
14. Both *Ragtime* and *Parade* won critical acclaim. In 1998 *Ragtime*, though nominated for thirteen Tony Awards, won but four; it lost out to *The Lion King* for Best Musical. In 1999 *Parade*, though closed by that time, received nine Tony Awards nominations and won two awards: Alfred Uhry won for Best Book of a Musical and Jason Robert Brown won for Best Original Musical Score. And where *Ragtime* ran 834 performances, *Parade* closed after eighty-five performances. As a side note, *Ragtime's* 2009 Broadway revival also received critical praise, but ran only sixty-five performances due to high costs and poor advance sales.
15. Interview with Hal Prince and Alfred Uhry, *Charlie Rose* (DVD), Charlie Rose with James Moll, Ronald Firestone, Irene Lisblatt and Tom Lantos; Hal Prince and Alfred Uhry (February 9, 1999).
16. Interestingly, Doctorow's *Ragtime* novel ends with a reference that eerily links it again with *Parade*: "And by that time the era of Ragtime had run out…The Anarchist Emma Goldman had been deported. The beautiful and passionate Evelyn Nesbit had lost her looks and fallen into obscurity. And Harry K. Thaw, having obtained his release from the insane asylum, marched annually at Newport in the Armistice Day parade." Doctorow, *Ragtime*, 270.
17. "Presentational" staging means that the actors speak directly to the audience, acknowledging their presence and hence involving them directly in the action of the play. It is the converse of "representational" staging in which the actors tend to "ignore" the audience and create the illusion that they exist in a time and place separate from that of the audience. In representational theatre the audience watches as voyeurs and what is onstage is assumed to be closer to real life, rather than theatre. The two contrasting aesthetics are both found in Shakespeare, where soliloquies are spoken directly to the audience whereas in the rest of the play the actors ignore the audience, blocking them out of the action.
18. Descriptions of the original staging of both *Ragtime* and *Parade* come from videotape recordings of each found in The Billy Rose Collection of The New York Public Library for the Performing Arts. The opening of *Ragtime* can also be found on *Broadway's Lost Treasures III: The Best of the Tony Awards* (DVD) (Acorn Media, 2005).
19. One of the students in my American Musical Theatre class, upon watching this, commented that this choreography anticipated the "Wheel of a Dream" song.
20. Steve Oney, *And the Dead Shall Rise: The Murder of Mary Phagan and the Lynching of Leo Frank* (New York: Pantheon Books, 2003); see also Leonard Dinnerstein, *The Leo Frank Case* (Athens: University of Georgia press, 2008).

21. Director Harold Prince deliberately cast Brent Carver as Leo Frank in an effort to replicate Frank's unsympathetic demeanor, thus placing the audience in a more difficult quandary than had he cast a more sympathetic actor in the role.
22. See Oney, *And the Dead Shall Rise*, 514–607.
23. Alfred Uhry spoke of his ties to the Frank case and his preparation on the *Charlie Rose* show (February 9, 1999).
24. The parallel to Franklin and Eleanor Roosevelt were made by Harold Prince on the *Charlie Rose* show interview (February 9, 1999).
25. See Oney, *And the Dead Shall Rise*, 514–607.
26. See *Charlie Rose*.
27. Abigail Progrebin, *Stars of David: Prominent Jews Talk About Being Jewish* (New York: Broadway Books, 2005), 296–299.
28. Prince's optimism was shared by Andre Bishop, the then artistic director of the Lincoln Center Theatre, whose season included both *Parade* and Michael John LaChiusa's *Marie Christine* (a multiracial version of *Medea* set in 1880s New Orleans). Bishop said, "Both *Parade* and *Marie Christine* are big, serious pieces, involving issues of anti-Semitism, racism and prejudice... . I just think that in the last year of the century it will be great to make a statement about the musical theater form. It is one of the great art forms of the century, and I love the idea of doing two big, serious shows in a row by young composer-lyricists." Quoted from Rick Lyman, "On Stage and Off; Lincoln Center Plans 3 Musicals," *New York Times*, found in nytimes.com (March 20, 1998), n. p.
29. A acknowledged example of this is Arthur Miller's *The Crucible* which, though set in 1692 Salem's notorious witch hunt, was in fact an indictment of the tactics used in the late 1940s and early 1950s by Senator Joseph McCarthy and the House Un-American Activities Committee.

7 FIDDLER'S CHILDREN

1. It was Robbins' first dance teacher Gluck Sandor who urged him to change his name. Gluck was himself Jewish and had changed his name from Samuel Gluck or Glick. Robbins later remarked that Sandor "... did a fine nose-job on his name, too." Perhaps significantly, years later Robbins cast Sandor in the role of the Rabbi in *Fiddler On the Roof.* I say "significantly" given Sandor's role in having Robbins Anglicized his name and now being cast as the shtetl rabbi, of all things. Amanda Vaiil, *Somewhere: The Life of Jerome Robbins* (New York: Broadway Books, 2006), 31–33.Jerry chose the name Robbins because his sister Sonia, also a dancer, had already begun to use it herself. As a side note, this was only four years after the premiere of the Al Jolson hit film (and first talking picture) *The Jazz Singer*, in which the protagonist's last name is also Rabinowitz, which he similarly does a "nose-job" on his name to

become "Jack Robin." This is probably only a coincidence, but is amusing to consider a relationship between the film and the future choreographer.
2. Vaiil, *Somewhere*, 220.
3. Robbins' own sister broke with him over his HUAC testimony, only reconciling near the end of his life. And Robbins' final work, never completed, was his *The Poppa Piece*, an autobiographical work composed of absurdist theatrics and dance that explored his conflict between self-acceptance and self-ridicule over his Jewish identity. It included strong references to himself and HUAC. Almost forty years after he testified, the incident still haunted him, as he wrote: "I cannot forgive myself. And I have no assurance within me that I would not capitulate again." Author Vaill commented on this *vis-à-vis The Poppa Piece* when she wrote, "Despite its name, then, *The Poppa Piece* wasn't really about Harry Rabinowitz; it was about Jerry's need to finally make things right with the father (and fathers) he felt he had betrayed." Quoted in Vaiil, *Somewhere*, 512.
4. This is particularly ironic given that Gilford was amongst those named by Robbins.
5. If Robbins had felt uncomfortable declaring his Jewish identity in the early 1950s, a decade later he had lost those qualms. Immediately after first hearing samples of the proposed script and score by Jerry Bock and Sheldon Harnick, Robbins shot off an exuberant telegram to a friend: "I'M GOING TO DO A MUSICAL OF SHOLEM ALEICHEM STORIES WITH HARNICK AND BOCK STOP I'M IN LOVE WITH IT IT'S OUR PEOPLE." Vaill, *Somewhere*, 361.
6. Robbins' later wrote of his prolonged visit to Rozhanka: "It was all lovely, all lovely. I do not remember one unhappy moment." Quoted in Vaill, *Somewhere*, 16. This experience clearly colored Robbins' heavily nostalgic approach when creating *Fiddler on the Roof*.
7. In 1960, the State Department arranged for Ballets: USA to tour Europe to generate goodwill. When Robbins and company performed in Poland he and a friend rented a car and drove in search of Rozhanka. They learned that all the Jews had been executed, the gravestones removed, the synagogue made into a stable By 1960 when they arrived in person, it was far worse: "There was nothing there." Vaiil, *Somewhere*, 319.
8. I ran across a clip on You Tube of an amateur Japanese production of the show, complete with yarmelkas and wigs, performed in a large gymnasium-like space. The look and sounds struck me as odd and more than a little disconcerting, but the cast nevertheless acted with verve and commitment, all in Japanese.
9. See Ben Brantley's review, *The New York Times*, January 21, 2005. Actually, the cast of the original *Fiddler on the Roof* only had a handful of Jewish actors; many of the leads were not Jewish, including Maria Karnilova (Golde), Julie Migenes (Hodel), and Austin Pendleton (Motl). Even the emblematic Fiddler

was not Jewish but rather Italian. But the strongly Jewish contributions of Robbins and of Mostel cemented its predominant warmth and Jewish tone, key elements reportedly missing in the 2004 revival. Also, on another topic, Fierstein as Tevye demonstrates America's changing attitudes towards difference. Here was a man who wrote pioneering scripts about gay life yet portrays a *pater familias*. And there is more than a little irony in it being he who struggles to preserve tradition while bemoaning the challenges of a wife and daughters.

10. Vaiil, *Somewhere*, 371. The "dancing menorah" description is Vaiil's.
11. Ossie Davis and Ruby Dee, *With Ossie and Ruby: In This Life Together* (New York: William Morrow and Company, Inc., 1998), 264.
12. The company included such notables as Julia Migenes, Morgan Freeman, Gerome Ragni. Both Anna Sokolov and Robert Wilson assisted Robbins as nonperformers. Robbins' approach was strongly influenced by traditional Japanese Noh Drama and also the experimentally stark actor work of Poland's stage director, Jerzy Grotowski. Vaiil, *Somewhere,* 387–388.
13. Vaiil, *Somewhere*, 391.
14. In fact, some have criticized *The Color Purple* for too harshly portraying the violence of black men.
15. Sanders reportedly said of the resemblance of *The Color Purple* to *Fiddler on the Roof,* "You watch this community change over a period of time... and also you have this incredible woman who is able to persevere and evolve despite what happens to her." Quoted in Jim Higgins, "Inspiring Journey," *The Milwaukee Journal Sentinel.* August, 10, 2008 [6].

8 LOVABLE MONSTERS: AN EPILOGUE

1. The trend is not limited to Broadway. The highly successful Harry Potter series featured teenage witches, far more wholesome than their mortal counterparts. Akin to this was the *Twilight* series of books, featuring the again teenage escapades of life amongst a most sympathetic group of attractive bloodsuckers. On Broadway this same combination of teen angst, eroticism and identity issues found expression in the 2007 musical *Spring Awakening,* albeit set in more conventional human terms.
2. A bialy is a flattened *role* sprinkled with chopped onion; the word is Yiddish and comes from the town where they were first made, namely "Bialystock," located in the once heavily Jewish populated northern Poland, near Belarus.
3. Bloom's name is no doubt a comedy reference to James Joyce's protagonist in his novel *Ulysses,* the Jewish Leopold Bloom.

Representative Bibliography

Michael Alexander, *Jazz Age Jews* (Princeton: Princeton University Press, 2001)
Richard Altman with Mervyn Kaufman, *The Making of a Musical* (New York: Crown Publishers, 1971)
Tyler Anbinder, *Five Points* (New York: Plume, 2002)
Brooks Atkinson, *Broadway* (New York: The Macmillan Company, 1970)
Bruce Babington and Peter William Evans, *Blue Skies and Silver Linings: Aspects of the Hollywood Musical* (Manchester, UK: Manchester University Press, 1985)
Stephen Banfield, *Sondheim's Broadway Musicals* (Ann Arbor: University of Michigan Press, 1993)
Mary Ellin Barrett, *Irving Berlin* (New York: Simon and Schuster, 1994)
Laurence Bergreen, *As Thousands Cheer: The Life of Irving Berlin* (New York: De Capo Press, 1990)
Henry Bial, *Acting Jewish* (Ann Arbor: University of Michigan Press, 2005)
Geoffrey Block, *Enchanted Evenings: The Broadway Musical from Show Boat to Sondheim* (New York: Oxford University Press, 1997)
Gerald Bordman, *American Musical Theatre: A Chronicle,* 2nd Edition (New York: Oxford University Press, 1992)
Judith Butler, *Gender Trouble: Feminism and the Subversion of Identity* (New York: Routledge, 1990)
Eddie Cantor, *My Life Is in Your Hands & Take My Life: The Autobiography of Eddie Cantor* (New York: Cooper Square Press, 2000)
Robert Dawidoff, *Making History Matter* (Philadelphia: Temple University Press, 2000)
E. L. Doctorow, *Ragtime: A Novel* (New York: Random House, 1975)
Ann Douglass, *Terrible Honesty: Mongrel Manhattan in the 1920s* (New York: Farrar, Strauss and Giroux, 1995)
Garth Drabinsky, *Closer to the Sun* (Toronto: McClelland & Stewart Inc, (1995)
Ken Emerson, *Always Magic in the Air: The Pomp and Brilliance of the Brill Building Era* (New York: The Viking Press, 2005)
Harley Erdman, *Staging the Jew: The Performance of an American Ethnicity, 1860–1920* (New Brunswick, NJ: Rutgers University Press, 1997)
Lewis A. Erenberg, *Steppin' Out: New York Nightlife and the Transformation of American Culture, 1890–1930* (Westport, CT: Greenwood Press, 1981)

222 Representative Bibliography

Henry Feingold, *A Time for Searching: Entering the Mainstream, 1920–1945* (Baltimore: Johns Hopkins Press, 1995)
Armond Fields and L. Marc Fields, *From the Bowery to Broadway: Lew Fields and the Roots of American Popular Theatre* (New York: Oxford University Press, 1993)
Hugh Fordin, *Getting to Know Him: A Biography of Oscar Hammerstein II* (New York: Random House, 1977)
Michael Freedland, *Jolson: The Story of Al Jolson* (London: Vallentine Mitchell, 1972)
Philip Furia, *Irving Berlin: A Life in Song* (New York: Shermer Books, 1998)
———. *The Poets of Tin Pan Alley: A History of America's Great Lyricists* (New York: Oxford University Press, 1990)
———. "America's Great Lyricists," *The American Scholar* (Summer 1997), 379–394
Neal Gabler, *An Empire of Their Own: How the Jews Invented Hollywood* (New York: Knopf Doubleday Publishing Group, 1989)
J. Ellen Gainor and Jeffrey Mason, ed., *Performing America: Cultural Nationalism in American Theatre* (Ann Arbor: University of Michigan Press, 1999)
Ira Gershwin, *Lyrics on Several Occasions* (New York: The Viking Press, 1973)
Sol Gittleman, *From Shtetl to Suburbia: The Family in Jewish Literary Imagination* (Boston: Beacon Press, 1978)
Herbert Goldman, *Banjo Eyes: Eddie Cantor and the Birth of Modern Stardom* (New York: Oxford University Press, 1997)
William Goldman, *The Season: A Candid Look at Broadway* (New York: Harcourt, Brace and World, Limelight Editions, 1969)
Jack Gottlieb, *Funny, It Doesn't Sound Jewish* (New York: State University of New York, 2004)
Bill Granger and Lori Granger, *Lords of the Last Machine* (New York: Random House, 1987)
Barbara W. Grossman, *Funny Woman: The Life and Times of Fanny Brice* (Bloomington: Indiana University Press, 1991)
Sabine Haenni, *The Immigrant Scene: Ethnic Amusements in New York 1880–1920* (Minneapolis: University of Minnesota Press, 2008)
Charles Hamm, *Irving Berlin—Songs from the Melting Pot: The Formative Years, 1907–1925* (New York: Oxford University Press, 1997)
Oscar Hammerstein II, *Lyrics* (New York: Hal Leonard Books, 1985)
Oscar Handlin, *The Uprooted* (Boston: Little, Brown and Company, 1975)
Hutchins Hapgood, *The Spirit of the Ghetto* (Cambridge, MA: Harvard University Press, 1967)
Lorenz Hart and Robert Kimball, *The Complete Lyrics of Lorenz Hart* (New York: Alfred A. Knopf, 1986)
Andrew R. Heinze, *Adapting to Abundance: Jewish Immigrants, Mass Consumption, and the Search for American Identity* (New York: Columbia University Press, 1990)

Amy Henderson and Dwight Blocker Bowers, *Red, Hot and Blue, A Smithsonian Salute to the American Musical* (Washington: Smithsonian Institution Press, 1996)

John Higham, *Strangers in the Land: Patterns of American Nativism, 1860–1925* (New York: Atheneum, 1981)

David Hirst, "The American Musical and the American Dream: from 'Show Boat' to Sondheim," *New Theatre Quarterly* (1985), 24–38

Thomas S. Hischak, *Word Crazy: Broadway Lyricists from Cohan to Sondheim* (New York: Praeger, 1991)

bell hooks, *Black Looks: Race and Representation* (Boston: South End Press, 1992)

Helen Lefkowitz Horowitz, *Culture & the City: Cultural Philanthropy in Chicago from the 1980s to 1917* (Lexington, KY: The University Press of Kentucky, 1975)

Irwing Howe, *World of Our Fathers* (New York: Simon and Schuster, 1976)

John Bush Jones, *Our Musicals, Ourselves: A Social History of the American Musical Theatre* (Hanover, NH: Brandeis University Press, 2004)

Kenneth Kanter, *The Jews of Tin Pan Alley: The Jewish Contribution to American Popular Music, 1830–1940* (New York: Ktav Publishing House, 1982)

Michael Kantor and Laurence Maslon, *Broadway: The American Musical* (New York: Bulfinch Press, 2004)

Robert Kimball and Linda Emmet, *The Complete Lyrics of Irving Berlin* (New York: Alfred A. Knopf, 2001)

Bruce Kirle, *Unfinished Business: Broadway Musicals as Works-in-Process* (Carbondale: Southern Illinois University Press, 2005)

Raymond Knapp, *The American Musical and the Performance of Personal Identity* (Princeton: Princeton University Press, 2006)

Mendel Kohansky, *The Hebrew Theatre* (New York: Ktav Publishing House, 1969)

John Lahr, *Honky-Tonk Parade: New Yorker Profiles of Show People* (New York: The Overlook Press, 2005)

Greg Lawrence, *Dance with Demons: The Life of Jerome Robbins* (New York: G. P. Putnam & Sons, 2001)

David Lehman, *A Fine Romance: Jewish Songwriters, American* Songs (New York: Nextbook, 2009)

Jerry Leiber and Mike Stoller with David Ritz, *Hound Dog: The Leiber and Stoller Autobiography* (New York: Simon and Schuster, 2009)

Alan Jay Lerner, *The Musical Theatre: A Celebration* (New York: McGraw-Hill, 1986)

Lawrence W. Levine, *Highbrow/Lowbrow: The Emergence of Cultural Hierarchy in America* (Cambridge, MA: Harvard University Press, 1988)

W. T. Lhamon, *Raising Cain: Blackface Performance from Jim Crow to Hip Hop* (Cambridge, MA: Harvard University Press, 2000)

Eric Lott, *Love and Theft: Blackface Minstrelsy and the American Working Class* (New York: Oxford University Press, 1995)

Arthur Mann, *The One and the Many: Reflections on the American Identity* (Chicago: University of Chicago Press, 1979)

Bruce McConachie, "The "Oriental' Musicals of Rodgers and Hammerstein and the U. S. War in Southeast Asia," *Theatre Journal* 46 (1994): 385–298

Albert F. McLean, *American Vaudeville as Ritual* (Lexington: the University of Kentucky Press, 1965)

Scott McMillin, *The Musical as Drama* (Princeton: Princeton University Press, 2001)

Jeffrey Melnick, *A Right to Sing the Blues* (Cambridge, MA: Harvard University Press, 1999)

Ted Merwin, *In Their Own Image: New York Jews in Jazz Age Culture* (New Brunswick: Rutgers University Press, 2006)

Harold Meyerson and Ernie Harburg, *Who Put the Rainbow in The Wizard of Oz: Yip Harburg, Lyricist* (Ann Arbor: University of Michigan Press, 1995)

Ethan Mordden, *Beautiful Mornin': The Broadway Musical in the 1940s* (New York: Oxford University Press, 1999)

———. *Broadway Babies* (New York: Oxford University Press, 1983)

———. *All That Glittered: The Golden Age of Drama on Broadway, 1919–1959* (New York: St. Martin's Press, 2007)

———. *Coming Up Roses: The Broadway Musical in the 1950s* (New York: Oxford University Press, 2000)

———. *Make Believe: The Broadway Musical in the 1920s* (New York: Oxford University Press, 1997)

———. *One More Kiss: The Broadway Musical in the 1970s* (New York: Palgrave, 2004)

———. *Sing for Your Supper: The Broadway Musical in the 1930s* (New York: Palgrave, 2005)

———. *Ziegfeld: The Man Who Invented Show Business* (New York: St. Martin's Press, 2008)

Andrea Most, *Making Americans: Jews and the Broadway Musical* (Cambridge, MA: Harvard University Press, 2004)

Michael Novak, *Unmeltable Ethnics: Politics and Culture in American Life* (New York: Transaction Publishers, 1995)

Julius Novick, Julius, *Beyond the Golden Door: Jewish American Drama and Jewish American Experience* (New York, Palgrave MacMillan, 2008)

Steve Oney, *And the Dead Shall Rise: The Murder of Mary Phagan and the Lynching of Leo Frank* (New York: Vintage Books, 2004)

Orlando Patterson, *Slavery and Social Death: a Comparative Study* (Cambridge: Harvard University Press, 1982)

Peggy Phelan, *Unmarked: The Politics of Performance* (New York: Routledge, 1993)

Abigail Pogrebin, *Stars of David: Prominent Jews Talk About Being Jewish* (New York: Broadway Books, 2005)

Richard Rodgers, *Musical Stages: An Autobiography*, Centennial Edition (New York: Da Capo Press, 2002)
Michael Rogin, *Blackface, White Noise* (Berkeley: University of California Press, 1996)
Jody Rosen, *White Christmas: The Story of an American Song* (New York: Scribner, 2002)
Deena Rosenberg, *Fascinating Rhythm: The Collaboration of George and Ira Gershwin* (Ann Arbor: University of Michigan Press, 1997)
Philip Roth, *Operation Shylock: A Confession* (New York: Viking, 1994)
Barry Rubin, *Assimilation and Its Discontents* (New York,: Random House, 1995)
Howard M. Sachar, *A History of Jews in America* (New York: Vintage, 1992)
Nahma Sandrow, *Vagabond Stars: A World History of Yiddish Theater* (Syracuse: Syracuse University Press, 1977)
Jonathan D. Sarna, *American Judaism* (New Haven: Yale University Press, 2004)
David Savran, *Highbrow/Lowbrow: Theater, Jazz and the Making of the New Middle Class* (Ann Arbor: University of Michigan Press, 2010)
Meryle Secrest, *Somewhere for Me: A Biography of Richard Rodgers* (New York: Random House, 2001)
———. *Stephen Sondheim: A Life* (New York: Alfred A. Knopf, 1998)
Ellen Schiff, *From Stereotype to Metaphor: The Jew in Contemporary Drama* (Albany: State University of New York Press, 1982)
Michael Schwartz, *Broadway & Corporate Capitalism: The Rise of the Professional Managerial Class, 1900–1920* (New York: Palgrave, 2009)
Stephanie E. Smallwood, *Saltwater Slavery: A Middle Passage from Africa to American Diaspora* (Cambridge, MA: Harvard University Press, 2008)
Robert W. Snyder, *The Voice of the City: Vaudeville and Popular Culture in New York* (New York: Oxford University Press, 1989)
Werner Sollors, *Beyond Ethnicity: Consent and Descent in American Culture* (New York: Oxford University Press, 1986)
Stephen Sondheim, *Finishing the Hat* (New York: Alfred A. Knopf, 2010)
Mark Steyn, *Broadway Babies Say Goodnight: Musicals Then and Now* (New York: Routledge Press, 1999)
Joseph P. Swain, *The Broadway Musical: A Critical and Musical Survey* (New York: Oxford University Press, 1990)
Robert C. Toll, *On With the Show: The First Century of Show Business in America* (New York: Oxford University Press, 1976).
Alan Trachtenberg, *The Incorporation of America: Culture and Society in the Gilded Age* (New York: Hill and Wang, 1982)
Amanda Vaiil, *Somewhere: The Life of Jerome Robbins* (New York: Broadway Books, 2006)
Donald Weber, *Haunted in the New World: Jewish American Culture from Cahan to the Goldbergs* (Bloomington: Indiana University Press, 2005)

Stephen J. Whitfield, *In Search of American Jewish Culture* (Hanover, NH: Brandeis University Press, 1999)

Max Wilk, *They're Playing Our Song* (New York: Da Capo Press, 1991)

Deborah Grace Winer, *On the Sunny Side of the Street: The Life and Lyrics of Dorothy Fields* (New York: Macmillan Library Reference, 1997)

P. G. Wodehouse and Guy Bolton, *Bring On the Girls!* (New York: Limelight Books, 1984)

Alexander Woollcott, *The Story of Irving Berlin* (New York: De Capo Press reprint of 1924 original)

Stacy Wolf, *A Problem Like Maria: Gender and Sexuality in the American Musical* (Ann Arbor: University of Michigan Press, 2002)

Robert Warshow, *The Immediate Experience* (Cambridge, MA: Harvard University Press, 2001)

Richard Ziegfeld, Paulette and Patricia Ziegfeld Stephenson, *The Ziegfeld Touch: The Life and Times of Florenz Ziegfeld, Jr* (New York: Harry N. Abrams, Inc, 1993)

Paul Zollo, "Sultans of Song" *Reform Judaism*, 31.2 (Winter 2002), 14–25

Index

Abbott, George, 72, 212n10
Abie's Irish Rose, 110
acculturation, 2–3, 98, 103, 116–17, 124, 152–7, 172–7
  limits of, 172–7
  the "salad bowl," 2
  in the twentieth century, See *Ragtime versus Parade*
  versus assimilation, 2–3
African American musicals, See *Dreamgirls*; *Ragtime*; *Shuffle Along*; Sissle and Blake
African Americans, 9, 48–52, 54, 57–8, 62–3, 103, 105, 110, 124, 132–4, 143, 145, 154–7, 166, 173, 176, 189, 196
  and Atlantic slave trade, 134
  and Irving Berlin, 48–52
  Jewish identification with, 9
  and musicals, See African American musicals
  and slavery, 133–9, 143–8, 150–1
Ahrens, Lynn, 154
Aleichem, Shalom, 179, 187–9, 193, 218n5
Alexander, Michael, 68
"Alexander's Ragtime Band" (song) (Berlin), 44
Alger, Horatio, 41, 46, 55, 66–7, 151
"All Alone" (song) (Berlin), 105–6
Allen, Woody, 202
"All the Wasted Time" (song) (*Parade*), 164

American Dream, 1, 4, 21, 28, 33–4, 36–8, 41–2, 54–5, 58, 61–102, 103–4, 108, 113, 120–1, 124, 128–9, 133, 137, 139, 142, 149, 152–3, 156, 166, 170, 172–4, 176–7, 194–5, 197, 199, 204
  and baby boom, 97–102
  and book musicals, 36–7
  and Cinderella, See Cinderella musicals
  and freedom, 67–8
  and gambling, 62–72
  and outsiders, 80–97
  and transformation, 4
  and unions, 72–88
  See also success; upward mobility
"An American in Paris," 9
American Museum, 8
American Theatre Lab, 190
Andrews, Julie, 103
And the Dead Shall Rise, 159–60
Animal Crackers (Marx Brothers), 3
Annie Get Your Gun, 16, 18, 44, 56, 83–6, 100
Anti-Defamation League, 166
anti-Semitism, 2, 32, 38, 46–7, 155, 161, 163–5, 167, 171, 180, 185, 203, 217n28
Anything Goes, 16, 20
Arnstein, Nicky, 63–5, 113, 212n5,6
Aronson, Boris, 186
"Ascot Opening Day" (song) (*My Fair Lady*), 126–7

Assassins, 171
assimilation, 2–4, 13, 15–39, 41–3, 46, 49, 57–8, 61–2, 65, 67–8, 70, 72, 80, 84, 87–8, 95, 97, 100–1, 105, 124–5, 128, 132, 152, 169, 176, 187–8, 192, 194–5, 197, 202–4
Astaire, Fred, 44, 48–50, 58, 110, 211n19
As Thousands Cheer (1933), 44, 48, 51
  and the book musical, 17
  and dramatic configurations, 15–30
  and Hart and Rodgers, 37–8
  and identity, 36–7
  and Jewish humor, 3
  and the "melting pot," 2
  and parody, 3
  versus acculturation, 2–3
  versus freedom, 67–8
  See also upward mobility
Atkinson, Brooks, 70
Auschwitz, 42
Avenue Q (2003), 201

Babes in Toyland, 4
baby boom, 32, 56–7, 97–102, 125
Balanchine, George, 182
Baline, Israel, 41–2
  See also Berlin, Irving
ballet, 17, 24, 33, 35–6, 107, 179–81, 218n7
Barnum, P. T., 8
Bat Boy: the Musical (1997), 201
Beauty and the Beast, 201–2
"Been a Long Day" (song) (*How To Succeed in Business*), 91
Beline, Israel, 58
Bennett, Tony, 202
Bergreen, Laurence, 58, 211n2
Berlin, Ellin Mackay, 47, 112
Berlin, Irving, 3, 8–12, 16, 37, 41–59, 84, 106, 112, 117, 119, 125, 183, 203, 206n10, 208n15
  and African Americans, 48–54
  and age, 58–9
  and American government, 44
  and assimilation, 42–3, 125
  and blackface/whiteface, 48–50
  changing context of, 55–6
  childhood of, 41
  education of, 9
  ethnicity of, 44–8
  four major career periods of, 44
  as Horatio Alger, 41, 46, 55
  and immigrants, 41
  name change, 41
  and the 1960s, 56–8
  personal life of, 46–7
  and popular music, 42
  and "Puttin' On the Ritz," 50–3
  and the "Rockefellers," 52
  and "sob ballads," 44
  songwriting career of, 12, 43–4
  as voice of immigrants, 41–2
  and war, 53–5
  wife of, 47
  See also *As Thousands Cheer*; *Call Me Madam*; *Carefree*; *Face the Music*; *Follow the Fleet*; *Mammy*; *Miss Liberty*; *Mr. President*; *On the Avenue*; *Puttin' on the Ritz*; *This is the Army*; *Top Hat*
Bernardi, Herschel, 188
Bernstein, Leonard, 36, 179, 181–2, 208n13
Berry, Chuck, 184
"Big News" (song) (*Parade*), 163
Bissell, Richard, 73, 77, 212n10
The Black Crook (1866), 17
blackface/whiteface, 48–50
Blake, Eubie, 51, 57, 110–11
Blazing Saddles, 202
Blitzstein, Mark, 72–3
"Blues: Feel the Rain Fall" (song) (*Parade*), 164
Blue Skies, 52, 55–6
"Blue Skies" (song) (Berlin), 11, 55
B'Nai Brith, 165
Bock, Jerry, 180, 189, 218n5

Bolshevism, 45
Bolton, Guy, 19–20, 107
book musical, 4, 8–9, 13, 15–19, 24, 32–7, 72–3, 114, 156, 168–9, 171–2, 207n11
   American versus British, 8
   and ballet, *See* ballet
   and the canon, 16
   and European culture, 34–6
   and the promise of America, 36–7
   and rise of ethnic cultures, 16–17
   and rock and roll, 32–7
   types of, 34
   See also *Oklahoma!*
Bow, Clara, 21
Boys In the Band, 6
Brand, Phoebe, 188
Brando, Marlon, 31, 184
Brecht, Bertolt, 73, 86
Brice, Fanny, 46, 62–5, 69–70, 84, 100, 112–15, 117, 212n6, 214n11
   See also *Funny Girl*
Brigadoon (1947), 27–9, 120
Broadway musicals, *See* musicals
Brooks, Mel, 3, 58, 202–3
   The Producers, 202–3
"The Brotherhood of Man" (song), 95–6
Brown, Jason Robert, 154
burlesque, 85–6, 110–11, 214n8
Burrows, Abe, 95
business-themed musicals, 61–102
   and baby boom, 97–102, See also *Company*; *Follies*; *Merrily We Roll Along*
   and cynicism, 70–2, See also *Pal Joey*
   and gamblers, 62–72, See also *Funny Girl*; *Show Boat*
   and insiders, 88–97, See also *How to Succeed in Business*
   and outsiders, 80–8, See also *The Music Man*
   and pluck and luck, 66
   and unions, 72–80, See also *Pajama Game*; *Pins and Needles*
   and women, 83–8, See also *Annie Get Your Gun*; *Gypsy*; *How to Succeed in Business*

Cabaret, 32, 171–2, 179
Call Me Madam (Berlin), 44, 56
Camelot, 120
Candide, 172
"Can't Help Lovin' That Man of Mine" (song) (*Show Boat*), 62–3
Cantor, Eddie, 111
Carefree, 49
Carnovsky, Morris, 188
Carousel (1945), 25, 27, 36
Carrie, 201
Chagall, Marc, 180
Chaplin, Syd, 64–5
chauvinism, 117–20, 123, 144
"Cheek to Cheek" (song) (Berlin), 8
Cinderella (1957), 103
Cinderella (1997), 103
Cinderella musicals (1919–1924), 103–29
   and acculturation, 103–4
   and diversity, 103
   end of, 109–10
   European versus American, 104
   and Galatea, 118–29
   and gender reciprocity, 115–16
   as Irish, *See Irene*
   as Jewish, 111–15
   and nativism, 108–12
   as paradigm, 104–12
   and Prince Charming, *See* Prince Charming
   and pygmalions, 117–28
   and reinvention, 116–17
   See also *Irene; Little Nellie Kelly; Sally*
Cinderella paradigm, 104–12
Cinders, 110
civil rights movement, 31–2, 57–8, 150, 174

classical composers, 182
Coalhouse Walker (character) (*Ragtime*), 131–42, 145–6, 148–52, 155, 158, 173–5
Cohan, George M., 3–4, 33, 44–5, 105, 108–9, 212n4, 214n5
The Color Purple, 101–2, 195–9, 219n14,15
"Come to Me, Bend to Me" (song) (*Brigadoon*), 28–9
commercialism, 5–7, 12
communism, 73–4, 76–7, 187
Company (Sondheim), 13, 97, 101, 172
"The Company Way" (song), 95–6
concept musical, 13, 15
conformity in the 1950s, 184
Cook, Barbara, 39
Coolidge, Calvin, 45, 166
Cooper, Gary, 31, 49, 52–3
Copland, Aaron, 182
The Count of Monte Cristo, 35
"A Couple of Swells" (song) (Berlin), 56
The Cradle Will Rock, 73
Crazy for You, 16
"Crime of the Century" (song) (*Ragtime*), 135, 158, 165
Crosby, Bing, 48, 55
Curtis (character) (*Dreamgirls*), 124–8
Cyrano de Bergerac (Rostand), 3
"*Cyrano de Bric-a-Brac*" (Harrigan and Hart), 3

Damn Yankees, 16
Da Silva, Howard, 188–9
Davis, Ossie, 189
Dean, James, 184
de Mille, Agnes, 35, 182
democracy, and musicals, 8–9, 17, 21, 39, 54, 120, 128
Democratic National Convention (1924), 45, 47, 109
Democratic Party, 45, 47, 56, 109, 166
The Desert Song (1926), 21–3
Desire Under the Elms, 35

diaspora, 13, 68, 131–2, 136–8, 141–6, 148–52, 166, 193
Doctorow, E. L., 131, 134–5, 146, 149, 152, 154, 169, 173–4, 216n16
"Doin' What Comes Naturally" (song) (Berlin), 8
"Don't Send Me Back to Petrograd" (song) (Berlin), 46–7
Dorsey, Hugh, 163
double couple motif, 18–24
    background evolution of, 19–24
    and ethnic prominence, 31
    and the foil, 18–20, 23
    and Hammerstein, 24–5
    popularity of, 19
    primary couple, 19
    secondary couple, 19
    See also operetta; vaudeville
double couple motif examples
    Anything Goes, 20
    Brigadoon, 27–9
    Carousel, 25, 27
    The Desert Song, 21–3
    Guys and Dolls, 29
    Kiss Me Kate, 30
    Of Thee I Sing, 23
    Oh, Boy!, 19–20
    Oklahoma!, 24–5
    Show Boat, 22–4, 26
    South Pacific, 26–7
    Very Good Eddie, 19–20
    West Side Story, 30–1
Douglas, Kirk, 31
Dowling, Eddie, 109
Drabinsky, Garth, 168, 170
Dreamgirls, 124–8
Driving Miss Daisy, 171
The Dybbuk, 188

Eastern Europe, 1, 21, 33, 45, 50, 109, 143, 166, 188
"Easter Parade" (song) (Berlin), 37, 43, 52–3, 58
"*East Side Story*," 181

The Ed Sullivan Show, 38–9
Eisenhower, Dwight D., 56
Eliza (*My Fair Lady*), 68, 118–27
Ellis Island, 1–13
Elsie, 105, 110
empathy, 8–9
Encyclopedia Judaica, 1, 205n1, 207n7
Erlinger, Abe, 111
ethnicity, 2–5, 12–13, 16, 21–39, 44–8, 50, 52, 54–6, 59, 61–3, 66–7, 73–4, 77, 79–82, 88, 104, 106–14, 116–17, 119, 126, 128, 131, 136, 138, 143, 154, 166, 168–9, 174, 176, 179–80, 182–8, 191–204, 205n5, 207n4, 210n9, 211n1, 212n10, 214n11, 215n3
   as encroaching, 108–12,
     See also nativism
   and identity, 12, 30–1, 33, 166, 169, 198–202
   and "monsters," 59, 202–4
   prominence of, 31–2
   twists to, 24–31
   See also acculturation; assimilation
Evita, 172
Exodus, 7

Face the Music (1931), 44, 48
Fancy Free, 181–2
Fanny (character) (*Funny Girl*), 62–5, 70, 84, 103, 111–14, 117, 129
Ferber, Edna, 62
Ferdinand, Franz, 145
Fiddler on the Roof, 170–1, 179–81, 184–200, 217n1, 218n6,9, 219n15
Fields, Dorothy, 84
Fields, Herbert, 35, 84
Fierstein, Harvey, 185
Fiorello! (1959), 31–2
Fisher, Eddie, 202
Flaherty, Steven, 154
Flower Drum Song (1958), 27, 31–2
Fokine, Michel, 182

Follies (1971) (Sondheim), 98–101, 111, 172, 214n10
Follow the Fleet, 44, 49
Ford, Henry, 132–4, 136–8, 152, 155
Fosse, Bob, 72, 77
Foster, Stephen, 10
Francis, Connie, 202
Frank, Leo, 152–5, 159–68, 170–1, 175–6
Freedman, Gerald, 190
Friml, Rudolph, 105
Funny Girl (1964), 62–5, 69–70, 84, 100, 112–15, 117, 212n6, 214n11

Gable, Clark, 31
Gabler, Neil, 48
Galatea, 118–29
Galati, Frank, 154, 156
gambling, 29–30, 62–72, 95–6, 113, 198, 204, 212n4
   See also *Funny Girl*; *Pal Joey*; *Show Boat*
Gelbart, Larry, 202
German ethnicity, 3, 33, 44–5, 54, 170–1, 179, 202, 208n13
German Jews, 33, 170, 179, 208n13
Gershwin, George, 9, 16, 23, 35, 106, 186–7, 208n13
Gershwin, Ira, 9, 16, 35, 37, 110, 206n9
Gilbert and Sullivan, 19, 46
Gilford, Jack, 183, 188, 218n4
The Gingham Girl, 110
"God Bless America" (song) (Berlin), 37, 55, 57
"golden age" of musicals (1940s–1960s), 1, 4, 15–16, 18, 21, 180
Goldman, Emma, 133–4, 140, 143, 147, 155, 157, 216n16
"Gonna Get That Man" (song) (*How to Succeed in Business*), 92
"Goodbye, My Love" (song) (*Ragtime*), 136
Great Depression, 48–9, 72–3

Greek culture, 3, 111
"greenhorn," 2, 9
Guys and Dolls (1950), 29, 68–70, 96–7, 169
Gypsy, 16, 85–8, 98, 183

H. M. S. Pinafore, 46
Hair, 184, 190, 191–3
Hairspray (2002), 201
Hamlet, 5, 20, 205n7
Hammerstein II, Oscar, 15–16, 20–2, 24–7, 31, 33–9, 62, 72, 98, 103–4, 112, 179, 191, 206n9, 207n4,5, 208n13
Harburg, Yip, 10, 206n9
Harlem, 48, 51–3, 136–8, 144, 155, 173, 211n22
"Harlem Nightclub" (song) (*Ragtime*), 136
Harnick, Sheldon, 180, 189, 218n5
Harrigan, Edward, 3, 45, 111
Harrigan and Hart (Irish), 3, 45, 111
Harris, Sam H., 3, 45
Harrison, Rex, 11
Hart, Lorenz, 9–10, 35
Hart, Moss, 44, 48
Hart, Tony, 3, 45, 111
"Heather on the Hill" (song) (*Brigadoon*), 28
Helen of Troy, New York (1924), 105, 110, 115
Hello, Dolly!, 7, 83
Henderson, Florence, 39
Herbert, Victor, 3–4, 107, 207n11
Herman, Jerry, 6–7
Higgins, Henry (character) (*My Fair Lady*), 118–28
"His Love Makes Me Beautiful" (song) (*Funny Girl*), 62
The History of the World, Part One, 202
Hitler, Adolf, 203
Hollywood, 7, 44, 48–9, 55, 153, 181–2, 202
Holm, Celeste, 39
homosexuality, 5, 7, 13, 38, 183, 197–9
honky-tonk, 9
Hope, Bob, 22
Horowitz, Vladimir, 182
Houdini, Harry, 134, 145, 155, 157
House Un-American Activities Committee (HUAC), 78–9, 183, 187–8, 217n29, 218n3
"How Can I Call This Home" (song) (*Parade*), 163
Howe, Irving, 42
How To Succeed in Business Without Really Trying, 74, 88, 90–7, 100, 213n11
HUAC, *See* House Un-American Activities Committee

"I Am What I Am" (song) (Herman), 7
"I Believe in You" (song) (*How to Succeed in Business*), 92–3, 95–6
"I Could Have Danced All Night" (song) (*My Fair Lady*), 119
identity, 2, 12, 22, 26, 28, 30–1, 33, 36–8, 66, 78–9, 89, 91, 100, 107, 122, 125, 131, 133–42, 144, 146, 153, 160–1, 166, 169, 181–4, 188, 191–203
and *Brigadoon*, 28
continental, 26
and economics, 66, 122, 125
escaping, 36–8
Irish, *See* Irish immigrants
Jewish, 153, 160–1, 166, 169, 181–4, 188, 203, *See also* Jewish immigrants
and *Kiss Me Kate*, 30
"masks" of, 22
and politics, 122, 153
and *Ragtime*, 134–42
sexual, 91

and slavery, *See* slavery
and *West Side Story*, 31
and women, *See* women
See also acculturation; assimilation; ethnicity
"If a Girl Isn't Pretty" (song) (*Funny Girl*), 114
"I'll Know" (song) (*Guys and Dolls*), 29
"I'm a Yankee Doodle Dandy" (song) (Cohan), 4
immigration, 1–13, 21, 33–4, 45–59, 61
See also Berlin, Irving; Irish immigrants; Italian immigrants; Jewish immigrants; second generation immigrants
Immigration Act of 1924, 45–6
"The Impossible Dream" (song) (*Man of La Mancha*), 123
"I'm Still Here" (song) (*Follies*), 101
In the Heights, 193–5
Into the Woods, 104–5
Irene (1919), 105–16, 120, 122, 129
Irene and Mary, 110
Irene O'Dare (Montgomery), 106
Irish immigrants, 2–4, 28, 31, 39, 44–5, 54, 67, 88, 96, 105–12, 115–16, 118, 135, 137–9, 144, 150, 155, 166, 171, 181, 209n3, 212n4, 214n7
and Cinderella, 105–12, 115–16, 118
See also *Irene*
Italian immigrants, 2–3, 45, 65, 111
"I've Grown Accustomed to Her Face" (song) (*My Fair Lady*), 119

jazz, 9, 24, 35, 43–4, 46, 48–52, 55, 110, 116–17, 136, 157, 182, 207n11, 217n1
Jazz Age, 116–17
The Jazz Singer (1927), 48, 55, 217n1
Jekyll and Hyde, 201
Jessel, George, 48–9
Jets, 181

Jewish
authenticity, 186–7
gangsters, 68–9
humor, 3
identity, 153, 160–1, 166, 169–70, 181–4, 188, 203
religion, 8–10
Jewish immigrants, 1–13, 21, 33–4, 61, 132, 180–1
and Broadway, *See* Jewish influence on Broadway
as natural actors, 2, 8
old world/new world conflict, 1–2, 18, 27
population statistics on, 1, 11
and professionalism, 69
second generation, 33–4
See also acculturation; assimilation; anti-Semitism
Jewish influence on Broadway musicals (1910–), 1–13
and classical composers, 182
and Cohan and Herbert, 3–4
and commercialization, *See* commercialism
as democratic, 8–9
and Ellis Island, 4–5
and Herman, 6–7
and lyrics, 9–10
and the mainstream, 5–6
and the minor key, 10–11
and religion, 8–10
transposing Broadway, 11–13
See also Berlin, Irving
Jewish National Fund, 43
Jolson, Al, 47–51, 55, 111, 217n1
Jones, John Bush, 111

Kallen, Horace, 166
Kaufman, George S., 23
Kelly, Gene, 49
Kennedy, Jacqueline, 88, 183
Kennedy, John F., 31, 88, 96, 183

Kern, Jerome, 15–16, 19–20, 42, 54, 62, 105, 107–8
Kerouac, Jack, 184
The King and I (1951), 8, 18, 27, 112, 179, 183, 207n4
King Kong, 58
"The King of Old Broadway" (song) (*The Producers*), 203
Kiss Me Kate (1948), 16, 30
Kiss of the Spider Woman, 153, 168, 172
Klezmer music, 9, 203
Kosher Kitty Kelly, 110
Koussevitsky, Serge, 182
Ku Klux Klan (KKK), 45–7, 109–10, 166, 187

La Boheme, 191
La Cage Aux Folles, 6–7
Lady, Be Good, 110
Lansky, Myron, 69
Lapine, James, 104
Larson, Jonathan, 7, 191
Last Night at Ballyhoo, 171
Latin musicals, 5, 13, 193–5
LaTouche, John, 72
Lazarus, Emma, 56
"Leave You," (song) (*Follies*), 98
Legally Blonde (2007), 201–2
Lerner and Loewe, 16, 27, 118–21, 157
"Let Me Sing and I'm Happy" (song) (Berlin), 47
"Let's Go Slumming" (song) (Berlin), 52
Lincoln Center, 153
Little Johnny Jones, 4, 212n4
Little Nellie Kelly (1922), 106, 108–9, 112–13, 115
Little Shop of Horrors, 201
Little Theatre Movement, 35
Loesser, Frank, 16, 29, 88, 92, 95–6, 213n11,13
logogenic, 10
Lott, Eric, 54
lovers, *See* young lovers

Love! Valour! Compassion!, 6
Lower East Side, 9, 33, 41, 53, 61, 132, 141, 144, 155
"luck and pluck," 41, 55, 66, 102
Lucky Luciano mob, 69
lyrics, and Jews, 9–10

Mackay, Clarence, 117
Magnolia (character) (*Show Boat*), 22–4, 26, 62–5, 211n2
Major Barbara, 95
major keys, 10–11
"Make Them Hear You" (song) (*Ragtime*), 135, 158
Making Americans: Jews and the Broadway Musical (Most), 42
Mame, 7
Mammy (1930), 47–9
"The Man I Love" (song) (Gershwin), 106
"Manhattan" (song) (Rodgers), 9–10
Man of La Mancha, 32, 122–8
"The Man I Love" (song) (Gershwin), 106
"Marie from Sunny Italy" (song) (Berlin), 37, 41
Marx, Groucho, 45
Marx Brothers, 3
Mary, 110
Mary Jane McKane, 115
McAdoo, William, 45
McCarthy, Joseph, 106
McCarthyism, 77–9, 188
McNally, Terrence, 134, 154
Mead, Shepherd, 95
melting pot, 2, 54
Merrily We Roll Along (1981) (Sondheim), 98–9
methodology, 13
middle class, 18, 66–9, 75, 80, 101–2, 133, 139, 144, 165, 173, 196
Milk and Honey, 7, 205n8
Miller, Marilynn, 107–8, 113–15

minor keys, 10–11
minstrel shows, 3
Miranda, Lin-Manuel, 193
Miss Liberty (Berlin), 56
Mr. President (Berlin), 56
Mitropoulos, Dmitri, 182
Model T Ford, 132–3, 137–8, 152
Molina, Alfred, 185
Monroe, Marilyn, 31
monsters, 201–4
Montgomery, James, 106
Morgan, J. P., 134, 155, 157
Morgan Library, 133, 140, 146–7, 155, 173
Morse, Robert, 96
Moses, 150, 202
Most, Andrea, 42
Mostel, Zero, 183–5, 189, 218n9
Most Happy Fella (1956), 31–2
"musical comedy," 15–17, 33, 35, 70, 109–10, 114, 116, 197, 203
musicals (Broadway)
  African American, *See* African American musicals
  and American character, 11–12
  and American skepticism (1970s), 5
  book musical, *See* book musical
  business-themed, *See* business-themed musicals
  canon of, 16–17
  and change, 5–7
  Cinderella, *See* Cinderella musicals
  and comedy, *See* musical comedy
  and commercialism, 5–7, 12
  concept musical, *See* concept musical
  as conservative, 5–6
  as cultural Ellis Island, 4–5
  as democratic, 8
  as entertainment, 5
  and escapism, 6
  and "fringe" groups, 5
  "golden age" of, 1, 4, 15–16, 18, 21, 180
  and integration, 4–5
  and Jews, *See* Jewish influence on Broadway
  and the mainstream, 5–6
  as "mongrel" in form, 17
  movin' on up, 33–7
  Pygmalion, *See* Pygmalion musicals
  and risk, 6–7
  and social change, 5–7
  transposing, 11–13
  and winning combinations, 15–32
  and youth culture (1960s), 5
Music Box Revues (1924), 45–7
The Music Man, 16, 68, 75, 79–82, 191
"My English Buddy" (song) (Berlin), 54
My Fair Lady, 11, 68, 103, 118–28, 157, 215n14

National Endowment for the Arts, 190
National Pencil Factory, 154
nativism, 45, 47, 75, 108–12, 156, 187
Nazi Germany, 27, 32, 171, 179–80, 204
Nesbit, Evelyn, 133–4, 140, 143, 155, 216n16
"The New Colossus" (Lazarus), 56
New Deal, 72
Newman, Randy, 154
New Rochelle, New York, 133, 136–7, 141–5, 155, 162
New York, 110
New York City
  and Broadway, *See* Jewish influence on Broadway
  and Jewish immigrants, *See* Jewish immigrants
  multicultural mix of, 44–5, 110–11, *See also* ethnicity
  neighborhoods, *See* Harlem; Lower East Side; New Rochelle
  population statistics, 1
  See also "golden age" of musicals

236 Index

The New York Times, 47
Niblo Garden Theatre, 17
Nixon, Richard, 57
Nusach, 10

Off-Broadway, 201
Offenbach, Jacques ("Jacob"), 17
Of Thee I Sing, 3, 23–4, 208n13
Oh, Boy!, 19–20
"Oh, How I Hate to Get Up in the Morning" (song) (Berlin), 53
"Oh My Pa-Pa" (song), 202
Oklahoma!, 8, 13, 15, 19, 24–5, 31, 33, 35, 38–9, 72, 169
"The Old Red Hills of Home" (song) (*Parade*), 162
"Once-a-Year Day" (song) (*Pajama Game*), 76–7
O'Neill, Eugene, 35
Oney, Steven, 159
On the Avenue, 49
"On the Street Where You Live" (song) (*My Fair Lady*), 120
On the Town, 179
On Your Toes (1936), 35
Operation Shylock (Roth), 43
operetta, 4, 17, 20–4, 28–31, 38, 49, 103, 120, 124, 159, 162, 164, 168
outsiders, 1, 8, 22–3, 25, 27–9, 61, 68, 80–97, 126–8, 132, 166–9, 192, 194, 196

Pacific Overtures, 172
The Pajama Game, 72–80, 88, 183
Pal Joey (1939), 16, 38, 70–2
Papp, Joseph, 190
Parade, 152–77
 and acculturation, 172–6
 and audience, 170–7
 construction of, 162–3
 costuming in, 161–2
 and facts, 165–8
 and *Fiddler on the Roof*, 170–1
 origins of, 153–4
 plot of, 154–6
 production of, 152–3
 style of, 159–61
 See also *Ragtime versus Parade*
Parade (1998–1999) (Lincoln Center), 153
parody, 3, 51, 214n8
Passion, 154
Passover, 8–9
Patterson, Orlando, 134
Peter Pan, 183–4
"The Picture Show" (song) (*Parade*), 163
Pins and Needles, 72–5, 213n11
Plain Jane, 115
Pogrebin, Abigail, 170
Porgy and Bess, 186–7
Porter, Cole, 16, 30, 33, 44, 203
postwar career women, 83–8
 See also *Annie Get Your Gun*; *Gypsy*
Presley, Elvis, 184
Prince, Harold, 154, 161, 167, 170–2, 175, 179, 181, 184, 217n21,24,28
Prince Charming, 104, 113, 115–20
Princess Theatre shows, 19–20
The Producers, 202–4
Public Theater, 190
Puerto Rican culture, 30, 120, 171, 181, 195
Puttin' On the Ritz (1930) (Berlin), 47, 50–3
The Producers (2001), 201
Protestant Work Ethic, 67, 79, 96
Purlie (musical), 189–90
Purlie Victorious (play), 189
Purple Gang, 69
Pygmalion musicals, 117–28
 and Curtis (*Dreamgirls*), 124–8
 and Don Quixote (*Man of La Mancha*), 122–8
 and Galatea, 118–29

Index   237

and Henry Higgins (*My Fair Lady*),
  118–28
and Jews, 126–8
and societal norms, 126–8

Quixote, Don (*Man of La Mancha*),
  32, 122–8

Rabinowitz, Jerome, 180–1
Ragni, Gerome, 190
Ragtime, 131–77
Ragtime (Doctorow) (1975), 131
Ragtime (film) (1981), 154
  and automobiles, *See* Model T Ford
  and collisions, 146–8
  construction of, 162–5
  costumes in, 161–2
  and diaspora, 131–2, 136–8, 141–6,
    148–52, 166
  and father and mother, 140–1, 173
  and fiction, 165–8
  and identity, 134–42
  language and music, 134–6
  and mid-passage, 132–5
  and Moses, 150
  and nation of immigrants, 143–6,
    151–2
  versus *Parade*, See *Ragtime versus Parade*
  plot of, 154–6
  and "quotation mark" style, 156–9
  and slavery, 133–9, 143–8, 150–1
  style of, 156–9
  use of non-names, 135
  See also Coalhouse Walker; Sarah;
    Tateh
Ragtime versus Parade, 152–77
  and acculturation, 172–6
  and audience, 170–7
  and costumes, 161–2
  and double fantasies, 154–6
  and the end of the century, 168–70
  fact versus fiction, 165–8

and Genesis, 153–4
and identity, 153, 160–1, 166, 169
productions of, 153–4
Raitt John, 39
Rat Pack, 31, 96
Ravenal, Gaylord (character) (*Show Boat*), 22–3, 62–5
Red Scare, 45, 54, 77–9, 109, 187
Reiner, Carl, 202
Rent, 7, 191–3
Richman, Harry, 47, 50–1
The Rise of Rosie O'Reilly, 115
Roach, Hal, 149
Robbins, Jerome, 179–90
  and American Theatre Lab, 190
  beginning career of, 183–4
  and Belarus, 185–6
  and blacklisting, 188–90
  and civil rights, 190–1
  and conformity, 184
  and HUAC, 187–8
  and Jewish authenticity, 186–7
  and name change, 180–2
  and National Endowment for the Arts, 190
  and Peter Pan, 183–4
  and tradition, 184–5
rock and roll, 15, 32–7, 56–8
Rodeo, 182
Rodgers, Richard, 8–10, 15–16, 25,
  27, 31, 33, 35–9, 70, 72, 103–4,
  110, 112, 179, 207n5, 208n13,
  209n16,18
Rodgers and Hammerstein, 15–16,
  25, 27, 31, 33, 35–9, 103–4, 112,
  179, 208n13
Rodgers and Hart, 70, 72, 110
Rogers, Ginger, 49
Romberg, Sigmund, 15
Rome, Harold, 72
Romeo and Juliet, 181
Roosevelt, Eleanor, 53, 167, 217n24
Roosevelt, Franklin Delano, 56, 72

Rose-Marie, 21, 35
"Rose's Turn" (song) (*Gypsy*), 85
Roth, Philip, 43
Rothstein, Arnold, 68–9, 214n17
Rubinstein, Arthur, 182
Runyon, Damon, 69
Russia, 9, 33, 41, 45–7, 55, 58, 77–8, 107, 132–3, 179–82, 208n13,15
Russian Jews, 33, 45, 55, 180–1, 208n13

Salinger, J. D., 184
Sally (1920), 84, 98, 103, 106–15, 117, 129, 214n5
Sally (character) (*Sally*), 84, 98, 103, 106–15, 117, 129, 214n5
Salvation Army, 69
Sampson, Jackie (character), 19
"Sarah Brown Eyes" (song) (*Ragtime*), 136
Sarah (character) (*Ragtime*), 131–3, 135–41, 146, 148–52, 155, 158, 173
Schultz, Dutch, 69
"Seasons of Love" (song) (*Rent*), 192
second generation immigrants, 32–4, 41, 57, 67, 77, 105–6
See also upward mobility
7 1/2 Cents (Bissell), 73, 77, 212n10
"7 1/2 Cents" (song), 75, 79–80
Shakespeare, William, 5, 19–20, 30–1, 35, 43, 70, 147, 161, 216n17
Sharif, Omar, 64–5
Shaw, George Bernard, 95, 118–19, 121, 127
"Sh'ma" (song) (*Parade*), 164
Show Boat (1927), 16, 20, 22–4, 26, 62–5, 69–70, 100, 106, 153, 172, 175, 211n2
"Show Me" (song) (*My Fair Lady*), 120
Shrek, 201

"A Shtetl Iz Amerieke" (song), 136
Shuffle Along, 51, 105, 110–11
Siegel, Bugsy, 69
Simon, Neil, 202
Sinatra, Frank, 88, 96
Sissle, Noble, 105, 110
Sissle and Blake, 105, 110
"Slaughter on Tenth Avenue" (song) (*On Your Toes*), 35
slavery, 133–9, 143–8, 150–1
See also African Americans
Smith, Alfred E. ("Al"), 45, 56
Sondheim, Stephen, 97–101, 104, 154, 171, 191
See also *Company*; *Follies*; *Merrily We Roll Along*
The Sound of Music (1959), 27
South Pacific (1949), 15, 26–7, 53, 112, 169, 179, 207n4,5
Spiderman (2011), 201
Springtime for Hitler, 204
State of Israel, 6–7, 12
"Steam Heat" (song) (*Pajama Game*), 77
Stein, Jerry, 189
The Story of Irving Berlin, 46
"Street of Dreams" (song), 202
Streisand, Barbra, 114
success in the 20th century, 61–102
and baby boom, 97–102
and gambling, 62–72
and outsiders, 80–97
and unions, 72–80
"Sue Me" (song) (*Guys and Dolls*), 29
"Supper Time" (song) (Berlin), 48
Sweeney Todd, 172

"Take Me For What I Am" (song) (*Rent*), 7
"Take Me or Leave Me" (song) (*Rent*), 7
The Tales of Shalom Aleichem, 188–9
Taming of the Shrew (Shakespeare), 30, 43, 69, 120

Tateh (character) (*Ragtime*), 132–4, 140–6, 149–51, 155, 158, 169, 173–5, 215n6
Tevye (character) (*Fiddler on the Roof*), 32, 179–80, 185–6, 189–94, 198, 218n9
That O'Brien Girl, 110
"There But For You Go I" (song) (*Brigadoon*), 28
"There's a Place for Us" (song) (*West Side Story*), 31
This Is the Army (Berlin), 44, 51, 53–5, 210n5, 211n22
Tierney, Harry, 106
"Till I Lost You" (song) (Berlin), 42
"Till the Clouds Roll By" (song), 20
Tin Pan Alley, 17, 44, 111, 205n1
Tomashefsky, Boris, 203
Top Hat, 44, 49, 58
"Top Hat, White Tie and Tail" (song) (Berlin), 58
Torah, 10
totalitarianism, 73
"Toy Land" (song) (Herbert), 4
transposing, 11–13
A Trip to Chinatown, 185–6
Trouble in Tahiti, 182
Tudor, Anthony, 182
Twain, Mark, 188
"Twinkle, Twinkle, Little Star," 12

Uhry, Alfred, 154, 159, 167, 170–1, 175, 216n14
upward mobility, 17, 21, 25, 32, 36–8, 41–2, 51–3, 57, 80, 104–5, 110
Uris, Leon, 7

Valentino, Rudolph, 21
vaudeville, 3–4, 8, 17, 21, 24, 28–31, 33, 48, 63, 70, 85–6, 88, 158–9, 163, 214n8
Very Good Eddie, 19–20, 31
Vietnam War, 57, 190–1

Walker, Alice, 195, 199
Warren, Lesley Ann, 103
Washington, Booker T., 146, 148, 155, 174
Watch Your Step (1914), 44
Waters, Ethel, 48, 51
Watson, Tom, 166
Weber, Donald, 3, 45, 111
Weber and Fields (Jewish), 3, 45, 111
West Side Story (1956), 16, 30–1, 171–2, 179, 181, 183, 208n13
"Wheels of a Dream" (song) (*Ragtime*), 131, 133, 136–7, 149, 158
White Anglo-Saxon Protestant (WASP), 2, 20–5, 30–1, 34–8, 47, 50, 53, 59, 62, 67, 73, 75, 84, 96, 105, 107–9, 111–12, 137, 141, 143–5, 149, 155–6, 158, 169, 211n1, 215n3
White Christmas (Rosen), 43
"White Christmas" (song) (Berlin), 37, 42–3, 55
"Why Can't The English Teach Their Children How to Speak?" (song) (*My Fair Lady*), 119
Wicked (2003), 201
Wilder, Gene, 58–9
Williams, Bert, 111
Winchell, Walter, 69
Winfrey, Oprah, 195–6
"Without You" (song) (*My Fair Lady*), 119
The Wizard of Oz, 201
Wodehouse, P. G., 19
women
 and business musicals, 83–8,
  See also *Annie Get Your Gun*; *Gypsy*
 and Cinderella musicals,
  See Cinderella musicals
 and Pygmalion musicals,
  See Pygmalion musicals
Woollcott, Alexander, 46–7, 57, 210n14,15

World of Our Fathers (Howe), 42
World War I, 45, 105, 145, 187, 207n7
World War II, 31, 44, 53, 69, 72, 120, 211n22

yeshiva buchers, 64
"Yiddisha Eskimo" (song) (Berlin), 46
Yiddish language, 2, 9, 25, 29, 33, 46, 54, 75, 114, 120, 134, 158, 188, 202–3, 205n2,8, 219n2
"Yiddle On Your Fiddle (Play Some Ragtime)" (song) (Berlin), 46
Yip, Yip, Yahank!, 44
"You Did It" (song) (*My Fair Lady*), 121–2
"You Don't Know This Man" (song) (*Parade*), 160
"You Gotta Get a Gimmick" (song) (*Gypsy*), 86–7
"You'll Never Walk Alone" (song) (*Carousel*), 25

The Young Frankenstein, 3, 58, 201, 211n27
young lovers, 15–39
and the canon, 16–17
double couple motif, 18–24
ethnicity, 24–32
and hegemony, 34–6
lessons and love, 18
and lost identity, 36–7
and the middle class, 18
and musical plays, 24
and rock and roll, 32–7
and transitions, 37–9
and vaudeville and operetta, 17
winning combinations of, 15–16
"Your Daddy's Son" (song) (*Ragtime*), 138, 158

Ziegfeld, Florenz, 34, 44, 62, 84, 100, 107–9, 111, 113–14, 117, 214n5
Ziegfeld Follies, 44, 107